Mainstre
Videoco

Mainstream Videoconferencing

A Developer's Guide to
Distance Multimedia

Joe Duran
Charlie Sauer

ADDISON-WESLEY

An imprint of Addison Wesley Longman, Inc.

Reading, Massachusetts • Harlow, England • Menlo Park, California
Berkeley, California • Don Mills, Ontario • Sydney
Bonn • Amsterdam • Tokyo • Mexico City

Acquisitions Editor: Thomas E. Stone
Associate Editor: Deborah Lafferty
Production Coordinator: Rosa Aimée González
Cover Designer: Diana C. Coe
Cover Art: Studio M D Inc.
Composition: American Stratford Graphic Services, Inc.

Many of the designations used by manufacturers and sellers to distinguish their products are claimed as trademarks. Where those designations appear in this book and Addison Wesley Longman, Inc. was aware of a trademark claim, the designations have been printed in initial caps or all caps.

The publisher offers discounts on this book when ordered in quantity for special sales. For more information please contact:

> Corporate & Professional Publishing Group
> Addison-Wesley Publishing Company
> One Jacob Way
> Reading, Massachusetts 01867

The complete volume(s) of the ITU material, from which the texts reproduced are extracted, can be obtained from:
General Secretariat-Sales and Marketing Service
Place des Nations- CH - 1211 Geneva 20 (Switzerland)
Telephone: +41 22 730 61 41 (English) / +41 22 730 61 42 (French)
Telex: 421 000 uit ch / Fax: +41 22 730 51 94
X.400: S = Sales; P = itu; C = ch
Internet: Sales@itu.ch

Library of Congress Cataloging-in-Publication Data

Duran, Joe.
    Mainstream videoconferencing : a developer's guide to distance
multimedia / by Joe Duran, Charlie Sauer.
        p.   cm.
    Includes index.
    ISBN 0-201-84747-7
    1. Videoconferencing.   I. Sauer, Charles.   II. Title.
HF5734.7.D87   1997
384.55′6—dc20   96-44237
                                                                                  CIP

Access the latest information about Addison-Wesley titles from our World Wide Web site: http://www.awl.com

Text printed on recycled and acid-free paper.

ISBN 0-201-84747-7
1 2 3 4 5 6 7 8 9—MA—00999897
First Printing, January 1997

To Susan, Alex, Blaise, David, Larry,
Michael, Caroline, and Liz

Contents

Preface

The initial, closed-circuit demonstrations of television in the 1920s provided us with a foretaste of videoconferencing. Modern interest in videoconferencing began with the "picture phone" demonstrations in the 1960s. Videoconferencing became practical during the 1980s, though, at this writing, videoconferencing is not yet pervasive. It is, however, inevitable that videoconferencing will be pervasive. Certainly, the science fiction writers see it that way. On the bridge of the *Enterprise,* the captain says "on screen" and the videoconference begins. Larry Niven postulates a future in which it is bad manners to turn the picture off when answering a phone call. Videoconferencing in fiction is at least as old as silent movies; Fritz Lang's classic, *Metropolis,* shows videoconferencing.

This book is about "mainstream" videoconferencing in that it describes what is practical now and in the near future, and in the sense of describing how videoconferencing will *become* mainstream and pervasive. Videoconferencing should become mainstream by the end of the 1990s; it is the intent of this book to accelerate the use of videoconferencing and help it become mainstream.

We hope that this work will be accessible and useful to a wide range of professionals who will either use videoconferencing or who will advance the state of the art. Potential users include most businesses, many organizations, and some homes. Professionals in communications, computer science, electrical engineering, entertainment, information technology, and other fields are likely to have an interest in videoconferencing and the ability to contribute to improving how it is designed and how it is used.

We think this book tells "how and why it works" and "what can I do with it." In some sense, we are trying to provide the book we wanted to read when we started working on videoconferencing. Very few books have been published on videoconferencing, and none of those few address the need we see.

We should make it clear that this is *not* a book on "how to" purchase and deploy videoconferencing. Products in the videoconferencing industry are changing rapidly, just as in the computer and communications industries that provide the basis for videoconferencing. We believe the manufacturers and suppliers of videoconferencing equipment, networking vendors, telecommunications companies, and others are the appropriate sources of "how to" information in this dynamic environment. By helping the reader understand "how and why it works" and "what can I do with it," we hope that the reader will be better prepared to read and evaluate the manufacturers' information and the "how to" books that do and will exist. We list sources of much of this information in Appendix II, and provide pointers through `http://www.aw.com/cp/duran-sauer.html`.

There has been much discussion in the trade press about "desktop" videoconferencing versus "room" videoconferencing. It is clear that the primary past usage of videoconferencing systems has been in room environments, and it is equally clear that the desktop will be dominant in terms of the numbers of future videoconferencing systems. However, there need be no "either–or" discussion of these environments. Both will be fundamentally important in the future of videoconferencing. The majority of the issues surrounding videoconferencing are the same in either environment, so we generally consider both desktop and room environments at the same time. One of us (Duran) has spent more than a decade focusing on room videoconferencing systems. The other (Sauer) has spent that same time developing workstations and personal computer systems. Thus we are confident that we are presenting a balanced view of both environments.

There are three main sections: *The Big Picture* is an extensive overview of videoconferencing in present and planned use. This should be accessible to all likely readers. *Behind the Curtain* discusses the technology in more depth. Those without sufficient engineering and software background might want to skip the second section. *Down the Road* gives our view of where videoconferencing capability and usage are headed. This third section is intended to be accessible to all likely readers.

This book is largely self-contained, but we have not repeated many of the details that are available in the published standards documents and in several fine books on video coding and audio coding. We have tried to provide what these books and standards do not. For example, we do provide a close look at how video flows through a standard system, since much of the necessary video processing is not described in the standards documents or in other books.

The Big Picture section consists of six chapters:

Chapter 1: "Why We're Here" is an introduction to videoconferencing. The purposes of the chapter are to begin establishing a sense of what people have expected and will expect from videoconferencing, to introduce some of the key technical issues and challenges, to describe the characteristics of some representative videoconferencing systems, to outline some of the applications of videoconferencing, and to suggest where the future of videoconferencing may lead. Chapters 2 through 6 expand on the introduction. Chapters 7 through 12, in the *Behind the Curtain* section, expand on the technical details, and Chapters 13 and 14 (*Down the Road*) expand on the future.

Chapter 2: "Where We Came From" gives a historical perspective on video-conferencing. We believe that some historical perspective on telephony, television, and videoconferencing will help the reader to understand the current state of the capabilities of videoconferencing and some of the inertia that affects the future.

Chapter 3: "Starting on the Desktop" begins to explore the technology of videoconferencing from the perspective of making a personal computer capable of sharing audio, video, and data in a conference.

Chapter 4: "Rooms with a View" builds on Chapter 3 from the perspective of a group of people separated into distant conference rooms. The emphasis is on the technology and characteristics needed to stretch the boundaries of the conference rooms so that the group can transcend the distances between the rooms.

Chapter 5: "All Together Now" extends the concepts of Chapters 3 and 4 to consider "multipoint" conferences with more than two sites.

Chapter 6: "Finishing the Picture" concludes the first section by delving into the applications of videoconferencing. Videoconferencing is not an application itself. Rather, distance meetings, telemedicine, distance learning, entertainment, and so forth are the real applications.

In the second section, *Behind the Curtain,* we explore the wizardry that makes videoconferencing practical today:

Chapter 7: "Analog, Digital, and Television" delves into the technology and boundaries of the analog systems used for most television and the digital realm used for most videoconferencing. A good part of the success of a videoconferencing product is in effective navigation of these diverse environments.

Chapter 8: In *"Communication Infrastructure"* we pursue further the most critical aspect of establishing videoconferencing. Videoconferencing has succeeded, so far, by clever utilization of a communications infrastructure that "isn't quite right." We must continue the trend of careful exploitation of a communications designed for other purposes if we are to see video-conferencing become mainstream.

Chapter 9: "Video" is our discussion of the fundamental mathematics that makes videoconferencing possible. The essence is "coding," in which we take a very "verbose" video signal and make it compact enough to travel across ordinary telephone and computer networking circuits. This chapter and the companion audio chapter contain the most challenging mathematics of the book. We have tried to limit the mathematics to the essentials, but nevertheless, this chapter will be daunting to many readers. We believe we have struck an appropriate balance between making this fundamental material accessible while not trying to make this the dominant portion of the book.

Chapter 10: "Audio" is in some sense the most important topic. Videoconferencing lifts the communication potential of a telephone call ("a picture is worth a thousand words"), but if the audio quality is lost in the process, the results will be failure. This discussion is the companion to the video chapter, and follows primarily because the mathematics needed for audio was more easily introduced in the video chapter.

Chapter 11: "Putting It Together with Multipoint" is the first of another two-chapter pair. Chapter 5 introduced the basics of multipoint conferencing. In Chapter 11 we continue the discussion with more technical detail on "bridging" audio and video among multiple sites, and conducting a multipoint conference. In addition, we cover some of the other protocols that are used to establish and manage conferences.

Chapter 12: "Multipoint Data" completes the pair by examining the protocols needed for sharing presentations and data across a multipoint conference. The bulk of the chapter is devoted to the International Telecommunications Union—Telecommunication Standardization Sector (ITU-T) T.120 recommendations for multipoint data conferencing.

Again, we realize that Chapters 7 through 12 will be too challenging for some readers. We encourage those readers to confidently skip all or part of these chapters and continue with the last section. *Down the Road* is our vision of the future of videoconferencing:

Chapter 13: "Barriers Breaking Down" is mostly about the current challenges to successful videoconferencing. With the technologies and developments we see on the near horizon, these challenges will be overcome, and mainstream videoconferencing will surely become a reality.

Chapter 14: "Things to Come" concludes our vision of where videoconferencing will take us, once videoconferencing is mainstream.

Appendix I "Summary of ITU-T Standards" lists the standards recommendations most important to videoconferencing and gives additional background on some of the standards.

Appendix II "Web Resources" lists some of the World Wide Web addresses that we consider valuable for readers to explore to learn more about videoconferencing. We intend to update periodically a version of this appendix at `http://www.aw.com/cp/duran-sauer.html`.

Since we have tried to make this book accessible to a diverse audience, it is inevitable that we have missed the mark for some readers and have wrongly assumed background in computers, or communications, or photography, or whatever. In the text, we try to compensate directly with explanations of basic concepts. We have also included an extensive glossary. When we first discuss a term in the glossary, we underline it in the style of links used by *World Wide Web* browsers. We hope readers will find this glossary to be a handy reference to unfamiliar concepts and terms.

In the next year or two, we anticipate dramatic proliferation of standardized videoconferencing using conventional telephone circuits and the Internet. We did not attempt to provide detailed coverage of these topics at this time, because these areas are seeing such rapid changes and so far there has been negligible deployment. We hope that reader acceptance of this book will be sufficient to justify a second edition that will cover these topics in detail. For now, we believe that we have provided the right foundation for understanding these topics, and intend to provide additional information at `http://www.aw.com/cp/duran-sauer.html`. We also would welcome e-mail addressed to `DuranSauer@aw.com`.

Acknowledgments

We are grateful to the many colleagues who have helped us develop and understand videoconferencing. We would like to thank those who have contributed greatly to this manuscript through their reviews and suggestions, including Rod Bond, Rick Flott, Bill Guthrie, Dave Hein, Bruce Kravitz, Arch Luther, Joon Maeng, Peter Salus, Barry Shein, Errol Williams, and a number of anonymous reviewers. We especially wish to thank our editors, Debbie Lafferty and Tom Stone of Addison Wesley Longman, for all of their help. We thank all those who have allowed us to reproduce figures, pictures, and text in this book. Finally, we acknowledge our debt to Charles Abbitt, Susan Combs, Caroline Sauer, and other family members who have provided not only encouragement and support but significant editorial assistance.

Joe Duran
Charlie Sauer
Austin, Texas
August 1996

PART 1

The Big Picture

Chapter 1

Why We're Here

1.1 VISIONS, METAPHORS, EXPECTATIONS, REALITIES

There are many visions of videoconferencing. The essence of most of them is that videoconferencing should transcend the geographical and physical boundaries between the participants through the use of shared audio, video, and other media. Ideally, a conferencing system provides the illusion that all of the participants are in the same room, sharing one space. Current products support this illusion to the extent that they provide appropriate audio, video, and multimedia communication and controls for the user.

To start thinking about how technology can be applied toward achieving this goal, consider two widely used metaphors for better communications devices—the "picture phone" and "desktop videoconferencing." The "picture phone," a telephone with video capability, has been a popular (though sometimes maligned) concept since the AT&T demonstrations in the 1960s. By themselves, a pair of picture phones is limited to two participants, and only partially transcends distance and physical boundaries. The need for a handset for sound, and the very small picture, relative to the people and surroundings, makes the participants very conscious that they are using a special device. (Use of the picture phone might be compared to use of a

3

telescope—there is noticeable benefit, but little illusion.) In the desktop videoconferencing approach, a personal computer or workstation provides augmented audio and video. As with the picture phone, there is little attempt to mask the obvious boundaries between sites and to present an illusion of shared space. However, the augmented computer provides tremendous communication capabilities, and will be the most cost-effective approach for many users.

We don't mean to imply that picture phones and desktop videoconferencing systems are inherently limited to a pair of participants. Just as it is possible to have conference calls with multiple telephones, various approaches may be used to extend the number of participants in picture phone and desktop conferences. Depending on the application, such "multipoint" conferences may be fundamental to effective communication.

To transcend the physical boundaries, first imagine an environment without the boundaries and then attempt to extend the environment beyond the normal limits. For example, try to think of "stretching" a conference room across multiple sites. First, we want audio provided in such a way that hands-free group discussion is possible. Typically, this means using multiple microphones and speakers with appropriate acoustic controls. Second, we need video cameras and large monitors to make the participants easily visible to each other. And, in many cases, we must provide for shared presentation materials, documents, marker boards, and so forth, so that most of the routine meeting facilities are shared across the multiple sites.

Similarly, imagine a classroom, or a medical practice, or a brokerage house stretched across multiple sites. We want to provide seemingly single-site facilities across multiple sites, in such a way that physical boundaries are not barriers to the participants in the activities.

These metaphors, and the notion that an illusion of shared space can be achieved, set a high level of expectation on system performance. Also, we are used to the audio quality levels established by telephones and radio and the video quality levels provided by commercial television. If the conferencing equipment does not have comparable audio and video quality, the illusion will be diminished.

Achieving this performance requires real-time transfer of large amounts of audio, video, and data—orders of magnitude more than the quantities associated with telephones. The transfer must be directed and often must be secure, so broadcast technology associated with television is not appropriate. Thus the biggest obstacle to pervasive use of videoconferencing is the gap between the communication requirements and the limitations of the available communication infrastructure. Much of our discussion in this book is about narrowing and eliminating that gap.

Despite difficult gaps between communication requirements and capability, videoconferencing is practical and rapidly growing in popularity. Business meetings are effectively conducted by joining desks and conference rooms with videoconferencing equipment. "Distance learning" across multiple classrooms and campuses is now a routine practice. "Telemedicine" enables specialists and general practitioners to collaborate, and provides medical care in rural areas to those who would otherwise do without. Employers and job candidates meet without either having to travel for a face-to-face meeting. Arraignments and other legal proceedings are conducted by videoconference. Few of the participants in any of these situations have the illusion that they are located at the same sites, but many of them find they can ignore the fact that they are at multiple sites and proceed as if they were all together.

1.2 BENEFITS, LIMITS, GROWTH

Why use videoconferencing? It is easy for some of us to take the benefits of videoconferencing for granted, but we should not do so. Usually, the first benefit cited is economic. A typical business meeting of people from different locations, even a short one, can easily cost thousands of dollars for travel and lodging. Other costs of such a meeting, for instance, the time the participants spend traveling, may be much more important than the direct travel costs. Depending on the circumstances, a videoconference may be a much more effective alternative, saving direct costs, avoiding travel time, and possibly enabling discussions that might not otherwise be possible—when travel is not possible the choices are either a teleconference or no meeting at all. It is relatively straightforward to add a person to a videoconference while it is in progress if the person is available at any of the locations participating in the conference. In a meeting requiring travel, asking another person to join the meeting is usually not practical. Videoconferencing enables individuals and organizations to manage time and opportunities that would otherwise be lost.

Let's take a closer look at direct costs. It is feasible to equip a conference room with a reasonable video system for roughly $20,000. Depreciating that amount over three years, the monthly equipment cost per room can be kept to well under $1,000. Costs of intracontinental long-distance communication for the video systems can easily be kept well under $100 per hour. Even if a room videoconferencing system is used only once a month, it is likely to cost less than direct travel costs for a meeting. These are fairly conservative figures; some users will see better cost benefits of videoconferencing. With more frequent use, the direct cost benefit clearly favors videoconferencing over travel. Similar arguments can be used to justify the costs of desktop videoconferencing systems. In this case, the cost benefit may be realized sooner, because desktop systems are much less expensive.

Of course, you could say it would be more cost effective to use telephones. But in many circumstances, telephones are insufficient. Visual contact between people may or may not be the qualitative difference that makes an activity effective. Those who participate in multiway telephone conferences know that communication is seriously impaired without visual contact between people and shared access to documents, visual aids, diagnostic equipment, stock tickers, and so on.[1] To help reduce these barriers, audiographics systems have been developed as a means to augment telephones with graphics such as shared documents. For some activities, audiographics may be sufficient. We believe that audiographics are a major aspect of videoconferencing, and that motion video is becoming sufficiently affordable such that most applications will include video. Much of the discussion in this book is not about motion video *per se*, but about the aspects of videoconferencing encompassed by audiographics.

Cost of travel versus cost of videoconferencing is often not the correct comparison. Videoconferencing is more than just travel replacement, it is an enabler of communication that otherwise would not take place. Physical meetings are necessary from time to time, but videoconferencing users can make more electronic "trips" in a day (or week) than they can physical ones, and with much less wear and tear. The telephone is still useful, but when it is insufficient, and a physical meeting is not possible, videoconferencing technologies allow meetings that would otherwise fail, or perhaps not even be attempted.

Some limits might not be overcome. Some individuals have a reluctance[2] to being "on camera" and resist the new technology, just as some avoid telephones and airplanes. The boundaries between sites of a conference are visible and inhibit some activities, e.g., side conversations during a meeting, and preclude others, e.g., physical contact.

As with other new technologies, estimating the extent and pace of growth is necessarily guesswork. Analogies to the computer industry have significant defects, but are still useful. Some have said that videoconferencing is of limited value and that few systems will be deployed. When IBM began making computers, there were serious questions of whether more than a few tens of computers would ever be sold and used! Rapidly increasing sales of videoconferencing contradict the minimal usage predictions. At the other extreme, some suggest that videoconferencing is the next "killer application"

---

[1] The first words of many multiway telephone conferences are "Does everyone have a copy of the faxed charts?"

[2] For most people, any such reluctance goes away with experience.

(in the sense that computer spreadsheets were the "killer application" that spawned the personal computer market) and that it will drive demand for computers and communication lines. For the next few years, at least, there are sufficient obstacles to deny the "killer application" scenarios. But it is reasonable to expect growth sufficient to strain the delivery capacity of equipment suppliers and communication lines. In the personal computer industry, local-area networks (LANs) seemed ready for widespread usage every year from 1984 forward. Each new year was declared "The Year of the LAN." LANs became pervasive by 1989. For several years now, analysts have forecast widespread availability of videoconferencing. Some year soon, the forecasts will have become reality, without a recognizable "Year of Videoconferencing."

1.3 TECHNOLOGY BOTTLENECKS AND BUMPS IN THE ROAD

Let us now consider the technology issues that are being resolved in anticipation of the "Year of Videoconferencing." As we said earlier, the biggest technical hurdle in videoconferencing is sending large amounts of data across existing networks that were designed for much smaller amounts. The existing networks are those intended for telephony, both local and long distance, and those intended for computer communication, primarily internetworked LANs. Computer communication across wide areas typically uses the networks originally developed for telephony. The first thing we want to talk about is sending sound and video across local and long-distance telephone networks.

Sounds audible to humans have a frequency range up to roughly 20,000 cycles per second, or Hertz, abbreviated Hz. The sounds required for speech use a much smaller frequency range, up to roughly 3,500 Hz. The telephone network is designed to transmit sounds in this smaller frequency range. Originally, this was done in terms of analog signals, where the strength of the signal on the telephone wires is directly analogous to the loudness of the sound, and the voltage of the signal alternates (between positive and negative) at the frequency of the sound. Most telephone service for residences and small organizations today uses the same analog conventions that were established early in the twentieth century.

Analog telephone service is not well suited to sophisticated connections of calls, either local and long distance. Also, when analog signals are sent long distance, the quality of the signals always degrades. For these and other reasons, long-distance telephone service and private branch exchanges (PBX) for connecting telephones within large organizations began converting to digital signals in the 1960s. Essentially all long-distance service is now digital, as is most PBX service.

For home telephones and other phones connected directly to the telephone company switching facility, "the last mile," the circuit from the home to the switching facility, is usually still analog. The telephone uses analog signals. These are converted to and from digital signals at the switching facility. When these circuits are used for fax and computer purposes, digital information must be converted to and from analog at both ends, because the switching facility is always performing the conversion. Fax machines and computers use <u>modems</u> (MOdulator/DEModulators) to perform the conversion. The maximum achievable data rate for modems using analog telephone circuits appears to be about 34,000 bits per second. (Higher rates can be achieved in one direction, under some circumstances, but conferencing usually requires equal rates in both directions.)

Digital representations of sounds use numbers, usually called <u>samples</u>, to represent the loudness of the sound. The signal-to-noise ratio is primarily determined by the range of numbers in a sample. Seven-bit samples are sufficient for speech, and 16-bit samples are sufficient for high-fidelity representation of music. Two samples per cycle of sound are sufficient to get good representation. Thus, for speech, roughly 8,000 seven-bit samples per second are enough. For music, roughly 40,000 sixteen-bit samples per second are needed for high fidelity; Compact Discs use 44,000 sixteen-bit samples per second, and professional recording equipment uses 48,000 sixteen-bit samples per second.

Digital telephone systems are designed to handle connection and transmission of many channels of 56,000 (8,000 × 7) or 64,000 (8,000 × 8) bits per second, each channel representing the sounds of a telephone conversation.[3] In the United States, 56,000-bit channels were used originally, but the trend worldwide is toward 64,000-bit channels. A 64,000-bit channel is referred to as a "<u>B-channel</u>" (B for "bearer"). A 56,000-bit channel is "restricted." A typical telephone line in urban areas is capable of transmitting a pair of B-channels. If video is going to travel on the telephone network, it should fit within a few of these B-channels. As we now see in discussing the components of video signals, transmitting video within a reasonable number of B-channels is a significant challenge.

A picture on a television screen consists of many small dots, called <u>pixels</u> ("picture elements"). These are intended to be small enough that only the composite picture is seen, not the dots, but the pixels are readily visible if one

---

[3] In the computer industry, it is normal to use "K" (kilo) and "M" (mega) to represent 1,024 and 1,048,576, respectively. In the communications industry, it is normal to use these to represent 1,000 and 1,000,000, respectively. For example, a 56,000 bit per second line would often be referred to as "56K." In general, we will limit our use of these abbreviations, so as to avoid confusion.

looks closely at the screen. For North American broadcast systems,[4] there is a maximum of roughly 360 to 400 pixels per row. Roughly 480 visible rows are broadcast, but most televisions show slightly more than half the rows. For videoconferencing (worldwide), a standard picture consists of 352-pixel horizontal resolution by 288-pixel vertical resolution. A single 352×288 picture is usually referred to as a "frame."

A 352×288 frame equals 101,376 pixels. To directly represent a full-color pixel 24 bits are required (8 bits for each of the primary colors of light, red, green, and blue). Thus one picture could take $101{,}376 \times 24 = 2{,}433{,}024$ bits. Motion requires 15 to 30 picture frames per second, so full-color, full-motion standard resolution video *could* require up to 73 million bits per second, well over a thousand B-channels! Fortunately, there are bridges across this apparent chasm.

By discarding less important information (for example, using far fewer than 24 bits of color per pixel) and coding the information (for example, only sending the differences between frames, not the entire pictures) it is possible to send a tiny fraction of those 73 million bits and still get good results. A pair of B-channels, across a telephone circuit, gives acceptable results for many uses. With today's coding technology, 6 B-channels (three telephone circuits) are enough to get very good results. Use of more than 6 B-channels, say, 12 or more, provides excellent results.

The most aggressive coding techniques have led to products intended for use with modems and analog telephone lines, using about 20,000 bits per second for the video. These products use lower pixel resolution, 176×144 or lower, and low frame rates. These products are becoming available in 1996 as a "bundled" aspect of personal computers sold for home use, so they are likely to be present in large quantities. It is unknown how well low resolution and frame rates will be accepted for home usage. For some families, even low-quality video will be a wonderful benefit if it allows members to see each other, whereas for other situations the resolution and frame rate will be too limited to be considered valuable. It is not likely that low resolution and frame rates will be considered sufficient for "serious" applications.

Coding techniques can also be used to reduce the bandwidth required for audio, but not by such dramatic factors. Instead of using a full B-channel for audio, as implied earlier, speech quality audio can be fit into as little as one-tenth of a B-channel.

The primary alternative to using the telephone network directly is to use the LANs and other networks designed for computer communication. The most overused phrase of 1994 was "The Information Superhighway," but we

---

[4] There are many differences in numbers of visible pixels, based on the broadcast standard in use (three standards are in use by different countries) and the design of the television receiver.

will abuse the phrase a few more times to depict the bumps in that road to videoconferencing! The telephone network is based on circuit switching, which means that once a telephone call (or videoconference) is established, circuits (B-channels) are dedicated to the call. Most computer networks are based on packet switching, which means that packets (packages) of data travel on the same network, much like boxes on a conveyor belt or on trucks on the highway. As long as the packets flow smoothly, a computer network is a very good highway for audio and video data, providing the capacity equivalence of many B-channels. However, there are almost always traffic jams on the information highway. When the jams are minor, audio and video can get through in time and things work well. When the jams are major, conversation is halted. Improving computer networks to manage traffic jams and improving videoconferencing technology to mask the effects of those traffic jams are major goals of current development.

In 1996 a plethora of products and prototypes for telephony have been introduced for the Internet. As Internet telephony becomes practical and standardized, this will benefit Internet videoconferencing. We discuss this further in Chapters 2 and 13.

1.4 REPRESENTATIVE SYSTEM CHARACTERISTICS

If (obviously, a "big if") adequate telephone or computer networks are available, then videoconferencing is practical for many individuals and organizations. Videoconferencing is capable of saving travel time and money, and enables communication that otherwise would not take place.

Figure 1.1 shows a representative roll-about videoconferencing system circa 1996. This is a good example to start with. From it we can consider the commonality and extensions to both desktop and larger room environments. A roll-about system is a medium-scale system intended for use by small groups in typical meetings. It is transportable from room to room, as long as the room has appropriate connections to telephone or local-area networks.

The cabinet under the television monitor houses a personal computer and additional equipment to support conferencing. In most cases, the additional equipment is installed inside the personal computer. The camera on top of the monitor is motorized to enable convenient positioning (pan, tilt, zoom in/out) by the participants.

The core technology is based on an industry standard personal computer, with added support for audio and audio coding, motion video and coding, and communication protocols and interfaces. We reap two major benefits by beginning with the PC. First, by taking advantage of the mass production

Figure 1.1 Roll-about videoconferencing system

and low cost of the PC, many of the conferencing functions can be provided using relatively low-cost PC hardware and software. Second, the integration of the PC makes its normal capabilities directly available to the conference participants.

The television monitor is very appropriate to motion video, but has relatively few pixels per inch (roughly 30) compared to a computer monitor (roughly 75 pixels per inch). With a group system and this relatively low resolution (pixels per inch) monitor, it is usually appropriate to devote the full monitor screen to motion video from the remote site(s). To display shared presentation materials, shared marker boards, shared computer applications, etc., either the monitor must be switched away from motion video or we must resort to overlaying video with these alternate images. (This is analogous to showing both a forecaster and a weather map on a newscast.)

For an individual, a desktop system is both more manageable in physical size and more functional. The user is usually sitting much closer to the monitor than with a group system. Rather than dedicating the full screen to motion video from a remote site, the remote site video is shown in a window, of perhaps 352×288 pixels out of a total of $1,024 \times 768$ pixels. The leftover

Figure 1.2   Desktop Windows example

screen pixels can be used for a local site ("preview") video window, shared presentation materials, computer applications, and other images. Figure 1.2 depicts a personal computer display with a collection of such windows.

For a larger scale room system, two or more monitors are used to allow for display of multiple sources of video, shared presentation materials, and computer applications. Figure 1.3 shows such a system.

1.5 APPLICATIONS

There are many current applications of videoconferencing, which will be discussed in coming chapters, especially in Chapter 6. The purpose of this section is to give a quick summary of some of the characteristics of current and near-term use.

Business Meetings. Larger companies with multiple locations have videoconferencing rooms at each of their locations. They may even have videoconferencing systems in most of their conference rooms. The systems used are typically midscale, larger than the roll-about shown in Figure 1.1, but not as complete as the system in Figure 1.3. The rooms and videoconferencing equipment are scheduled as part of the overall meeting scheduling.

Figure 1.3 Large-scale videoconferencing system

Use for intracompany meetings is probably much more prevalent than for meetings involving other companies. One of the explanations for the prevalence of internal meetings is familiarity of the participants with each other. People seem to be more comfortable using videoconferencing with people they already know than as part of a first meeting. Once companies become familiar with videoconferencing capabilities, they use it extensively. A large financial institution installed systems in two large cities 1,500 miles apart. The company anticipated use for certain emergencies, and dedicated communication circuits were already in place. The systems quickly came into use six hours per day for collaboration among groups that had been unable to get travel funds to visit each other. One large multinational company reportedly spent $500,000 on long-distance charges for videoconferencing in 1994. That figure leads to a guess that that company keeps dozens of videoconferencing facilities busy at least half the business day.

Distance Learning.   Most state universities in the United States have multiple campuses, typically a primary campus and several additional campuses, and most of these have videoconferencing facilities for instructional purposes. It is often the case that a single instructor can conduct a class simultaneously across several of the campuses by videoconference. The precedent has been set for decades by broadcast lectures sent from a central site.

There are obvious limitations with the broadcast approach, for example, interaction between the instructor and students, shared use of marker boards, etc. Current videoconferencing approaches can overcome these limitations and also provide capabilities analogous to traditional classroom facilities. For example, student response terminals can be used not only to give the effect of "raising hands," but also to communicate specific responses. The same approaches apply outside of universities, of course, in corporate, government, and other learning and training environments.

Professional Conferences.   Is a professional conference a business meeting or a learning event? In many cases it is both of these and more. The number of conferences is both daunting and tempting for many of us because there are many more interesting conferences than we can attend. (We can't spend full time going to conferences.) Fortunately, it is more and more common for major portions of technical conferences and similar meetings to be available, at least with audio and video, on the Internet. With Internet video availability, I can easily (and discreetly) attend the most interesting portions of a technical conference without leaving my office.

Telemedicine.   Medical practice is tending toward higher degrees of specialization, along with increasing numbers of general practitioners. In rural or remote areas, there may be no physicians at all. Videoconferencing is being used to allow specialists and generalists to collaborate more effectively in diagnosis and treatment, not only by allowing physicians at different sites to view a single patient, but also to share radiographic and other diagnostic information and instrumentation. Even in urban areas, videoconferencing systems are useful for patient monitoring, potentially allowing patients to remain at home. Again, it is not just motion video that would be communicated in a patient/physician visit, but diagnostic information (heart rate, blood pressure, temperature, etc.) from instruments that can be jointly managed during the visit.

Financial.   There is an obvious surge toward electronic funds transfer, automated teller machines, and home banking services via telephone and personal computer. On the other hand, some services (for example, opening/closing accounts, loan application, and so forth) still seem to require human intervention, possibly with more senior personnel. In many instances, these activities can be handled at a branch location via videoconferencing kiosks. In brokerage firms, traders often have a plethora of computing and information devices on their desks. One of these devices is likely to be a videoconferencing system, used for contact with other brokers, with clients, and with sources of information.

Product Support. Remote support of products by telephone is routine in many industries, covering everything from household appliances to manufacturing systems. In many cases, the customer problems are much more readily resolved if the support person can see the product and/or the customer can see visual examples from the support person. For sufficiently expensive products, manufacturers find it worthwhile to include videoconferencing equipment with the products to better enable remote support.

Legal. Some preliminary legal proceedings, such as arraignments and depositions, are handled by videoconference. The New York district attorney's office uses desktop videoconferencing systems for arraignments. Rather than requiring the arresting officer to appear in person in court, the officer participates by videoconference, lessening travel, scheduling, and other difficulties.

Employment Interviews. Travel for employment interviews is often a significant impediment for both applicant and employer, especially for initial interviews. By using videoconferences for initial interviews, the employer is able to better evaluate a pool of candidates, then have on-site interviews as warranted.

Sales Kiosks. Direct sales of many kinds of merchandise via telephone and television have been a significant trend in recent years. The customer *and* the salesperson often desire better communication than is achievable with a telephone call, and they desire an interactivity not possible with the television shopping networks. Videoconferencing kiosks allow the centralization efficiency of telemarketing, with added communication benefits for both parties.

1.6 THE FUTURE

Communication Infrastructure. Better telephone service, better data communication, the entertainment potential of video on demand, and interactive home video are all creating demand for a "faster, better, cheaper" communication infrastructure. The deployment trend toward pervasive, high-capacity communication (the "superhighway") is likely not as rapid as was predicted in the merger and partnership frenzy of 1993, but it also seems inevitable. Since adequacy of communication infrastructure is the biggest issue in implementation of videoconferencing, continuing improvements in the infrastructure are a major catalyst for videoconferencing.

System Costs. Semiconductor and computing performance and cost–performance ratio continue to improve without foreseeable barriers. These trends have a twofold benefit to the effectiveness and cost of videoconferencing equipment. First, the capabilities and costs of specialized hardware follow the general trend. Second, the capabilities of mass-produced computers more adequately match the needs of videoconferencing, reducing the need for specialized equipment.

New Applications.   As availability and capability improve, many new applications will be found. Telecommuting will become a reality for a noticeable fraction of the workforce. Entertainment and social events will be augmented by, or even based on, videoconferencing.

New Approaches.   The increase in communication and computing capability will stimulate improvements in providing the illusion of shared space. For example, with current technology, conferences among multiple sites typically allow only one or a few of the sites to be seen concurrently, often in an unrealistic fashion. Better technology will enable more sites to be visually active, and may allow "virtual reality" approaches to presenting the many sites as a shared space.

Chapter 2

Where We Came From

This chapter introduces the most important historical background for video-conferencing. To grossly oversimplify, videoconferencing is the addition of television to telephony, so we need to talk about basics in both telephony and television. It also helps to consider the influences from the vendors of video-conferencing products and the computing industry. The final topic of this chapter is an introduction to the standards that make it possible for different vendors' products to interoperate.

2.1 TELEPHONY

The telephone system provides (1) stiff competition with videoconferencing (if a phone call is good enough, why bother with more?); (2) the circuits frequently used for videoconferencing; and (3) a set of expectations for audio quality, ease of use, responsiveness, reliability, etc.

For the near future, an optimistic view of videoconferencing might predict that there will be a few videoconferencing systems for every thousand telephones. Videoconferencing will be used more and more where the telephone is not good enough. Why might the telephone not be good enough? If I need to gauge your reaction to what I am saying, I may want to observe your facial expressions and body position. If you are reading from a document, then

I need to be looking at the same pages. Without videoconferencing, I might say "wait a minute while I fax this to you." It is not too far a stretch to say that faxes and electronic mail are "clumsy audiographics."

Many types of telephone circuits are relevant to videoconferencing. The most important type of circuit is basic rate ISDN, also known as BRI. ISDN stands for Integrated Services Digital Network.[1] To oversimplify, ISDN is a standardized approach to providing digital service from digital telephones. Unlike conventional telephony (Plain Old Telephone Service, POTS) with a mixture of analog telephones, analog circuits, and digital circuits, ISDN is digital at the end points all the way across a fully digital network. Since ISDN has standardized definitions, any manufacturer's ISDN phone should be configurable to work with any other manufacturer's PBX, etc. Such standardization is unlike pre-ISDN digital phones and PBXs, that is, non-ISDN digital phones must be designed to match a specific manufacturer's PBX. BRI circuits are intended for connection of individual telephones. At this writing, ISDN service is readily available in Australia, Europe, Hong Kong, Japan, and Singapore, and is becoming readily available in the United States. A BRI circuit has two 64,000 bits/second B-channels and one 16,000 bits/second D-channel. The D-channel is used for dialing and other signaling.

For telephony, the advantages of BRI over conventional analog circuits include (1) the general benefits of digital approaches, for example, audio quality; (2) the availability of a second audio channel; and (3) the features and flexibility of using the D-channel for signaling. In spite of these advantages, inertia favors continued use of analog phones. Also, some of the benefits of the D-channel can be provided through innovative use of analog phones. (Signaling features such as Caller ID and Call Waiting are more elegantly implemented using the D-channel, but can be provided with analog circuits.) However, ISDN availability and usage has gained momentum with recognition of applications and requirements that cannot be satisfied by existing analog circuits. For example, analog circuits are used frequently for communication between personal computers. A modem is used to convert the computer's digital information to audio tones at the sending end and to convert from audio back to digital at the receiving end. It is quite impressive that inexpensive modem products achieve up to 33,600 bits/second on a conventional analog circuit, since this rate is close to the theoretical maximum. However, a BRI line allows more than four times faster transfer, with greater

---

[1] Widespread availability of ISDN has been anticipated by some since the mid-1980s. Skeptics would say that ISDN stands for "I Still Don't Know." Robert Metcalfe, co-inventor of Ethernet, said, in early 1995, that 1994 was the "Year of ISDN" and that ISDN stands for "Information Superhighway Delivered Now."

reliability. A rate of 128,000 bits/second with BRI is enough for a reasonable quality videoconference; 33,600 is not.

We must acknowledge that many manufacturers are providing products for videoconferencing on conventional analog telephone lines. These POTS products are likely to proliferate to the point where there are far more of these than any other form of videoconferencing product. However, we believe the bandwidth limitation is just too great to ever achieve good quality video. For this reason, we generally do not discuss these products in this book.

Many other types of telephone circuits are relevant to videoconferencing. Of special interest are Switched 56, T1, and PRI. These and others are discussed in detail in Chapter 8, but it is useful to describe them here briefly:

- Switched 56 is a 56,000 bit/second circuit, designed for dial-up customer use, which became available in the United States before ISDN. Though similar to BRI, Switched 56 is harder to attach to than BRI, because of the equipment needed at the customers' premises. A typical videoconference requires two Switched 56 circuits versus one BRI to get comparable bandwidth. As BRI becomes readily available it is expected that use of Switched 56 will diminish.

- T1 is a higher speed circuit used in the United States for dedicated connections, capable of 1,544,000 bits/second. The electrical connection uses two pairs of telephone wires. T1 circuits are widely used for connecting PBXs to central telephone offices. T1 circuits are also used to connect distant LAN segments. Similar E1 circuits, capable of 1,928,000 bits/second, are used in Europe and Asia.

- PRI (primary rate ISDN) is electrically similar to T1 and E1, but can be switched (dialed). A PRI circuit has 23 B-channels and a 64,000-bit D-channel for signaling (1,536,000 bits/second) in the United States, and 30 B-channels plus a D-channel in Europe and Asia.

Perhaps most important are the user-visible characteristics set by the telephone systems in the industrialized parts of the world. By dialing, at most, a country code, an area code, and a local number, it is possible to reach essentially any telephone. The dialing is essentially the same whether the phones are conventional analog, proprietary digital, ISDN, or cellular, and calls can go through without regard to the types of phones at the opposite ends. The delay between dial and ring is usually a few seconds. A failed call is usually due to the called party's phone being either in use or not answered. Audio quality, though not high fidelity, is typically more than adequate for conversation. Though seemingly basic, these characteristics required substantial engineering and standardization to achieve. Providing equivalent characteristics for videoconferencing is not trivial and, as of this writing, is not always achieved.

2.2 TELEVISION

2.2.1 The General Experience

Just as telephones are ubiquitous in industrialized countries, so are televisions. Group videoconferencing systems typically use television sets as monitors. So it is inevitable that the conscious and subconscious reactions to videoconferencing will be in comparison to television. We already discussed resolution and frame rate parameters in Section 1.3. Though resolution and frame rate must be acceptable in comparison to television, the more daunting comparisons relate to the studio production of commercial and public television. Whether the program is documentary or entertainment, a production crew and an array of equipment produce the sounds and images that captivate viewers. In a typical videoconference, either there is no equivalent of the production crew or some of the conference participants attempt to operate the equipment to improve the sounds and images at each end. In television production, there are usually several (sometimes, many) microphones so that all sounds are captured properly. One of the crew operates an audio mixing console to turn microphones on and off at appropriate times and to adjust the volume levels associated with the microphones. It is not hard to provide several microphones in a videoconferencing room, but where is the equivalent of the audio engineer? From the users' perspective, videoconferencing equipment should handle audio mixing, etc., without human intervention. Correspondingly, a television studio has several cameras, an operator for each camera, a video engineer that controls the switching and mixing of the images from the cameras, and a director that instructs the camera operators ("move in on her face" or "pan over to the hallway") and coordinates the activities of the crew members. To be fully effective, videoconferencing equipment should handle these activities. Though videoconferencing equipment cannot achieve the production quality of a television studio (if it could, the studios would use the same equipment!), it can automate or partially automate many of these functions.

2.2.2 Color Representations

Beyond user perceptions, television has had a strong influence on the technology of videoconferencing equipment. The video cameras, recorders, and receivers that are mass produced for consumer and professional use are suitable for videoconferencing. Further, videoconferencing equipment needs to be compatible with television equipment. For example, it must have the ability to connect to a VCR to play a videotape or record a conference. Third, many of the technical issues that had to be solved in the development of modern television are similar to issues that had to be solved for videoconferencing, and the solutions are similar. In particular, the representation of color in videoconferencing is more like the handling of color in television than representation of color in computer graphics.

RGB Representation. Initially, computer graphics used monochrome (black and white), before color was affordable. The next step was grayscale, where each pixel could have a range of luminance (brightness intensity) values from black, through many shades of gray, to white. To represent color, computers normally use the primary colors of light, red, green, and blue. This is known as RGB. Appropriate mixtures of these primary colors can be used to represent any color. For example, black is represented by R(ed), G(reen), and B(lue) all at zero intensity, white is R, G, and B all at a value of one (full intensity), yellow is B at zero, R and G at one, etc. This representation facilitates the design of both hardware and software for manipulation of images and colors at the pixel level. But RGB does not fit so well with either traditional television design or the coding needed for videoconferencing, for reasons we consider next.

Luminance Representations. Television also began as monochrome. Development of color television had to allow for strict compatibility between color signals and monochrome receivers so that color broadcasts could be received well on the televisions already in use. With RGB representation, this is very difficult. It is more natural, both from an engineering perspective and a human physiology perspective, to emphasize luminance first and then provide additional information to represent color properly. Assuming this additional information does not interfere with reception on a monochrome television, this is the most direct approach to providing compatibility between color broadcasts and monochrome reception. This approach recognizes that our human perception of images is primarily dependent on brightness. In a very dark or very bright environment, our recognition of color is limited or lost, but we can recognize shapes and motion.

In addition to luminance, the additional information is hue, the relative proportion of green and red, and saturation, the intensity of color in the image. These three components are usually directly controllable on a television set. The luminance control is often called "picture." The hue control is often called "tint," and the saturation control is often called "color." Hue and saturation are often referred to as the chrominance components.

Several similar but mathematically different luminance-based representations are used in television, each of which is preferred in particular countries and continents. The luminance component is consistently represented by the variable Y, but there are subtle differences in the symbols and values used for representation of hue and saturation. The preferred approach for television in Europe is the YUV representation used in the PAL (phase alternating lines) television broadcast standard. YUV is also the preferred representation, worldwide, for coding of video for videoconferencing. The preferred approach for television in North America is the YIQ representation used in the NTSC (National Television Standards Committee) broadcast standard. It is a simple computation to convert among RGB, YIQ, and YUV (see Chapter 7).

Color Representation in Videoconferencing.   A typical videoconferencing system uses either NTSC or PAL cameras for input, uses YUV representation inside the system, and uses RGB, NTSC, or PAL for output. The choice of input and output devices depends on the type of system and where in the world it is used. A system using computer monitors for display provides RGB output, while one that uses television monitors will use the representation incorporated in local television.

For coding motion video, there are immediate opportunities available with the luminance-based representations that are not available with the primary color representations. The color (U and V) components can be represented with less precision than the luminance (Y) component, reducing the amount of information transmitted without significantly reducing quality. This imbalance of precision is used in television, where much more of the broadcast channel is dedicated to the luminance, and roughly one-fourth as much of the channel is used for the color components. Another common coding technique is to transmit luminance information for individual pixels, but to average the color information across a group of nearby pixels and only transmit the averages.

Electrical Signals.   A final aspect of television component technology worth mentioning is the composite video versus S-Video signals used to connect components electrically. Most inexpensive cameras, VCRs, and televisions use composite video, where luminance, hue, and saturation are multiplexed on a single signal wire on the sending end and separated at the receiving end. Composite video usually uses single-pin "phono" connectors, the same as the ones that are typically used for audio connections. S-Video keeps the luminance and chrominance component signals separate on separate signal wires, using multipin connectors. S-Video leads to higher image quality, because the degradation of combining and separating the components is avoided.

2.3 NEC, CLI, PICTURETEL, VTEL, INTEL, . . .

The earliest practical room videoconferencing systems across switched digital networks were Nippon Electric Corporation (NEC) systems developed in the early 1980s. These required six million bit/second channel capacities for good performance. The equipment cost for a single system was well over $100,000. Soon afterward, Compression Labs (CLI) introduced systems that produced good results using T1 circuits. However, the systems were still very expensive—both for the equipment and the T1 circuits. PictureTel pioneered systems with lower cost equipment and substantially lower cost circuits. The PictureTel systems were the first to work well with a pair of Switched 56 circuits. These systems made dial-up conferences practical, whereas the predecessor systems typically required preestablished connections. VTEL introduced systems that supported presentation materials and shared computer applications and integration of peripherals, extending the capabilities beyond audio and video. In general, the vendors' approaches were not able to communicate with each other and the vendors recognized the need for standards that would allow communication between different systems. This is a short summary, but it does highlight the major developments of the 1980s.

In the 1990s the omnipresence of the personal computer as a primary business appliance was well established. Most of the major videoconferencing vendors developed products intended for use with personal computers. Some of these were based on room system technology and were compatible with those systems, and some were based on unique, incompatible technologies. Many other companies, including large companies such as AT&T, IBM, and Intel, began developing products for desktop environments.

At this writing, the videoconferencing industry is reacting and growing, based on these influences. Literally dozens of approaches to desktop conferencing are vying for mind-share and market share. The need for standardized approaches is stronger than ever, and consensus is forming around definitions for intervendor communications. As the longer established videoconferencing vendors address both desktop and room system products, the trend is to base as much of the technology as possible on personal computer components. From this computing base, it is possible to develop compatible, lower cost products that apply to both environments.

2.4 ROLE OF COMPUTING

The personal computing industry has undergone unprecedented growth rates in capabilities and unit volumes, from the hobbyist systems of the mid-1970s to the Apple II, to the IBM PC, the Macintosh, and, most recently, the phenomenal growth of systems based on Microsoft Windows™ and the Intel 386, 486, and Pentium™ family of processors. A large portion of the professional workforce depends on personal computers for their normal work activities and a large portion of these people depend on personal computers for electronic mail, faxes, shared data, and other communication. Personal computers are becoming common in homes—for working at home, for education, and for entertainment. Communication via electronic mail and information services such as America Online and dial-up access to the Internet are also significant aspects of home computer use.

Though there have been, and are, numerous applications for personal computers, many view the arrival of the computerized spreadsheet, first with VisiCalc on the Apple II, then with Lotus 1-2-3 on the IBM PC, as the "killer application" that catalyzed the mid-1980s growth of the personal computer industry. Computer companies ever since have sought the next application that would spur even higher customer acceptance and growth rates. Much of the focus has been on increasing the communication capabilities of the computers and enabling them to handle multimedia, that is, audio and video. Apple, Intel, Microsoft, and others have been especially successful at promoting a vision of the personal computer as a multipurpose information and communication appliance.

Capabilities for generating sounds have been part of PCs since the early days, but the growth of the PC as an entertainment and communication device has led to significantly higher quality and capability, from "bloops and beeps" to high-fidelity stereo. Though the bare bones PC may still be at the "bloop and beep" level, many of the newly purchased systems include audio capabilities suitable for sophisticated entertainment, including music with CD quality. Unfortunately, audio support on PCs is often only half-duplex, that is, suitable for either input or output but not both simultaneously. Full-duplex (simultaneous input and output) support is a requirement for effective audio communication, whether by telephone or full videoconference.

The growth in processing power, memory sizes, and storage sizes in personal computers has been so rapid that it seems revolutionary, even though it has been evolutionary at any particular time. Two areas have seen more revolutionary jumps in characteristics: removable storage and connectivity. For many years, the primary removable storage device on a PC was a diskette. Though these grew in capacity from 160 kilobytes (KB) to 1.44 megabytes (MB) and more, the recent radical transition has been from diskettes to CD-ROMs, with a capacity of 650MB. For many years, office PCs were stand-alone machines. By the late 1980s, the typical office PC was connected to a local-area network with a nominal transfer rate of 10 megabits (Mb) per second. At this writing, 10 Mb/second is painfully slow, relative to processor and memory speeds, but a widespread jump to the next level of network performance seems as frustratingly far away as 10 Mb/second seemed in the mid-1980s. (Dial-up connectivity for personal computers is based on the modems and BRI lines discussed in Section 2.1.)

All of the capabilities discussed thus far beg for another—digital motion video. The PC industry continues the search for the right way to support motion video, one that is both effective and inexpensive. Part of the problem is the recognition of at least two different requirements—for stored video and for interactive videoconferencing. Stored video is intended primarily for later viewing, whether for entertainment, training, or some other purpose. It is usually assumed that such video is stored on a CD-ROM, or a file server. If it is acceptable to use special equipment or take extra time to code the video, then additional techniques are available that are not practical when "real-time" coding, as required for videoconferencing, is needed. A plethora of coding methods has been proposed for stored video on the PC, most notably the Motion Picture Experts Group (MPEG) standard and Intel's Indeo™ algorithms. The QuickTime™ software for the Macintosh and Video for Windows for the PC have made stored video readily accessible on personal computers.

2.5 ROLE OF STANDARDS

The objective of videoconferencing is communication. The historical tendency of the major vendors of room videoconferencing systems was to develop systems with unique protocols that would not communicate with other vendors' systems. The International Telecommunications Union–Telecommunication Standardization Sector (known as the ITU-T, formerly known as the CCITT) establishes "recommendations" for standard protocols, and the major vendors, having helped develop them, adopt these standards. Most of the major U.S. vendors' products support both proprietary and ITU-T modes, and much of the actual usage is in proprietary modes. Most of the major Asian and European vendors' products support only ITU-T modes.

The ITU-T recommendations are numerous. Some are primarily applicable to videoconferencing, and some apply to related technologies. The main family of videoconferencing recommendations for ISDN is H.320, "Narrowband Visual Telephone Systems and Terminal Equipment," which encompasses most of the other recommendations by citations. In principle, all of the capabilities described in this book are covered by current recommendations or will be covered by planned recommendations. In practice, only a subset of the capabilities is likely to be standardized by ITU-T and other capabilities, for example, some of those most closely tied to personal computers and the Internet are likely to be dominated by *de facto* standards and standards established by the Internet Engineering Task Force. Some of the major recommendations encompassed by H.320 include the following:

H.261: "Video Codec for Audiovisual Services at Px64 Kbit/s" has been known informally as "P × 64"[2] because it defines video coding based on *P* 64,000 bit/second channels. (*P* is typically 2 or more.) Codec is a term for "coder/decoder." We consider H.261 in Chapter 9.

H.221: "Frame Structure for a 64 to 1920 Kbit/s Channel in Audiovisual Teleservices" defines the usage of *P* B-channels to transmit multiplexed audio, video, other data, and control signals. We discuss aspects of H.221 in Chapters 3, 8, and 12.

H.242: "System for Establishing Communication between Audiovisual Terminals using Digital Channels up to 2 Mbit/s" defines initiation of communication between systems and "capabilities negotiation." Capabilities negotiation allows dissimilar systems to recognize their common capabilities and communicate using those capabilities.

H. 230: "Frame-Synchronous Control and Indication Signals for Audiovisual Systems" defines simple multipoint (more than two system) control and communication network maintenance functions.

These are the basic standards explicitly cited by H.320. There are literally dozens of related standards either completed or in definition stages. Some of the most important include G.711, G.722, and G.728, which define audio coding of varying qualities and bandwidth requirements, and the T.120 "User Data Transmission Using a Multi-Layer Protocol (MLP)" series, which defines protocols appropriate to shared presentations, applications, and other capabilities beyond audio and video. We devote most of Chapter 12 to T.120.

The main family of videoconferencing recommendations for POTS is H.324, "Terminal for Low Bitrate Multimedia Communication." Although H.324 includes H.261 as part of the recommendation, all current H.324 products emphasize H.263.

H.263: "Video Coding for Low Bitrate Communication" includes additional techniques to obtain improved video (compared to H.261) at low bit rates, say, 20,000 bits/second. H.263 is discussed in Section 9.2.9.

In place of H.221 and H.245, H.324 uses, respectively,

---

[2] Read as "P times 64."

H.223: "Multiplexing Protocol for Low Bitrate Multimedia Communication."

H.245: "Control Protocol for Multimedia Communication." It is anticipated that H.245 will displace H.242 in a future version of H.320.

H.324 uses a lower bit rate audio coding method, G.723, which achieves speech-level quality in 6,300 bits/second or less. G.723 is discussed in Section 10.1.5. T.120 is used with H.324 for the same purposes as with H.320. [See SCHA96 for comprehensive discussion of H.324 videoconferencing.]

The main family of videoconferencing recommendations for IP networks is H.323, "Visual Telephone Systems and Terminal equipment for Local Area Networks Which Provide a Non-Guaranteed Quality of Service." H.323 uses both H.261 and H.263 for video. H.323 uses H.225, "Media Stream Packetization and Synchronization on Non-Guaranteed Quality of Service LANs," in place of H.221. It also uses H.245, G.711, G.722, G.723, G.728, and T.120. A major aspect of the H.323 definition is provision for gateways to allow interoperation between H.320 and H.323 equipment.

As mentioned in Chapter 1, there are many competing approaches to Internet telephony. H.323 allows for Internet telephony between systems that do not support video. Many companies and individuals are advocating H.323 as the appropriate reconciliation of the plethora of Internet telephony approaches.

Appendix I includes a list of the primary ITU-T recommendations regarding videoconferencing. See, also, the sources listed in Appendix II through `http://www.aw.com/cp/duran-sauer.html`.

The International Standards Organization (ISO) has adopted several standards that are related to videoconferencing, in particular the Joint Photographic Experts Group (JPEG) standard for coding of still images and MPEG. These are discussed further in Chapter 9.

REFERENCE

SCHA96   Schaphorst, Richard, *Videoconferencing and Videotelephony: Technology and Standards,* Artech House, Norwood, MA, 1996.

Chapter 3

Starting on the Desktop

Conferencing with Personal Computers

Many of the videoconferencing technical issues—communication, audio coding, video coding, document sharing, etc.—are much the same in desktop and group conferencing systems. The remaining issues are associated primarily with group environments. This chapter focuses on issues common to both environments and on a few that are primarily associated with the desktop systems.[1] Chapter 4 expands the discussion with additional issues associated with group conferencing. We prefer, here, to begin with a modern desktop computer and provide the enhancements, for both hardware and software, needed for conferences.

The enhancements likely to be required are

1. Hardware and software to enable connections to other systems in the videoconference.

2. Input/output devices, hardware and software to provide telephone-like, or better, audio capabilities.

3. Camera(s), hardware and software for video capture and coding, and

4. Software to enable collaborative use of the "normal" computer capabilities.

Figure 3.1 illustrates the enhancements added to the computer. The figure implies separate expansion cards for each function. However, it is increasingly likely with newer computer products that most or all of the hardware

---

[1] Most of the discussion of desktop issues is the same, whether the desktop system is a PC, a Macintosh, or a UNIX workstation. Where the issues are specific to these different platforms, we assume PC systems based on Intel 386 compatible processors that are using Microsoft Windows.

29

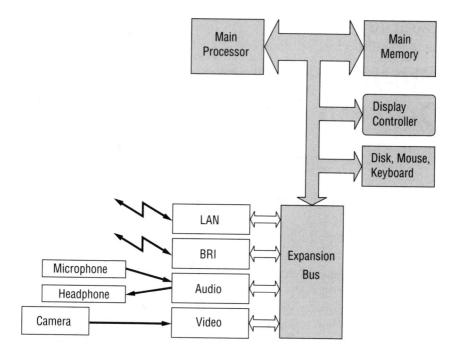

Figure 3.1 Enhancements for videoconferencing

enhancements will be included. Where hardware enhancements are needed it is likely that several of the functions will be included on a single expansion card. The following sections discuss each enhancement in turn.

3.1 ESTABLISHING CONTACT

3.1.1 Local-Area Network Connections

The first conferencing requirement is connection between the computers. Some sort of wiring (or wireless equivalent) needs to be provided to transport the audio, video, and other data. There are two likely candidates for establishing hardware connection. One candidate is a local-area network (LAN)—a desktop computer is probably already connected to a LAN, probably an Ethernet LAN. An Ethernet connection is nominally rated at 10 million bits per second, and can likely sustain half that rate in actual use. So a dedicated Ethernet connection will be far more than is needed for the video and audio traffic described in Chapter 1.

However, Ethernet LANs are usually shared; a single LAN may have several dozen computer connections. If the computers to be conferenced are on the same LAN, then the biggest problem is the level of congestion on the network, since the computers are sharing the nominal 10 million bits per second. Computer access to an Ethernet LAN can be likened to indestructible vehicles attempting to gain access to a highway. An indestructible vehicle might charge onto the highway, not knowing for sure that there will not be a collision, but if there is a collision, it can back off and try again. When a computer tries to place a packet of information on an Ethernet LAN, it cannot be sure that no other computer is using the LAN. If there is a collision between two computers as they each attempt access, they try again after waiting a random period of time.

Ethernet LANs can have several different physical wiring schemes. The originally dominant schemes used a single coaxial cable with stations spliced or tapped in at appropriate points. More recently, so-called 10BaseT twisted-pair wiring to a hub in a star configuration has become the preferred wiring scheme. We find it easier to illustrate using classical Ethernet, so our figures imply traditional coaxial schemes.

More often than not, the computers to be conferenced will not all be on the same LAN. If the computers are on the same Ethernet, then the people would be more likely to meet face to face, since they are all in the same local area. Within medium and large organizations, multiple Ethernets are usually connected, "internetworked," and Ethernets of distinct organizations are often connected by the Internet[2] (see Figure 3.2). When the Ethernets are physically close together, in the same buildings or campus, the connections between nets is at Ethernet speeds or better. When the Ethernets are more distant from each other, the connections between nets are at slower speeds, frequently T1 (1,544,000 bits per second), and often as slow as 56,000 bits per second. There are two potential reasons why internetworked Ethernets may not be sufficient for conferencing. First, the traffic congestion problems are likely to be worse, in general, and especially worse for traffic across the slower interconnections. Second, the interconnections between the particular Ethernets of interest may not exist at all or may be too limited (too many "hops" across the internetworking, or too slow a connection between two of the Ethernets) to be usable for conferencing.

The LAN interface hardware in the computer is almost certainly sufficient for conferencing. When LAN connections are inadequate, it is usually because of congestion on a single LAN or poor internetworking between multiple LANs. The desktop computer does not need connection hardware

---

[2] The proper noun "Internet" and the common noun "internet" are carefully distinguished in the Internet development community. Before the Internet became known in the popular press, Internet developers established a convention of using "Internet" as the proper name for the network that evolved from the 1970s ARPANET to become a worldwide internet. Private internets within a single organization are often called intranets.

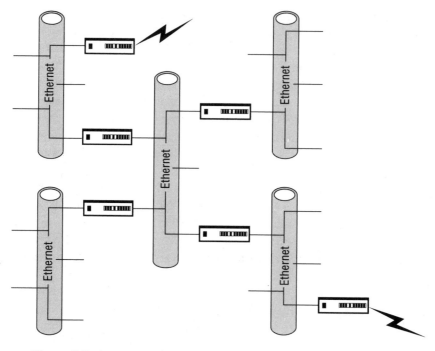

Figure 3.2   Internetworked Ethernets

enhancement for LAN-based conferencing. The LAN interface hardware manages the physical interface to the LAN, for example, the collisions on an Ethernet LAN. The LAN interface also unpackages data in memory from "packets" (several hundred bytes) into the series of bits that travels on the LAN, and packages the data from the LAN's bit-serial form to packets in memory. The packets are more suitable for handling by the main processor; software running on the main processor converts from/to the packets to/from structures suitable for internetworking and for higher level applications, such as conferencing.

3.1.2 ISDN Connections

The other primary hardware candidate for connections is a BRI (basic rate ISDN) interface, using the telephone system. Though BRI connections have been much less prevalent than LAN connections, they are rapidly becoming more available. An ISDN connection provides much more predictable behavior than a LAN connection. LAN and BRI hardware are not mutually exclusive—it is reasonable for a computer to have both types of connections.

With BRI, the pair of telephone wires entering the premises needs to be connected to a termination device, called an NT1 (network terminator one). The NT1 device converts the two off-premises signal wires to four wire connections suitable for an ISDN telephone. An NT1 is often designed to support more than one of these four wire connections, for example, one for a telephone and one for a fax machine. Though the NT1 device could be placed inside the computer, it is often an external device.

The primary circuitry that must be added to the computer is the logical equivalent of part of an ISDN telephone, called a terminal adapter, or TA. The TA must enable the computer to manage dialing and answering the call (using the D-channel) and convert the bit-serial data on the B-channels to and from a form suitable for management by the conferencing software. These are the minimum requirements for the BRI hardware that is added to the computer. (Some computer manufacturers' products include BRI TAs as an integrated part of the computer, but this is atypical.) Increasingly, TA products are including the NT1 device internally, without making a four-wire connection available for another TA. This saves space and money, but makes it impossible for, say, an ISDN phone and an ISDN videoconferencing system to share an ISDN line.

An ISDN phone would usually use only one of the two available B-channels, but a videoconference will use both. Dialing and connection for one B-channel is largely independent of the other, and must be managed as such. Once the channel connections are established, the communication software must manage the aggregation of the two channels to make the combined bandwidth available. Different protocols (vendor proprietary, ITU-T, and others) use different approaches to aggregating the channels. Some, including most proprietary schemes, interleave data at the packet level, sending a packet on one channel and then a packet on the other. Others, primarily ITU-T H.221, interleave at a finer granularity, sending some bits on one channel and then some bits on the other. The ISDN hardware added to the computer may perform this aggregation; at a minimum, it must enable the main processor to perform the B-channel aggregation efficiently.

3.1.3 Addressing and Delivery

Having the hardware (the wiring) in place is only the first step to enable connections. The audio and video subsystems need facilities, call them "delivery services," to send data across the wiring, with the data arriving at the intended destination(s), and not arriving at unintended destinations. (Since the wiring is shared among many computers, it is certainly possible that the data would go to the wrong computers. There may be dozens, thousands, or even millions of computers with physical connections to an internet of LANs. Just as people depend on postal services to keep contents of packages private and deliver packages to specified addresses, LAN users depend on software delivery services to keep order in the midst of potential chaos.)

With LANs, the physical connection between the computers is normally semipermanent. (Temporary, dial-up connections are used with LANs, but such connections are often too slow for conferencing. Broader use of BRI connections for *ad hoc* connections to/among LANs is becoming more common. Even so, congestion on a shared BRI connection may limit the available bandwidth to a level insufficient for conferencing.) Assuming there is a physical path between computers that can be used for a conferencing connection, there must be ways for the computers to identify a logical path between the computers on which the audio/video subsystems can depend. With typical protocols for LAN connection, for example, TCP/IP and IPX/SPX,[3] the logical path is established by addressing analogous to postal addressing. The audio/video subsystems package up portions of data, mark them with an address, and give the packets (packaged data) to the LAN software. It is up to the LAN software to see that the packets reach the destination address. (The LAN software provides delivery services analogous to the postal service.)

There are typically three, equivalent, addresses assigned to a computer. First, there is a large number (a 48-bit number for Ethernet connections) that uniquely identifies the LAN interface hardware. (The manufacturer of an Ethernet interface provides the unique 48-bit number in the interface as part of the manufacturing process.) Second, there is another large number (32 bits for TCP/IP) that also uniquely identifies the LAN interface, but in a format that is consistent for all interfaces used with that protocol. Third, there is a mnemonic name that humans are more likely to use. For example, one of Charlie's computers has Ethernet address 00-AA-00-3E-24-59 (hexadecimal), Internet numeric address 192.150.109.27, and Internet name chs.vtel.com.

Consider the simple internet shown in Figure 3.3. To establish a conference across this internet using TCP/IP, a user gives the mnemonic name, perhaps asking for a conference with chs.vtel.com (or asking for a specific person who is using chs.vtel.com). The conferencing software sends a query to a name service to get the equivalent numeric address, for example, 192.150.109.27. The end-to-end connections across the internet use Internet addresses; e.g., the destination of a packet is given as a numeric Internet address, while in each subnetwork of the internet (each of the Ethernets), the

---

[3] TCP/IP (Transmission Control Protocol/Internet Protocol) is the name usually used for the family of protocols used on the Internet and in many other networks. IPX/SPX (Internet Packet eXchange/Sequenced Packet eXchange) is the name usually used for the family of protocols used on NetWare networks. (Some NetWare networks use TCP/IP instead of IPX/SPX, and many NetWare networks use both families of protocols.)

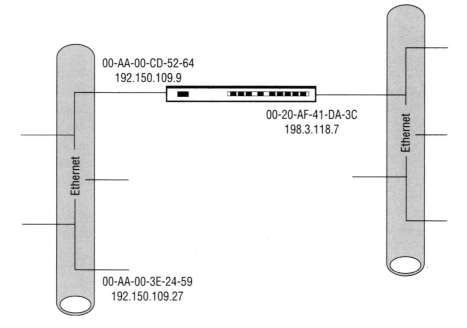

00-AA-00-CD-52-64
192.150.109.9

00-20-AF-41-DA-3C
198.3.118.7

Ethernet

Ethernet

Ethernet

00-AA-00-3E-24-59
192.150.109.27

Figure 3.3 Addressing in internetworked Ethernets

Ethernet addresses are used. Continuing the postal analogy, it is as if there is a package inside of the package. The inside packages are labeled with Internet addresses. The outer packages are labeled with Ethernet addresses. The Ethernet address is sufficient to get the packet to the local router. The router strips off the Ethernet address (removes the outer package), sees the Internet address (on the inner package), determines which interface to use, puts on a new Ethernet address (outer package), and sends the new package on its way. This unpackaging and repackaging is repeated by the other routers until the packet reaches the destination. A specific path may never be established between conferencing sites, and different packets may take different physical routes. The software in each system uses the delivery services without attention to the details of how packets get transported across the internet.

With BRI, a connection directly analogous to a telephone call is established for each B-channel when one computer dials the other. The software that establishes the connections provides a delivery service for the audio/video subsystems. Establishment of the connections is similar to establishment of other telephone calls. The connection software must recognize dialing states (on hook, dialing, ringing, busy, connecting, . . .) and react accordingly. This is done for both B-channels, usually one channel and then the other.

Just as with delivery of physical packages, the delivery services may make strong guarantees about delivery, or may make no guarantees beyond "best efforts." Without guarantees, it is quite likely that packets will arrive out of order. On an internet, the different packets may take different paths, so some packets will take longer than others to get to the same destination. With BRI, data on one B-channel may get ahead of data on the other. The delivery service can maintain records to guarantee that packets are delivered in sequence, depending on the guarantees expected by its "customers." Worse than arriving out of order, some packets will be lost entirely. Loss of packets on LANs and/or telephone circuits is inevitable, due to noise, congested routers, etc. A delivery service is always expected to recognize a damaged packet, and will discard damaged packets. However, a delivery service that makes guarantees of delivery can keep careful records of the packet traffic and acknowledgments of receipt. When packets seem to have been lost, such a delivery service will resend packets until they get through.

Audio and video subsystems usually tolerate inexpensive delivery service with limited guarantees; the primary objective is high throughput at low cost. If small amounts of audio/video data are lost, this will usually not be a problem for the users. The audio and video subsystems keep sufficient records to keep the good data in sequence. Subsystems for shared presentations, shared applications, etc., usually need fully dependable delivery. In this case, it is natural to use a more expensive delivery service that is able to make guarantees.

The delivery services for videoconferencing are usually also responsible for multiplexing the different kinds of data (audio, video, etc.). With many delivery services, including TCP/IP, IPX/SPX, and most of the videoconferencing vendor proprietary protocols developed for telephone networks, the multiplexing is implicit. The audio, video, and other subsystems give packets to the delivery subsystem and the delivery system sends packets (possibly as pieces of the given packets) containing only audio or only video or only other data. With H.221-based systems, the delivery service manages multiplexing by explicit channels, each of which uses a reserved portion of the connection bandwidth, with the channels specifically synchronized with each other. H.221 multiplexing of channels has the advantage that dependable channels of known bandwidth are allocated to each data type. H.221 multiplexing is very difficult to adapt to LANs, which are typically asynchronous, with fluctuating bandwidth available to individual connections. Thus a major part of the H.320 standard is generally considered not readily adaptable to LANs.

With the wiring and delivery services in place, other subsystems can send audio, video, and other data that make the conference real.

3.2 DO YOU HEAR ME?

As we discussed in Chapter 2, even computers with relatively sophisticated entertainment audio capabilities may not be ready for audioconferencing. Figure 3.4 illustrates the functional components that are needed for audioconferencing.

From the outside of the computer looking in, the first requirements are for an input device, a microphone for capturing sounds, and an output device for generating sounds: speakers, headphones or equivalent. The choice of input/output devices can affect the requirements for the rest of the audio system. Where speakers are used for output, it is likely that sounds from the speakers will be picked up by the microphones, resulting in echoes. Where headphones or earpieces are used for output, the sounds produced are unlikely to be captured by the microphones, and echoes are not a problem. Thus the choice of audio input/output devices is very significant in determining whether echo cancellation capability is needed in the computer.

On the inside of the computer, there are three main functions: (1) conversion between analog representations used by the input/output devices and digital representations used by the computer and the delivery services, (2) echo cancellation, and (3) coding.

Analog-to-digital conversion consists of filtering followed by the actual conversion. Frequencies that cannot be sampled must be filtered out of the analog signal, or they will result in noise, called "aliasing." (A high-frequency sound results in lower frequency noise, thus the term "alias.") Since the maximum frequency that can be sampled is half the sampling rate, for example, 4,000 Hz (cycles per second) for 8,000 samples per second, and since filter cutoff frequencies are not precise, the filtering starts at some frequency below the maximum, say, at 3,500 Hz per second for a 4,000-Hz maximum. From a digital perspective, the filtering has not reduced the amount of data, since there are the same number of samples, each with the same number of bits, as without filtering. Each filtered sample is passed on to the echo

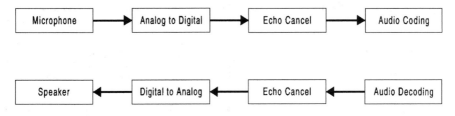

Figure 3.4 Audio subsystem functions

cancellation and coding functions. At the other end, the decoding process produces samples that are converted back to analog signals. The filtering, if done properly, results in better sounding analog signals.

The analog-to-digital and digital-to-analog conversion must work both ways at the same time, both converting analog signals from the microphone(s) to digital and converting digital signals to analog for the headphones/speakers. Converting both ways at the same time allows people to speak and listen at the same time and adjust their behavior accordingly, for example, for one person to stop so another can continue. The simultaneous bidirectional capability is called "full duplex," as opposed to "half duplex." With half duplex, the circuitry can convert in either direction, but only one direction at a time.[4] With half duplex, if one person is speaking and another tries to speak, the first person does not hear the attempted interruption. Also, with half duplex, echo cancellation is not needed because echoes cannot occur. (This is a primary reason that low-cost speakerphones have often been half duplex, to avoid the cost of echo cancellation.) Many PC audio systems have been designed with the assumption that they are to be used primarily for playing back sounds, and the designers have left out full duplex capability to save cost.

Echo canceling works by "remembering" what signal has been put through the speaker, and then subtracting it, appropriately attenuated and delayed, from the signal entering the microphone. The difficulty is in attenuating and delaying the correct amount. Echo cancellation requires much computation, and is likely to add costs in terms of processor capability to perform the cancellation algorithms. Echo cancellation is discussed in depth in Section 10.2.

Audio coding approaches range from the very simplistic, such as the G.711 algorithm mentioned in Chapter 2, which requires very limited computation, to relatively complex approaches with higher computational requirements, such as the G.728 algorithm associated with H.320. Depending on the processor capability of the computer and the algorithm(s) to be used, additional processor capability may be needed for audio coding.

For G.711, a simplistic algorithm, the coding improves the signal-to-noise ratio (SNR), so that noise will be less noticeable when the audio is relatively quiet. The input audio signal is converted from analog to 12-bit digital format. A 12-bit sample provides relatively good SNR, but requires more transmission bandwidth than needed; 7 or 8 bits will suffice. By encoding based on logarithms of the sampled values, it is possible to retain relatively precise information about signal level for smaller signal levels, and discard accuracy

---

[4] Another mode of operation is "simplex," one direction only. Simplex is not relevant to this discussion.

about signal level for stronger signals (louder sounds). Two different encoding formulas are commonly used. The μ-law ("mu-law") formula is associated with telephony in North America and Japan and is therefore typically used for G.711 in those places. The A-law formula is associated with telephony in Europe and is typically used with G.711 there and in the rest of the world. G.711, G.728, and other audio coding algorithms are discussed in detail in Section 10.1.

In a typical desktop system, if a card must be added for conferencing audio it will include, at least, connections for the input/output devices, and the circuitry for conversion of analog to/from digital. The same add-in card might also have circuitry for video and/or for BRI.

Another major consideration for audio is synchronization with video, "lip-sync." Let us return to this topic after considering video implementation.

3.3 CAN YOU SEE ME?

In some sense, the handling of video is the same as audio. There must be an input device, a camera, and an output device, usually the computer display. There are also significant differences. Though the camera is probably not otherwise part of the computer, the display certainly is normally part of a computer. The camera will normally not capture the image from the display, so there is no need for "video echo cancellation."

The major video coding functions are illustrated in Figure 3.5. First, excess visual detail is filtered from the signal to avoid aliasing noise, analogous to the filtering of high-frequency audio signals discussed earlier, and the signal is digitized. As with audio filtering, this filtering does not reduce the amount of digital data, but, if the filtering is done properly, the result is better decoded pictures.

Next, the video is converted from the resolution and color space assumed by the camera to the YUV representation discussed in Chapter 2. Conversion to YUV while retaining full chrominance (color) components normally reduces the bits per pixel from 24 to 16. Using lower precision for the chrominance, as is usually done, reduces the number of bits per pixel to 12 or even 9, an overall effect of 2 to 1 or better.

Depending on the transmission bandwidth available, it may not be possible to transmit 30 frames per second at full resolution. If so, there is no need to even attempt to code every input frame.

Scaling is the process of converting resolution. Typical scaling, if performed, would be to reduce resolution from 352×288, Common Interchange

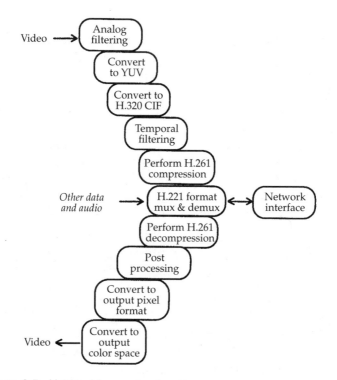

Figure 3.5 H.320 video coding functions

Format (CIF) resolution, to 176 × 144, one-quarter of the pixels of CIF. This quarter CIF resolution requires one-fourth the transmission bandwidth.

Temporal filtering, dropping frames and otherwise filtering excess detail across successive frames, is also done at this point. If, for example, every other frame is dropped out of 30 frames per second, this results in 15 frames per second and half the data rate.

Once the preceding steps are completed the really intensive computational work begins. The most ambitious and effective aspect is motion estimation—estimating which pixels in a frame are different from those in the previous frame. Rather than transmitting each entire frame, it is usually much more efficient to transmit only what has changed from frame to frame. Motion estimation and other interframe coding techniques divide successive frames into corresponding blocks (8 pixels × 8 pixels, or sometimes 16 pixels × 16 pixels or other sizes) and compare the differences. If the differences are "small," then no data are transmitted for this block, and the decoding process will use the pixels from a previous frame for this block. The determination of differences between the corresponding blocks in different frames may occur both before the intraframe coding process described later and during that process. If it is determined before the transformation process that the block will not be transmitted, then most of the computation for intraframe coding for that block is avoided. Where motion has occurred, it may still be possible to represent the motion concisely by representing shifting of the block of pixels to a different portion of the picture, and reducing the amount of data transmitted. Motion estimation can reduce the data by a factor of at least 5 to 1, depending on the motion in the pictures.

Intraframe coding is the most discussed, and most diverse, aspect of video coding. There has been, and continues to be, major research and development efforts to determine methods that (1) retain high picture quality, (2) dramatically reduce the amount of data needed for representing a picture, and (3) require relatively small computational effort. A variety of approaches is discussed in some detail in Chapter 9. In current practice, the most popular implementations, including H.261, are based on discrete cosine transforms (DCTs). Intraframe coding approaches reduce the amount of data transmitted by factors of up to 5 to 1.

To summarize the data reduction effects:

1. YUV conversion and reduced chrominance precision yields at least a 2:1 reduction.

2. Scaling down to quarter CIF resolution yields a 4:1 reduction.

3. Dropping frames from 30 to 15 frames per second yields 2:1, if performed.

4. Interframe coding yields at least a 5:1 reduction.

5. Intraframe coding yields up to a 5:1 reduction.

The total reduction from effects 1, 4, and 5 is roughly 50:1, going up to 400:1 with reduced resolution and frame rate. But this is not enough! In Chapter 1 we said we needed to get 73 million bytes per second down to a couple of B-channels. A reduction of 50:1 leaves a requirement for roughly 23 B-channels and 400:1 still leaves a requirement for roughly 3 B-channels. For full resolution and full motion, the reality of current technology is that 23 B-channels (a PRI connection) are required and that for quarter CIF and 15 frames per second, 2 B-channels (a BRI connection) are not quite enough. However, if motion in the captured video is limited, interframe coding may be able to achieve factors significantly better than 5:1 without noticeable degradation in quality and substantially less bandwidth may be enough. In any case, it is the responsibility of the video coding system to limit the coded video data to match the available bandwidth. If this means coding fewer blocks, or dropping frames entirely, so be it. Coding fewer blocks may result in visual artifacts (discrepancies) where motion occurs, but for most applications occasional artifacts are acceptable.

After the encoding steps are completed, the data are multiplexed, and if appropriate, time-stamped to enable synchronization of audio and video at the decoding station. H.221 interleaves audio and video to provide implicit synchronization, without time stamps, and requires bit-synchronous transmission. Any transmission delays thus have an equal effect on audio, video, and any other multiplexed data. With other delivery services, it is likely that audio and video packets will have different transmission delays, and explicit synchronization is appropriate. Typically, audio and video packets are both stamped with the time of capture. At the decoding station, priority is given to preserving time consistency of the audio data. Video data are matched to the audio data. If either the encoding or decoding station gets behind on the video, it may drop video frames or take other special action to assist in maintaining synchronization.

The decoding process is the inverse of the encoding process, but the steps are simpler computationally. For example, motion estimation requires extensive searching at the encoding station, without any corresponding effort at the decoding station. The computations for intraframe decoding are simpler than those for coding, and so forth.

Let us finish the subject of hardware enhancements needed to enable a personal computer for conferencing. The most important enhancements for video are circuitry to convert analog video input to digital[5] and dedicated computational capability for video coding. With the recent advances in the main processors of personal computers, the relatively simple decoding computations can be readily performed on the main processor. At lower resolutions and frame rates, a typical main processor may handle the encoding chores as well. At higher resolutions and frame rates, it is likely either a very high performance main processor is needed or that a processor specially designed for video coding should be used.

Now, let's consider sharing computer data during the conference.

---

[5] Cameras are available with digital outputs instead of the traditional analog outputs, and these cameras are especially well suited for desktop videoconferencing applications. However, at this writing, cameras with analog outputs are more likely to be used, and, even when digital output cameras become widely used, there will still be a need for analog-to-digital conversion for input sources such as VCRs.

3.4 MY COMPUTER WILL GET BACK TO YOU

One of the primary advantages of using a personal computer for videoconferencing is getting the benefit of shared access to the computers' facilities. Personal computers are widely used for preparing documents, spreadsheets, and presentations; for design, development, and manufacturing in many fields ranging from architecture to computers to entertainment; and for education, financial planning, and on and on. For all of these uses, the computer activities are often multiperson activities; it is natural to include them in conferences. The most popular approaches are file transfer, document sharing, and program sharing.

File transfer is a common facility in Internet, remote access, and remote terminal environments. The use of file transfer in conferencing is conceptually the same.

Document sharing approaches provide a specific program designed to allow the participants to view and manipulate the same document. The program is conceptually the same as the many drawing programs that allow free-form drawing and text entry in a window representing a document. The primary difference between a generic drawing program and a generic document sharing program is that the document sharing program allows more than one person, each on different computers, to draw and/or enter text simultaneously. In the simplest cases, the document begins as a shared drawing area, and the participants mark on the drawing area with a mouse and type on the area with the keyboard. For an electronic equivalent of a chalkboard, these programs are a natural approach. However, for dealing with existing documents, this approach may be less effective. One problem is simply converting an existing document to a format recognized by the shared document program. This problem is readily solvable in a variety of ways: The operating system is likely to allow "cut and paste," copying from the program providing the document source to allow pasting in the shared document program. The shared document program probably is able to "import" document files from popular programs. The shared document program may be able to emulate a printer so that the program providing the document can "print" the document into the shared drawing space. All of these solutions can be effective and appropriate. However, none of them is the same as directly manipulating the document with the program that produced the document. This is especially noticeable when the complexity of the document dominates the simplicity of the concept of a shared drawing area.

Program sharing allows more than one person, each on different computers, to use the same copy of the same program, working with the same document and seeing the same displays on screen (see Figure 3.6). At first, this

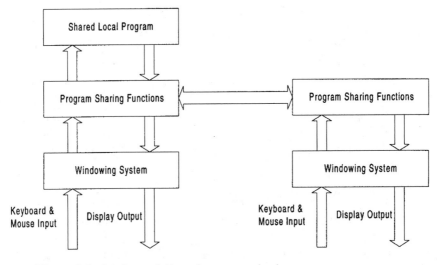

Figure 3.6   Implementation of program sharing

seems like an impossibility, and in some cases it is infeasible where the program has unique characteristics that invalidate the "tricks" used to share programs. In practice, it is a general approach that works well across a variety of application domains and programs. Program sharing in this sense is not a difficult distributed processing problem; there is only one copy of the program running on only one computer, just as there would be without program sharing. (There need not be a copy of the shared program on the other computers, and if copies exist on the other computers, the copies are not used.) There is only one copy of the document(s) manipulated by the shared program; these copies are accessed just as if program sharing were not involved.

Program sharing depends on being able to intercept, at the operating system level, output from the program, so that it can be displayed at each site in the conference, and mouse/keyboard input from each site, so that it can be supplied to the program as if it came from a local mouse and keyboard (see Figure 3.6). Widely used operating systems are not typically designed specifically to enable intercepting input and output in this manner, but the widespread use of windowing systems has led to operating systems where the interception is possible. The operating system needs to be able to redirect mouse input and keystrokes to any of the visible windows, so the program sharing facilities take advantage of this redirection, both to receive the input and to pass the input on to the shared program. Similarly, the operating system must be able to capture the output from a program and direct it appropriately to a window, if the designated window is visible. The program sharing facilities intercept the output and send it both to the local window and to the remote system window.

Where program sharing is provided, the document sharing program is unnecessary. If the conferees want to have a shared drawing, they can use a conventional drawing program as a shared program, a program that is a more familiar program to the users, and therefore more productive.

As conferencing becomes a more important aspect of computing, operating system suppliers will provide integrated facilities to enable program sharing across a conference. Microsoft has already begun to supply program sharing capabilities for Windows 95 and Windows NT.

Program sharing is very attractive because the capability is general and applies to most computer applications. However, the process of intercepting program actions at a level close to the input/output devices and communicating those actions across a network incurs very substantial overhead. For many common computer applications, the overhead is acceptable. For some, for example, computer-assisted design (CAD) applications, it is likely that the overhead is prohibitive.

Another approach, *object sharing,* as demonstrated by VTEL's ObjectShare program, can provide much of the generality of program sharing without the overhead. If the operating system and application adhere to an appropriate object model, then the facilities of that model can be used to share object viewing and manipulation in a conference. Because the actions are high-level actions, designed to be appropriate for the objects at hand, most of the overhead of program sharing can be avoided. For example, Microsoft's Component Object Model (COM) suggests that an object provide methods for rendering the object on a display device. In a conference, the file representing an object, say, a CAD drawing, can be transferred between sites using standard file transfer mechanisms. A general-purpose object sharing program at each site can determine the kind of object and invoke the object's rendering methods to display the object at each site. With program sharing, the display of the object might have involved transmission of many display actions, perhaps at a pixel granularity. With object sharing, these are replaced by a single-action "display object." The object sharing program may provide additional facilities, for example, to invoke a program that can modify the object.

As the World Wide Web becomes increasingly dominant in the use of computers, it is natural to use Web facilities for communication during a conference. Without special software, the participants in a conference can independently point their browsers at the same addresses (URLs). Conferencing software can automate and coordinate browser access. Appropriate software can also facilitate creation of Web content for use as presentations and tailor browser behavior to achieve the best presentation in a distance meeting.

Chapter 4

Rooms with a View

Rooms for Group Videoconferences

In a group conference, people expect audio and video to be distributed throughout the room. Users want the same ease as when listening to recordings or watching television, not the awkwardness of using a telephone handset or a portable television. In many circumstances, even meeting audio and video expectations is not enough; we must also have facilities equivalent to presentation easels, overhead projectors, and chalkboards. We use notebook computers (and larger computers) in business meetings, so a group conference needs to allow for use of computers, including specialized devices attached to computers.

In this chapter we address technology issues for group conferences: audio/video suitable for a conference room, support for shared discussion media, and integration of computers into group conferences. We will tend to assume we have conference rooms and groups of people at all of the conference sites, but we don't wish to make it seem like this is the only interesting situation. Many times, a conference will occur between a group system and a desktop system, and what we say here also applies to these types of conferences.

4.1 STRETCHING THE CONFERENCE TABLE

When all participants in a meeting with us are present together in a single conference room, we take for granted that we can be anywhere in the room, hear nearly all of the normal conversation, and be heard when we want to be heard. Similarly, we can usually see most everything in the room, except for minor obstructions. (For example, if we are sitting on opposite sides of an overhead projector we may have to tilt our heads to see each other around the post supporting the projector's mirror and lens.) A videoconferencing system needs to maintain this level of aural and visual contact, as though our conference table has been virtually stretched across a country or a continent.

In the subsections that follow we discuss specifics in these areas:

- Cameras and camera operation,
- Video display characteristics,
- Microphones and loudspeakers,
- Communications connections with bandwidth for high-quality audio/video, and
- The user interface.

4.1.1 Cameras

The cameras and video displays provide our view of the people in the different rooms. The cameras need to capture not just any picture of the far site, but a view that would be chosen by those of us viewing the picture on the display. A camera provides a restricted, targeted view, compared to the human eye, with the extent of the targeting dependent on the focal length of the lens. With a variable focal length ("zoom") lens, it is possible to adjust a camera's field of view from a relatively wide-angle view to a narrowly targeted, telephoto view. The narrowly targeted view is desirable for capturing the nuances of facial expressions and gestures, but for only one person at a time. With the wide-angle view, it is possible to capture several of the participants, but with less visible details. Even in wide-angle mode, the camera has no equivalent of our human peripheral vision; there is a large portion of the room that is not captured by the camera. Either the camera must be pointed in different directions, in a manner analogous to our looking in different directions, or there must be several cameras to select from, or some combination of these capabilities. In a television studio, there would be an operator for each camera who would point the camera, zoom in and out, and adjust focus and other settings. In addition, there would be at least one person responsible for switching among the cameras. In a typical videoconferencing system, some of these functions will be automated and we, the meeting participants, must handle the rest of the camera operation and selection (see Figure 4.1).

Automated focusing is standard technology in general photography and is usually incorporated in video cameras. However, continual adjustment of focus may be a detriment to the video in that it can interfere with motion estimation and video coding. It is usually beneficial to enable autofocus when a camera is moved and disable autofocus at other times. Similarly, automated control of the camera's iris (exposure in still photography) is standard

Figure 4.1 Television studio and cameras
(Photo courtesy of KVUE-TV, Inc., Austin, Texas)

technology incorporated in video cameras. Again, it is usually beneficial to selectively enable auto-iris capability.

Video cameras used in group conferencing systems will usually be motorized to enable positioning by remote control.[1] The "remote control" may be effected by someone in the same room as the camera, by someone viewing from a distance, or by a tracking system that attempts to automatically point the camera at the person speaking. In some cases, the actual device used for remote control may be specific to the camera and handled by those close to the camera, similar to the remote controls used for televisions and VCRs. It is usually simpler for us to manage the overall system when the controls for the cameras are part of the devices used for establishing connections and managing other conference functions.

In general, we prefer to have the camera and microphones coordinated so that the camera can move to point at the person speaking. Research prototypes, and even custom-made products, have demonstrated encouraging

---

[1] Control signals for camera positioning are naturally included in the other data multiplexed and sent between sites. The signals require tiny fractions of the available bandwidth, and can be transferred between sites with no noticeable effect on video or audio.

progress in providing this capability, but video follows voice for conference room cameras is not yet available in standard products. For specific environments, it is possible to automate the pointing with simple mechanisms. A lecturer can carry an infrared or radio transmitter and the camera can adjust position to point at the transmitter. The students in a classroom can use push buttons to effectively "raise their hands" and the camera can point at the first one to push the button. [This assumes the camera(s) are calibrated in advance to be able to point at the button locations.]

4.1.2 Displays and Resolution

At the viewing end, the meeting participants will likely be across the room from the display(s). Large cathode-ray tube (CRT) displays (at least, say, 27 inches on the diagonal) or projection displays are necessary to provide large enough images of the other sites of the conference. For video at 352×288 resolution, the CRT displays and projection displays used for television give good results and are very cost effective. For display of documents and computer-generated images, television resolution is marginal. High-resolution large CRT and high-resolution projection displays are not produced in nearly the volumes of smaller computer displays and televisions, so a significant cost premium is involved with using high-resolution large displays for conferencing.

Nearly all displays used for television and for personal computers have a 4:3 aspect ratio, that is the ratio of the width of the visible display to the height of the display area is 4:3. For example, a nominal 20-inch display, measured diagonally, has an approximate width of 16 inches and height of 12 inches. Personal computers normally use pixels such that the ratio of horizontal pixels to vertical pixels is also 4:3, for example, 640×480 resolution or $1,024 \times 768$ resolution. These pixels are square, since each pixel represents a square area on the display. Television and the common resolutions used in videoconferencing, such as 352×288, arrange the pixels with a slightly lower aspect ratio, approximately 1.22:1. The pixels in these resolutions are rectangular, in that they cover a rectangular area on the display. Videoconferencing equipment must carefully respect these different pixel shapes and adjust accordingly if images are to appear in proper proportions.

Consider a display that is 640 mm wide and 480 mm high. (The diagonal measure is therefore 800 mm, so these dimensions correspond to a nominal 32-inch display.) If a 640×480 computer resolution is used on this display, then the pixels will be 1 mm square. If a 352×288 resolution is used, then the pixels will be approximately 1.82 (640/352) mm $\times$ 1.67 (480/288) mm. Suppose a 4:3 aspect ratio image is captured by the equipment with pixels in this format, then presented on the display in 640×480. The top half of Figure 4.2

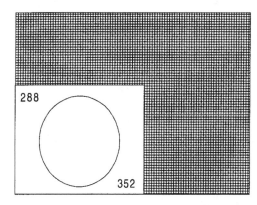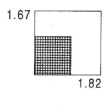

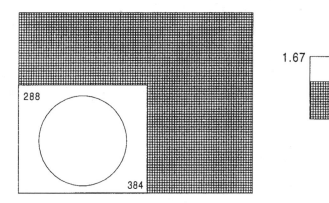

Circle captured with rectangular pixels and displayed with square pixels

Circle captured with rectangular pixels, then scaled horizontally for display with square pixels

Figure 4.2 Pixel shape

illustrates this scenario. The image will be presented as slightly narrower than its proper proportion, for example, a circle would appear as a vertical ellipse. In order for the image to appear proportioned properly, additional horizontal pixels must be added to the image (or vertical pixels removed) so that the pixels in the image will be in 4:3 ratio. For example, if the 352 horizontal pixels of the image are spread across 384 pixels of the computer display, then the 4:3 ratio exists and the image will appear properly proportioned. If a 384×288 resolution were used across the full display, the image would have pixels approximately 1.67 mm square. The "scaling" techniques used for adjusting pixel shape and resolution are discussed in more detail in Chapter 10.

If the conferencing hardware is an augmented personal computer, as suggested in Chapter 3, one (and, likely, the only) video output from the computer will be VGA or similar output designed for a computer display, not the S-Video output most appropriate for a television display. If so, a device known as a scan converter can be used to convert the computer output to S-Video. This device must perform the appropriate scaling to convert the square pixels and computer resolution to rectangular pixels and television resolution, as well as converting between the VGA and S-Video electrical signals.

Common practice at this writing is to use multiple displays, typically two, in each conference room (see Figure 4.3). One display is devoted to video from the remote site(s). The other display is used for shared presentations, for monitoring camera selection and positioning, and other auxiliary purposes. Of course, equipment costs can be reduced by using a single display. It might also be desirable to duplicate displays within a single room, so that participants can see the displays more easily.

4.1.3 Microphones and Loudspeakers

It is a significant challenge to provide and position the right microphones and loudspeakers to enable people to speak to each other without consciously considering whether the others are in the same room or stretched across the country.

Figure 4.3 Dual display configuration

Microphone Characteristics.   A single microphone usually has noticeable directional and proximity effects. It may be useful to think of a typical microphone in analogy to a camera lens, in that it "looks" primarily in one direction and "sees" best the sounds coming from that direction.[2] Use of only a single microphone favors those near the microphone. Sounds from "off-axis," from a direction other than the "pointing" direction of the microphone, are not as loud as those from in "front" of the microphone. Tonal quality is noticeably different based on the distance and direction from the microphone. Bass frequencies are captured strongly when the sound source (a person's voice) is near the microphone and captured less well at a distance. More importantly, sound sources at a distance from a microphone are obscured by sounds from other sources. Some of these sounds are sounds that should be captured, such as other persons' voices, but others, such as voices reflected off of walls, sounds of office equipment, ventilation systems, traffic, etc., usually should be considered noise to be avoided or suppressed.

Microphone Mixing.   Just as a television studio has personnel to control cameras both individually and collectively, a television studio has an audio engineer responsible for mixing the sounds from the microphones, and may have people responsible for repositioning microphones. Corresponding operation of the audio for a conference should be preset or controlled automatically, to the extent possible. In many circumstances, it will be sufficient to position several microphones around the room and mix the audio signals equally. More complex room environments may require unequal mixing of microphones, but may still allow the settings to be preset and forgotten.

Noise Suppression.   Common technology from sound reinforcement and recording environments may be used to provide some level of automated control of audio sources. As the number of microphones increases, it becomes more and more important to suppress extraneous sounds picked up by the microphones. Otherwise, the combined extraneous sounds become a dominant component of the audio signal. A microphone with a noise gate can effectively turn itself off when the sounds entering the microphone are below a predetermined threshold (and thus likely to be "extraneous") and turn itself

---

[2] This discussion assumes so-called "unidirectional" microphones. So-called "omnidirectional" microphones and other types of microphones have less prominent directional effects in some cases, or are designed to have more complex directional effects in others. Such microphones tend to exacerbate echo cancellation problems and cause more dramatic problems with ambient noise, so they have been less frequently used for group conferences. With sufficient echo cancellation and noise reduction technology, omnidirectional microphones can be used to more evenly capture the participants' voices.

on (instantly) when louder sounds are present (when someone is speaking near the microphone). If each microphone has a noise gate, then only the microphones near persons speaking will be on at any given time. "Push to talk" microphones are sometimes used for similar reasons. However, requiring the user to remember to press a button to speak invites the user to either forget to push the button or to leave the button pressed at all times—neither of these situations is conducive to an effective distance meeting.

Automated Volume Control.   Another problem is fluctuation in sound levels as a person speaking moves closer to and away from a microphone. Audio dynamic range compression circuitry and signal processing software can decrease amplification when signals become stronger and increase amplification when signals are weaker, thus reducing the overall dynamic range of the signals. Compression can be applied to each microphone signal individually, or to the mixture of microphone signals. (Excessive compression may produce undesirable effects, such as increasing the amplification of extraneous sounds.)

Other Audio Sources.   Microphones are not the only sources of audio that may be important to a conference. It may be that one or more participants must call in from an ordinary telephone, so the ability to add a telephone participant is important. Sounds from a computer, a conventional audio recording, a VCR and/or other sources may also be part of the conference. Except for telephones, which have potential for echos and other issues with the telephone microphone, the technical issues in incorporating these sources are usually easy to handle, much easier than selecting and positioning microphones.

Loudspeakers.   The preceding discussion emphasizes sources of sound input. A successful conference experience also depends on loudspeaker quality and placement. Since the frequency range of the audio signals is limited, it is possible in principle to use speakers with limited capabilities without impairing reproduction, but in practice it will usually be cost effective to use loudspeakers suitable for unrestricted frequency ranges. A sufficient number of loudspeakers should be placed so that participants around the room can hear easily. At the same time, loudspeakers should generally be placed away from microphones, to minimize microphone pickup of sounds from the loudspeakers.

4.1.4 "Better than BRI" Connections

Though useful videoconferencing is possible with only two B-channels, the quality of the video increases quite noticeably with the addition of a few more B-channels. Unfortunately, "adding a few more B-channels" is easier said than done. Electrical interfaces and dialing protocols for basic rate ISDN are relatively standardized[3] and accessible. Electrical interfaces and switching protocols for higher bandwidth connections are much more diverse, with significant differences across regions, nations, and continents. Where BRI is not available, these issues also apply to Switched 56 connections. Some of the specifics are discussed in Chapter 8. However, it is often the case that the preferred solution is to use several BRI lines to gain access to more B-channels. For example, using three BRI lines gives a total of six B-channels. To use multiple BRI lines, some mechanism is needed to present the multiple B-channels in a form suitable for use by the videoconferencing system. This is usually done with a device called an <u>inverse multiplexer</u> or <u>IMUX</u>, which can readily be built in.

4.1.5 Control Mechanisms

As much as possible, we would like to have "no user interface" by avoiding any need for conference participants to control the conference. However, it is inevitable that participants (or operators acting on behalf of the participants) will need to control the conference to some extent. At a minimum, we need ways to establish a conference (the equivalent of picking up a telephone and dialing), to end a conference, to adjust the volume of the loudspeakers, to temporarily shut off the cameras/microphones for the sake of privacy, and so forth. When we have the typical levels of automation provided in today's products, we may also want to select which camera signal is to be viewed and the position of that camera to manipulate devices such as VCRs, and to control other equipment and aspects of the conference.

Let us consider some of the control mechanisms that might be provided. In doing so we will cite deficiencies of all of these mechanisms. Given our assertion that the conference equipment should be self-controlling insofar as possible, we should assume that all of the mechanisms discussed have significant deficiencies and that the importance of the deficiencies will vary with the people using the equipment and the ways they want to use the equipment. However, in spite of these deficiencies, the example mechanisms have been well received by users and should be considered successful approaches.

A telephone typically has all of the controls on a keypad as part of the instrument. It would usually be impractical to place the controls of a conferencing system on the main cabinet, since that cabinet is usually out of the participants' reach. However, it is quite practical to provide a keypad similar to that of a telephone as a separate device for the participants to use. This device

---

[3] Unfortunately, there are several conventions for dialing protocols for BRI.

may be placed on a table in the midst of the participants or placed out of the way where an operator would want to use it (see Figure 4.4). Such a device may have additional buttons for camera control, volume, and the other most frequently used functions. Conceptually, it is a natural equivalent of the telephone keypad and thus potentially easy for users to adjust to. There are several limitations to this approach. First, one has to learn (and remember) how to use the buttons. Second, it is difficult to customize the capabilities of the control unit, and customization likely will aggravate learning/memory issues. Third, with such a keypad it is difficult to provide integrated facilities for drawing and/or for the equivalent of a computer mouse. (Pointing devices of the sort used with portable computers might be included in the keypad for these purposes.)

Most of us control our television sets with a hand-held remote control device. We can use a similar control device for videoconferencing, as shown in Figure 4.5. Except that the control device is portable, it is the logical equivalent of a tabletop keypad of the sort we just discussed. The portability alleviates the potential problem of forcing seating to adjust to the location of the device, but allows for the probability that the control device will be misplaced from time to time, will need new batteries, etc., just like a television remote control.

A variety of devices have been devised for controlling specific computer environments or other equipment. Two such devices that are commonly used with videoconferencing equipment are graphics tablets and touch panels (see Figures 4.6 and 4.7, respectively).

A graphics tablet, such as the one in Figure 4.6, can be similar to the keypad, in that it has icons that are pressed with the pen. These tablets are widely used for computer-aided design applications. With use of replaceable

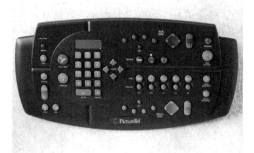

Figure 4.4 PictureTel Venue 2000 control keypad
(© PictureTel Corporation. Reprinted with permission.)

Figure 4.5 Compression Labs hand-held remote control
"The CLI *eclipse* Remote Control Unit makes videoconferencing as easy
to use as a television set."
(Courtesy of Compression Labs, Inc. (CLI))

overlays, it is possible to customize the functions of the tablet for specific users or classes of users. However, such usage may require more hand–eye coordination than with a keypad or hand-held remote device. A fundamental benefit of using the tablet is the availability of the pen for use in drawing and annotation, and for use as a mouse surrogate in computer applications.

For our purposes, a touch panel may be thought of as a programmable graphics tablet. It allows the customization benefits of the graphics tablet, and adds the benefit of direct visual feedback to simplify hand–eye coordination. However, there is no straightforward way to get the fine control of a pen or mouse with such a touch screen—it is usually necessary to augment the touch screen with a graphics tablet, a mouse, or a mouse surrogate such as a trackball.

Except for the graphics tablet, none of the approaches discussed provides directly for integration of personal computers and computer applications in

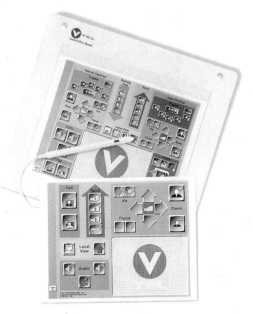

Figure 4.6   VTEL control tablet

the conference. Yet we know that use of computers has become a major aspect of many meetings. It is possible to integrate computer concepts and conferencing concepts. AppsView™ (Figures 4.8, 4.9, and 4.10) provides a control interface that fits naturally with the sense of watching television by having a translucent icon serve as a "gateway" to the latent capabilities of the control system. When people are conversing and watching, not needing controls, the icon is on the screen but relatively unobtrusive, appearing to be one

Figure 4.7   AMX touch panel

Figure 4.8 AppsView™ dormant state

of the translucent logos ("bugs") ubiquitous in commercial television. When a user moves a graphics pen, a mouse, or equivalent device, the cursors on the screen change and indicate the ability to move the camera to point higher or lower, pan from left to right, or zoom in and out. Figure 4.9 illustrates two such cursors, one for zoom-in and one for tilt-up. When the gateway icon is selected (with the pen or mouse), more icons appear and enable additional control of the system. As with the graphics tablet, these additional controls can visually stimulate the intended usage and can be customized for specific circumstances. An obvious drawback of having controls on the screen in this

Figure 4.9 AppsView™ camera control cursors

Figure 4.10   AppsView™ toolbar

fashion is that they may be distracting to the conference participants. One way to deal with this problem is to provide a separate display for control purposes, allowing the main displays to be used only for meeting content. For example, the sort of display used with notebook computers could be provided as a tabletop control interface.

4.2 "MULTIMEDIA"

The term "multimedia" has been used in so many contexts in the computer and communication industries that we should be very careful about its use. In some contexts, "multimedia" has been used to mean only adding "digitized motion video" to a PC screen. We want to discuss a "multiplicity of media types," so the term is literally descriptive.

Business meetings and class environments usually depend on visual aids such as an easel with flip charts, a chalk or marker board, a projector for transparencies, paper copies of materials, videotapes, and so forth. Some of these visual aids may be adequately captured by pointing a video camera at the item (perhaps at the item and a person next to it) and transmitting the video to the other sites in the conference. For some visual aids, for example, an easel with flip charts, the approach of using the main video capabilities is likely the most appropriate, and may be the only feasible approach. However, in many other cases, significant detail of the visual aid will be lost if the main video capabilities are used to share the visual aid across the conference, and alternatives that are specifically designed to support sharing of the visual aid are likely to be more appropriate.

4.2.1 Shared Overhead Projectors

One of the most common forms of visual aid used in business meetings and other environments is a transparency shown on an overhead projector. In a videoconference, a document stand with a built-in video camera (see Figure 4.11) and the displays used for motion video can substitute directly for the overhead projector. In the simplest implementation, the document stand camera is simply used as an alternate video input, rather than the camera(s) pointed at the meeting participants, and the transparency (or paper) placed on the stand is shown in the video displays. There are two big drawbacks to this approach: (1) The people at the other sites cannot see us when we select the document camera as the motion video source, and (2) the resolution (say, 352 × 288) used for the motion video is likely not sufficient to show enough detail in the transparency (or piece of paper).

In principle, we could avoid the first drawback from a display perspective by having the other sites use a second display, or a window on the first display, to show our motion video images while showing the documents as well. However, that would require two streams of motion video coming from

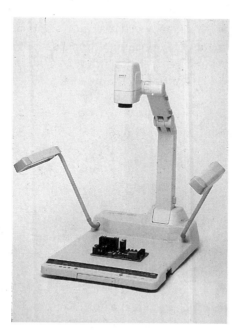

Figure 4.11 Document stand and camera
(Photograph courtesy of VCS Division of Canon, USA, Inc.)

our site, requiring significant additional communication bandwidth between the sites and significant additional video coding/decoding capability.

Since the use of overhead projectors (or equivalents) is so common in meetings, it is natural to provide explicit support for an effective alternative for use in videoconferences. The document stand camera and video display are not the primary cause of the drawbacks with the simple approach. The drawbacks are the result of the treatment of the document camera—unnecessarily—as a motion video source, when motion on the document stand occurs every few seconds, or even less frequently. Thus it is reasonable to treat the document camera as a source of still images. With most products, a person must explicitly indicate to the conference equipment that the image has changed, so that the equipment will transmit the new image. It is possible for the conferencing equipment to detect changes directly and transmit automatically. "QuickView" in the VTEL TC system does this by analyzing motion in the video from the document stand.

Treatment of the document camera image as a still image means that the other camera(s) can be used as the source of motion video to be transmitted to the other sites, except perhaps for brief periods when the image from the document camera is "captured" so that it may be coded and sent to the other sites separately from the motion video. Of course, "there is no free lunch"; some of the communication bandwidth must be used to send the document image. But this usage is brief and need not cause significant disruption of the motion video. Treatment of the document camera input as a still image also allows the documents to be sent at significantly higher resolution, such that the displays are likely the limiting factor in the perceived image resolution at the receiving sites.

More explicitly, the following steps would happen. These steps are closely related to the discussion surrounding Figure 3.5, so a review of that figure and discussion may be helpful. First, the document camera is selected, at least temporarily, as a video input. To ensure that the camera is in focus and set to the right focal length, and that the document is positioned properly on the stand, this video input would be shown on one of the displays, or in a window on one of the displays. Image filtering and YUV conversion are performed. Temporal filtering is typically not performed. The image is scaled to the desired resolution, likely higher than 352×288, probably 640×480. Coding of the image uses intraframe techniques similar to those used for H.261, but interframe coding is not appropriate and not used. The coded image is sent to the other sites, which decode the image and present it on a display. In the case of H.221, a fraction of the bandwidth of the communication channel(s) would be temporarily reserved for the still image transmission, reducing the bandwidth available for motion video, and after transmission, the temporarily removed bandwidth for video would be restored for video usage. In other communication link protocols, similar steps would allow video to be temporarily deprioritized so that the still image could be transmitted.

In many cases, the documents that are viewed on an overhead projector are computer generated. If the conferencing system is itself a computer capable of manipulating the source files for the documents, then it can be visually preferable to bypass making a physical copy of the pages, bypass the document camera, and use the computer-generated image as the input to the coding process. From that point on, the implementation is the same as outlined in the previous paragraph, so at the receiving end the implementation does not need to be sensitive to whether the source was physically present and seen by a camera or contained within the computer.

As we said before, the display resolution may be less than needed to properly show fine detail of the documents. The cost of higher resolution large displays may be justified by the need for better visibility of detail. Such displays may be devices designed for computer displays, high-resolution television, or other higher resolution image requirements in other applications, or they may be devices specifically designed for conferencing.

Polycom has developed a device similar to an overhead projector that is capable of capturing images of paper documents at higher resolution ($1,024 \times 768$) and providing a projection display at that resolution (see Figure 4.12). The Polycom ShowStation™ can be used like a conventional overhead

Figure 4.12 Polycom ShowStation™
(Courtesy of Polycom, Inc.)

projector, can be used with a speakerphone and a pair of telephone lines for a distance meeting without video (a good example of "audiographics"), or can be connected to a videoconferencing system to augment that equipment for higher resolution still images. Some applications require much higher resolution than 1,024 × 768; we discuss this situation further in Chapter 6.

If the documents are computer generated, then it may be desirable to use a program sharing capability, as described in Section 3.4, to share the document generation program among the conferees. Depending on the visual appearance of the program and the familiarity of the participants with the program, this may be preferable. This approach may allow the participants to partially overcome limitations in display resolution by using the program to display smaller portions of the images at a time, effectively increasing the resolution available for those portions.

4.2.2 Annotation of Shared Presentations

When transparencies are used for presentations, the presenter, and maybe others, will often mark on the transparencies to emphasize, clarify, or augment the discussion. Videoconferencing equipment must provide such annotation capabilities for presentations shared across the conference. There are at least three approaches available, based on things we have already discussed. One approach is to let the participants at one site mark on the physical copy, then transmit that copy as a new image, a so-called "sketch and send" operation. This requires no additional capabilities for the equipment, but is a significant limitation on the dynamics of a meeting. Another approach is to use a document sharing program as described in Section 3.4. Such programs normally include substantial annotation capabilities, and can handle images that are produced by camera input, as well as computer-generated images. Third, a program sharing capability may be appropriate, as discussed in the preceding paragraph.

4.2.3 More Media Types

Both because of the importance of the shared presentation materials in typical meetings, and because of the implementation effort that has gone into videoconferencing equipment to support shared presentations, it was important to devote the previous section to shared presentation material. But many other forms of media are important in typical meetings.

It is routine for a meeting to begin by one of the participants handing out paper copies of a document to be discussed in the meeting. This document might also be presented as projected transparencies, or it might be read silently by the participants. In some circumstances, it is necessary for all of the participants to have paper copies of materials. The technology discussed so far does not address this need, but there is a straightforward solution: the fax machine. A fax machine could be used independently of the videoconferencing equipment, but with the communication already established between sites, it is undesirable to ask participants to exchange fax numbers, go to a separate room to use the machines, etc. Some of the communication bandwidth of the conferencing connection can be diverted temporarily and allocated to conventional fax machines connected to the videoconferencing systems.

Similarly, it is common in meetings to ask the participants to view a videotape, and not unusual to make a videotape recording of a meeting. Since a VCR uses the same video interfaces as the conferencing equipment, the VCR can be used as if it were a camera, as a source of video to be sent to the other sites. Correspondingly, the signals that go from the conferencing equipment to the video displays can also go to a VCR for recording the portions of the conference that appear on that display. It may be desirable to provide additional video switching and mixing circuitry so that the VCR can capture the signals from multiple sites. The audio signals must be addressed in a compatible fashion. All of these capabilities are feasible to implement with off-the-shelf VCR accessories, assuming the conferencing equipment includes the essential input and output connections. The main efforts that would be specific to implementation for videoconferencing would be aimed at making the VCR an easy-to-use part of the environment.

Instead of, or in addition to, a VCR, it may be appropriate to save some of the coded audio and video on a computer disk. The saved form of the audio and video might be retrieved for viewing instead of videotape, might be more easily indexed and searched, might be sent to the other sites, etc. We can provide this "video mail" to others with compatible equipment, in lieu of videotapes.

Other equipment may also be connected to the video inputs or outputs of the conferencing system. For example, the meeting participants may want to use 35mm transparencies in the meeting. It is likely infeasible to use a conventional 35mm projector directly in a video conference, but there exist devices that will accept 35mm slides and produce a video signal that the video conferencing equipment can accept as if it were just another camera.

Inevitably, there will be pieces of equipment that are specific to a particular meeting, or a particular environment, that the participants would like to be able to share across a video conference. Often, the equipment will have been designed to connect to a computer's serial ports, since the ports are provided on the computer to enable the connection of additional pieces of equipment. If the videoconferencing equipment is based on a computer, then the serial ports exist and the main implementation effort is in making the serial ports on the equipment available across the conference. This, in turn, is mainly a matter of diverting communications bandwidth from that allocated to motion video. In some cases, the equipment connected to the serial ports will be equipment specifically designed to enable distance meetings. The Polycom ShowStation described earlier is one such example. Several companies have developed equipment that is designed to physically appear to be an ordinary marker board hanging on a wall, but by use of special markers and erasers, the board can capture the markings on the board and transmit them to a personal computer for display at another location. Such equipment can be easily connected to the serial ports on videoconferencing equipment for use in distance meetings.

4.3 COMPUTERS

Most of the earlier discussion has been oriented toward meetings where human interaction and traditional visual aids are dominant. However, personal computers, especially "notebooks," are rapidly becoming a routine aspect of meetings. In many environments, a presenter may reasonably assume that he or she can bring a presentation on only a notebook computer and use display facilities in the conference room to show the presentation. Meeting participants bring notebook computers as sources of reference material, as a tool for capturing and manipulating data during the meeting, and for the computerized equivalent of "doodling," pretending to be involved in the meeting while actually working on something else or playing a computer game.

Where the computer is "just another visual aid," there are at least two approaches already discussed that can be used to include them in the conference. A "scan converter," as discussed as a means of converting computer format video output to television format, can be used to directly convert the display output from a notebook computer for use as if it were another camera. This is closely consistent with the expectations a presenter would have who is using a notebook for a presentation. The conferencing equipment takes the notebook output and presents it on a large display. From the presenter's perspective, it is almost a side effect that the display is in multiple rooms, some of them a great distance away.

Most notebook computers have serial ports intended for connecting to other devices and computers. It is possible to connect the notebook to the conferencing equipment using serial ports, and then use document sharing or program sharing capabilities between the systems.

More and more notebooks now have Ethernet capabilities. It may be more appropriate to connect the notebook to the conferencing system by an Ethernet connection, achieving much higher communication speeds than a serial port, and use document sharing or program sharing capabilities across an Ethernet connection.

At this writing, notebook computers are not quite as ready for direct use in videoconferencing as are desktop computers. However, high-performance notebook computers are capable of videoconferencing using the approaches described in Chapter 3. As such notebooks become commonplace, there will be new perspectives on how computers are used in meetings, and the equipment used for group conferences will enable such usage. In some sense, this will be natural evolution, but it will also be the case that some group conferences will be even more "computer centric." Depending on the people in the conference, the subject of the meeting, and so forth, conferences will range from those where the equipment must be as transparent as possible, so that it appears to the participants that they are in a "stretched room" with a "stretched table," to those conferences where the participants want to be directly involved with the conference equipment as just another part of their computer systems and networks. A challenge for the videoconferencing industry is to meet both of these extremes of expectation and need, as well as other variants on these two scenarios that will likely become the "typical" meeting scenario.

Chapter 5

All Together Now

Introducing Multipoint Conferencing

In the previous chapters for the most part we discussed conferences conducted between exactly two systems. Though it is simpler to implement equipment with only two-way conferences in mind, it is often important to connect more sites. As desktop systems become more prevalent, relative to group conferencing systems, it becomes even more natural to have multiway capabilities, if the total number of participants is to remain roughly the same. Conferencing with more than two sites is usually referred to as multipoint.

5.1 THREE IS NOT A CROWD

Brute force support for multiway conferences, that is, integrating point-to-point conferences between each pair of systems, is potentially expensive in terms of additional communication links and additional coding capabilities (see Figure 5.1). If each site is to be connected to each other site, then each site needs $N-1$ connections, where N is the number of sites. Within a local-area network (LAN), this may be practical, since only one physical connection is needed per system to support the $N-1$ logical connections. (The network bandwidth consumed may still be a problem if N is more than a few.) Outside of a LAN, either with ISDN connections or with internetworked LANs, providing $N-1$ connections for each system is generally impractical. The audio/video coding is also expensive in the brute force approach. Each site must be able to encode its own audio and video and decode the audio and video from the other $N-1$ sites. The support for decoding audio and video from the other sites will be prohibitively expensive for large N. On a LAN, brute force multipoint conferencing is practical for several, say, four, participating sites.

The alternative to brute force direct connections that is usually used, especially with ISDN connections, is to have specialized equipment, a

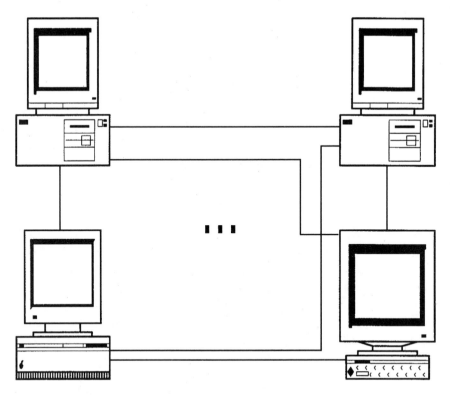

Figure 5.1   *N* fully connected systems

"multipoint control unit" (MCU), serve as a network focal point for the conference. Rather than connecting each system to each other, each system connects to the MCU (see Figure 5.2). Rather than having each system handle decoding *N*–1 audio and video streams, largely duplicating efforts at the other sites, the MCU can decode the audio/video from all of the sites, and send each site audio/video streams appropriate to that site. The collective computational effort can be much smaller.

MCUs are typically implemented to be able to handle a fixed number of connections. Twenty connections are a typical maximum, though some products allow more. Those connections may be spread across many conferences. For example, an MCU with 20-connection capability might simultaneously support three four-way conferences and an eight-way conference, each of these conferences occurring simultaneously and independent of each other. MCUs can be cascaded, so that two 20-connection MCUs could be combined to provide support for a 39-connection conference.

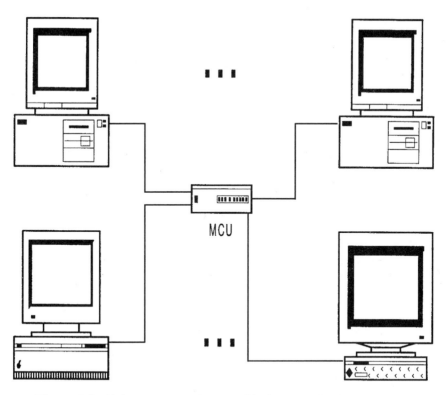

Figure 5.2 *N* sites connected to a multipoint control unit

5.2 AUDIO INDEPENDENCE

Whether fully connected, as in Figure 5.1, or connected to an MCU, all of the conference sites must participate more or less equally in audio.

In the fully connected case, each site must decode the audio from each of the other sites and mix these separate audio signals. Except for the issues already cited, the communications bandwidth required and the computation required for decode processing, there is nothing difficult to implement. If the communications interface is to a LAN, then one interface should suffice for connection to all of the other sites. If ISDN connections are needed, then a terminal adapter will be needed for each of the other sites.

In the common case where an MCU is used, with ISDN (or similar) connections, the MCU will have a terminal adapter, or equivalent network interface, for each site of the conference. Figure 5.3 shows the functional elements of a typical MCU. (In product implementations, multiple functions may be handled by a single element. For example, one processor might handle both

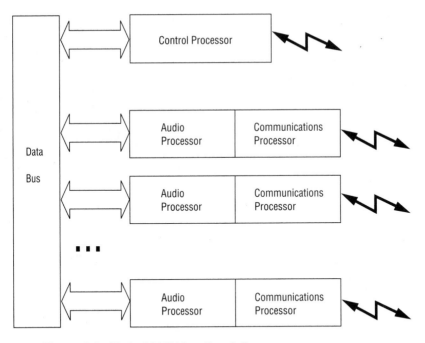

Figure 5.3   Typical MCU functional diagram

communication and audio chores, or one processor might handle communication for several sites.) From each site, the MCU receives multiplexed audio and video streams, and, potentially, additional streams of control and data (for example, for camera control and shared presentations). The communications processor demultiplexes each of the incoming streams. The audio processors receive coded audio streams and decode these audio streams to produce digital audio streams in a form suitable for mixing. The digital audio streams are placed on the data bus. Each audio processor takes the streams from the other sites of the conference from the data bus, mixes the audio streams together, and encodes the mixed audio stream for transmission to the other sites. These steps may require active involvement of the control processor. At a minimum, the control processor must indicate to the audio processors which streams are included in their respective conferences. [Since the MCU may be handling several independent conferences, the audio processors must be able to distinguish between (1) their own audio streams, (2) other streams from their conference, and (3) other streams from other conferences.]

Just as mixing signals from many microphones can allow extraneous noises to dominate the audio from a single site, as discussed in Section 4.1.3, mixing the signals from many sites in a multipoint conference can lead to unacceptable SNRs. It is typical in an MCU to mix together only some of the audio signals. An MCU might mix the strongest six or eight, ignoring the weaker ones, or it might mix the current strongest signal with the five or seven that most recently had their turn at being strongest.

The decoding, mixing, and re-encoding of the audio potentially degrades audio fidelity. If MCUs are cascaded to enable conferences with many sites, the signals from a subordinate MCU are treated as if they were from a single site. Both the subordinate and dominant MCUs are decoding, mixing, and re-coding audio signals, so an audio signal might be encoded and decoded four times. (For sites connected to the subordinate MCU, the audio is encoded at the originating site, decoded/re-encoded at the subordinate MCU, decoded/re-encoded at the dominant MCU, decoded/re-encoded again by the subordinate MCU, and finally decoded by the receiving site.) One of the measures of effectiveness of an audio coding algorithm is whether it preserves fidelity with repeated encoding/decoding.

5.3 VIDEO CONTROL

Assuming extraneous sounds are not a problem, it is possible for an MCU to mix the audio from many sites. However, there are two problems with video that make it harder to include video from many sites simultaneously. First, video requires substantially higher data rates and computational power for coding, so it is more difficult and expensive to support many video streams simultaneously. Second, it is visually difficult to present many video streams simultaneously. Each video stream requires its own window on the display, so as more streams are added, there is a smaller and smaller number of pixels available for each stream. Because of these problems, multipoint conferences normally display video from only a limited subset of the conference sites.

Three approaches are commonly used:

1. Continuous presence refers to the attempt to make video from many of the sites continuously present on the screen. The number of sites present is limited by the problems cited earlier, typically to at most four sites being visible at a time. Which sites are seen can be determined by either of

Figure 5.4 Controls available to conductor

the approaches discussed next. Without an MCU, each site is responsible for decoding the video streams and displaying them. With an MCU, the MCU is responsible for selecting the streams to be displayed, decoding those streams, producing a new video stream including the selected streams, say, as four quadrants of the combined stream, and encoding the composite stream. This requires significant, but likely acceptable, video decoding and coding capability in the MCU. The decoding/coding can add significant delay.

2. <u>Voice-activated switching</u> refers to conferences where the sites generally display the video from the site with the strongest audio signal, with that site seeing the video from the previously selected site. If implemented properly, the sites generally see the person speaking, and the person speaking sees the previous speaker. The MCU (or the individual sites, in a fully connected environment) must be able to select the strongest signal and avoid switching too frequently, but simple heuristics are usually sufficient to handle these decisions well. Perhaps the most important characteristic is that the MCU does not need to decode the video streams at all! The MCU need only recognize the coded video streams coming from the selected sites (the current and previous speaker) and route these streams to intended destination sites.

3. <u>Conducted</u> (sometimes called "chaired" or "chair-controlled") conferences allow one site to be designated as the conductor of the conference. A person at this site acts as the chairperson of the conference and selects the video that will be seen by the other sites. One of the other sites in the conference may "request the floor," asking to be made visible, and the conductor may select this site to be displayed or ignore the request. If a conductor site has not been established, or if the conductor relinquishes that role, then an individual site may ask to be made the chair, or may simply ask to be seen by the other sites. These control mechanisms are straightforward to implement, both at the individual sites and at the MCU. As with voice-activated switching, the MCU does not need to decode the video streams, just route the proper streams to the proper sites (See Figure 5.4).

The last two items are slightly overstated with regard to video switching. If a decoder is receiving coded video, and suddenly receives arbitrarily different coded video, obvious distortion of the decoded video will occur. The distortion will be temporary, but very noticeable and undesirable. An MCU can avoid the distortion by observing the structure of the coded video streams and switching at points that will be least problematic for the decoders. Observing the stream structure does not require decoding.

5.4 HARDER STUFF

Multipoint audio and video is challenging because of bandwidth and performance issues. Product implementation requires attention to detail such as switching video streams without causing problems for decoders. These issues aside, the handling of audio and video in multipoint is not conceptually harder than in point to point. Some of the issues associated with other shared facilities in multipoint can be a little harder, sometimes more for conceptual reasons rather than technical ones. For example, in annotating a shared presentation, do all of the sites simultaneously mark on the image? In managing remote cameras, who gets to move which cameras? There are also implemenation issues that are harder. How does fax support work, for example? The answers depend, in part, on whether the conference is conducted or not. In a conducted conference, some of the challenges are easier because it can be assumed that the chair can resolve issues of contention.

Shared Presentations.   An image captured from a camera or computer program can be "broadcast" to all of the sites, either across a LAN or through an MCU. The image is coded at the originating site and decoded at the receiving sites in the same manner, whether the conference is two way or multipoint. The differences for multipoint potentially arise with regard to annotation. Are all of the sites allowed to type and draw on the shared image at the same time? If so, each site can broadcast its additions and erasures and expect the other sites to update their copy of the shared image accordingly. There are potential problems with "race conditions"; for example, if one site is marking a spot on the image and the other site is erasing that area at the same time, what is the net effect? Such problems may be perceived as minor and acceptable. On the other hand, it may be desirable for only one person to have the virtual chalk and eraser, and it may be appropriate to enforce this characteristic. This can be done using the same or similar mechanisms as those for managing a conducted conference and for managing a potentially conducted conference when no site has assumed the conductor role.

Program Sharing.   If we forget that program sharing, as discussed in Section 3.4, is *not* distributed computation, then multipoint program sharing applications may seem daunting. But remember that the program is running on only one computer, using only the program files, memory, and data files on that computer, and we see that multipoint program sharing is not complicated. The issues are the same as those for annotation, which we just discussed. Can every site use the keyboard and mouse at the same time? If not, conductor mechanisms are needed, but these are the same mechanisms already needed for other purposes.

Faxes. Conventional fax machines are designed for two-way usage, with "handshaking" and error control protocols that assume a pair of fax machines. Using such machines in a broadcast mode is infeasible. However, it is feasible, in a conducted multiway conference, to have pair-wise connections between sites for fax purposes. With those pairs established, faxing can work in multiway conferences.

Serial Ports. Similarly, most devices intended for connection through serial ports are designed assuming pair-wise connection. As long as the pairs are established properly, these devices can work in a multipoint conference, ignoring the other sites.

5.5 GETTING CONNECTED

Establishing a multipoint conference requires additional steps, both because of the additional participants, and, assuming an MCU is used, because of the need to connect to the MCU instead of connecting directly to another site. Some level of prearrangement is normal for a multiway conference. For example, the participating sites may be instructed to dial numbers corresponding to assigned ports of the MCU at the designated time. Such arrangements are sometimes called a "meet me" conference. An alternate prearrangement would be to have the participating sites waiting for the MCU to call and establish the conference. It is reasonable to expect that *ad hoc* multipoint conferences will become normal, as well. A participant might call an MCU and request to join a conference already in progress, and be added to the conference if authentication and authorization criteria are met.

With several conference rooms, an MCU, possibly some communication links, possibly some portable equipment, etc., needing to be prearranged for a multipoint conference, it is natural to have much of the prearrangement handled by scheduling software. This software is analogous to software often used for managing schedules of individuals and groups in an organization, but in addition to administering the reservations, resolving conflicts, etc., the software can take an active role in controlling an MCU and equipment at the conference sites.

Chapter 6

Finishing the Picture

How We Use Videoconferencing

We now expand on the ideas in Section 1.5 to look in more breadth and depth at the opportunities made possible by videoconferencing. We intend to show the potential for videoconferencing to enhance everyday activities and make people more effective.

But first, we seek inspiration from Sherlock Holmes! In the early pages of "The Adventure of the Cardboard Box," Holmes and Watson are sitting in the same room. Watson believes that Holmes is not paying attention to him. After prolonged silence, Holmes tells Watson what Watson has been thinking, based on the visual clues from Holmes' observation of Watson during the silence. Predictably, Watson is amazed and Holmes represents his observations as "very superficial." Though fiction, the Holmes stories are replete with examples of the usage of all senses, particularly vision, to gain understanding. Attempts at a distance meeting with only audio seem like sensory deprivation. This is a conscious phenomenon for someone used to using videoconferencing. For others, the deprivation is no less real, but less likely to be consciously recognized.

6.1 EVERYDAY MEETINGS

(Would you rather spend your time on airplanes or on TV?)

Sometimes it seems that the activity of having meetings, in itself, is the primary goal of modern organizations. Many people say they cannot get their work done because they are always going to meetings.

Videoconferencing won't make meetings go away. Nor can it make people define and stick to meeting agendas. And people who don't like meetings will not suddenly feel differently because of videoconferencing. A meeting that is a waste of time is a waste of time whether all of the participants are in the same room or different rooms.

However, videoconferencing *can* make distance meetings more effective.

In some cases, a videoconference will be seen as a more formal event, and that formality may enable better meeting discipline. Having shared video and shared presentation materials can make the difference between a productive distance meeting and time wasted in an ineffective telephone discussion.

6.1.1 Scheduled Meetings

Videoconference meetings are typically scheduled and coordinated in advance, for a variety of reasons:

1. A videoconference in lieu of a face-to-face meeting that requires travel probably is important enough to merit advance planning.

2. A meeting of more than a very few individuals requires advance notice to ensure the desired participants are present. Person-to-person telephone calls are usually, but not always, unscheduled. (As a counter example: "Let me call you back at eight.") Multiperson telephone calls are usually, but not always, scheduled. (Counter examples: "I'm going to put you on the speakerphone." "Let me see if I can get Mary on the line.")

3. Meeting rooms that are used must have videoconferencing capability. Otherwise, video-capable rooms must be rented. Copying centers and hotels are two likely locations for such rental facilities.

4. The nature of the equipment and communication links required may make it necessary to reserve facilities in advance, obtain other equipment, locate administrative assistance, establish/test a connection before the scheduled starting time, and so on.

Face-to-face meetings often start late or otherwise do not "get going" until the participants have adjusted to each other and the physical environment. Similarly, the first few minutes of a videoconference meeting may be spent, for example, establishing connections, adjusting sound levels, explaining the equipment if the participants have not used it before, etc. This "overhead" will diminish with experience and familiarity.

6.1.2 Unscheduled Meetings

One-on-one videoconferences will eventually be as easy and spontaneous as telephone calls are today. First, however, more people will need to have videoconferencing capability. They will need to recognize the option, and to relish the value of video communication. Just as people can carry around a cellular phone and not remember they have omnipresent telephone capability, people will need to adjust to having videoconferencing as an available, attractive, and routine means of communication. Video numbers will become the fifth "address" on business cards, after postal, telephone, fax, and electronic mail addresses. Pagers will not need to change to support paging for video calls, but equivalents of voice mail and call waiting will emerge.

6.2 EMPLOYMENT RECRUITING

We would be making an overstatement if we suggested that videoconferencing is sufficient for typical pre-employment interviewing. In a typical interview, even after both employer and candidate have given their best efforts and have reached a formal agreement, there are usually significant surprises in store for both. However, videoconferencing used early in the process can enable employers to evaluate a larger group of candidates and thereby potentially identify better candidates for open positions. Video interviews are likely to yield more information and more substantive discussion for both parties than the typical alternative, the cursory telephone interviews that screen candidates before asking them to travel for face-to-face interviews. The additional information results partly because of the visual communication itself. Also, the parties are likely to treat the video interview more like a formal interview and less like initial telephone contact. This better communication earlier in the process is beneficial to both parties. For example, candidates obtain a better sense of the employer's environment and expectations.

However, although the employer may have appropriate equipment, the candidate likely does not. Even if that person's current employer has conferencing equipment, ethics and privacy issues make it likely that other equipment will be needed. So the candidate will likely need to use rental facilities. Also, a recruiter should have equipment available for these purposes.

6.3 LEGAL

Some legal procedures cannot reasonably be performed remotely. The more weighty and formal the proceedings, the less likely that alternatives to traditional approaches will be accepted. Surprising alternatives, such as punishment by confinement to a convict's residence by electronic surveillance, are being accepted, and it is reasonable to expect videoconferencing-based procedures to become more prevalent. Remote testimony is one example. Arraignments are often viewed as a necessary evil by an arresting police officer, and in some jurisdictions, many crimes go unprosecuted because the arresting officer does not appear at arraignment of the suspect. In some jurisdictions, the arresting officer can participate in the arraignment by videoconference from his/her usual station, with much less impact on other duties. Remote arraignment is likely to be acceptable to both prosecution and defense because it allows faster resolution and earlier release on bond. Depositions are given by videoconference, and it is plausible that videoconferencing will be used for testimony in some trials, at least in civil proceedings. Bell Atlantic Corporation, VTEL, and others offer products specifically targeted at supporting video arraignment.

6.4 PRODUCT TECHNICAL ASSISTANCE

When a user of a product needs assistance with the product, it is often expensive, possibly impractical, to have on hand an expert familiar with the product. This is true for different kinds of products: manufacturers of computers, machine tools, and appliances all provide technical assistance by telephone. When it is easy to describe the support issues, telephone support can be very successful. On the other hand, verbal descriptions may be difficult, inaccurate, even grossly misleading. Visual information, either of the prod-

Figure 6.1 Video arraignment

uct usage, or of procedures to identify a suspected malfunction, can overcome the limitations of verbal descriptions. "Fax-back" services frequently help the user get diagrams, pictures, and other product information.

Videoconferencing is a natural step beyond telephone technical support and fax-back services. It may not be important for the support person and the user to see each other, but it can be enormously helpful for the support person to see the product, to see where the problem lies. Seeing a properly installed/functioning product can be a revelation to the user. We are assuming it is possible to point the camera(s) at the products and/or move the products within the field of view of the camera. In some cases, it may be economically appropriate to include videoconferencing equipment with the product, to ensure that support is possible.

6.5 MANUFACTURING

Similarly, a manufacturing organization will likely have both experts and relatively unskilled workers. Their activities may be spread across a single large building, several co-located buildings, or across substantial distances. When problems arise, telephone may not be effective enough, and travel won't be fast enough. Video communications can make the difference between efficient operation and significant production delays. Companies such as Wheaton Industries in Millville, New Jersey, have made extensive use of videoconferencing for their own products' production, and provided videoconferencing production equipment to other manufacturers [STRA94].

6.6 KIOSKS

Kiosks for automated teller machines, information booths, remote sales, and so forth are being augmented by videoconferencing capability. At an automated teller machine, videoconferencing can enable the financial institution to offer more complex services, such as account establishment, loan processing, and investment counseling, which would otherwise be inhibited without visual contact. The customers and the bankers all want the clues that come from video.

6.7 TRADING FLOOR

Brokers in securities, commodities, and options, and other financial traders, are always looking for more information to give themselves and their clients an edge. It is not unusual to see five or six computer monitors at a trader's workstation. These monitors are used for conventional personal computing, for monitoring prices and indices, for monitoring financial and general news, etc. More and more, videoconferencing is a significant aspect of these environments, for contact with customers, corporate investor relations departments, and other traders.

One of the frequent activities of securities analysts is gathering information on individual companies in order to estimate financial performance of those companies. For an analyst that closely follows a particular company, this may include occasional visits to the company's facilities. Videoconferencing allows an analyst to virtually visit such companies more frequently.

Most public companies have large multiway telephone conferences with financial analysts when they are announcing financial or other news, to be sure that the analysts understand what the company is doing. These conferences can be more effective for all concerned when data conferencing is used to present the company's announcement materials, and when videoconferencing is used to ensure understanding between the participants.

6.8 CLASSROOMS

It seems that "distance learning" is *the* primary application of videoconferencing, especially group conferencing systems:

- In the United States, most universities, especially state universities, have significant networks and installations of videoconferencing equipment.

- Large instructional networks have been established by government and military organizations.

- Internal training and external instructional offerings are a major portion of business usage of videoconferencing.

- "Telemedicine" installations are often used for continuing medical education.

Video has been used for instructional purposes since the initial availability of commercial television receivers, and many of the earliest videoconferencing installations were for educational purposes, so it is not surprising that distance learning is dominant in videoconferencing application.

Distance learning will continue to be a dominant application of video. Just as personal computers have transitioned from novelty status to pervasiveness in educational institutions, with acquisition of equipment and connections, videoconferencing will become a routine aspect of primary and secondary education.

Distance learning is a sufficiently broad and dominant application that it would be misleading to presume that videoconferencing is mandatory for distance learning. Before videoconferencing was practical, before television was commercial, distance learning existed with correspondence courses. The modern equivalents of those courses may be very similar to their predecessors, or they may depend on mailing computer media instead of paper, or they may depend on electronic mail and Internet repositories. For some subjects, instructors, and students, audio and video contact may be of secondary interest. For other situations, audio and video make distance learning possible. The discussion here emphasizes those situations.

6.8.1 Local Classroom Characteristics

Instructors are primarily concerned with the class content and engaging the students. In a Socratic style, the instructor seeks an active dialog. In a lecturing style, the instructor needs to capture the students' attention so that they absorb the material and ask questions when they need to. Instructors find it effective to wander around the room, especially when students work on in-class assignments. In doing so, he or she expects to stay in the students' sight and hearing and hear and see the students. Watching the students helps the instructor gauge their comprehension, and allows the students to get the instructor's attention to comment or ask questions.

Instructors outline the material on a chalkboard or marker board, and use transparencies prepared in advance to lead the discussion. They use laboratory equipment, videotapes, and computer programs to illustrate the material. Field trips allow the class to see subject material firsthand.

There are written handouts of class notes, excerpts from published sources, reading lists, and other study materials. Material is needed from libraries, private collections, and publications. Homework, quizzes, and exams are part of the instructional process as well as gauges of comprehension and progress.

6.8.2 Virtual Classroom Characteristics

In a distance learning context, instructors need to retain all of the above capabilities and characteristics. They require specific facilities to break down the physical boundaries and distance and to attempt to re-create the characteristics of a single classroom. Specific facilities include the following:

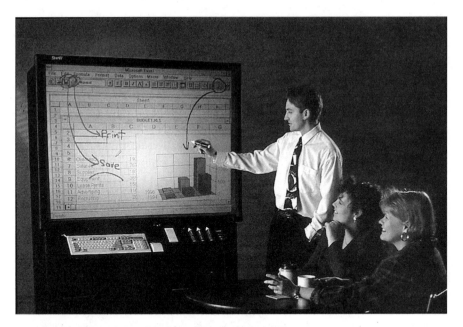

Figure 6.2 Rear projection SMART Board™
(Photograph courtesy of SMART Technologies, Inc.)

- *Audio.* An instructor needs to *hear* and be heard. The lack of two-way audio is one of the most significant limitations of traditional television-based approaches, whether the television is transmitted by broadcast, satellite, or private circuits. For an instructor to hear the students, many microphones may be needed. Push-to-talk switches or noise gates are often used on microphones, each keeping the cumulative noise from being a problem. The instructor should have a wireless microphone or equivalent device that allows freedom of movement without loss of sound pickup.

- *Video of the instructor.* In an instructional setting, the requirements for camera tracking and video display may be much stronger than in a business meeting. The instructor should be able to wander around the classroom[1] and remain visible to the students. There are several ways to enable a camera to follow the instructor. One way is to have the instructor wear a locator device, for example, a very low power radio transmitter, that cam-

---

[1] This discussion assumes the instructor is in a conventional classroom, with students present in that classroom. Other scenarios are certainly feasible. For example, if none of the students is geographically near the instructor, it may make sense for the instructor to stay in an office, conducting the class from a desktop system.

era mechanisms can track. There are several commercial implementations of such camera tracking facilities. Another possibility is to use multiple microphones to estimate speaker location to position the camera. Similarly, it is possible to estimate speaker location as part of the video coding processes and use that information to position the camera. There are research prototypes of both of these approaches, the multiple microphone approach and the video processing approach.

- *Video of the students.* Some (or all) of the students are in different rooms from the instructor. There may be more rooms than locales if there are too many students for specific rooms. The instructor wants to see all of the students, when appropriate, <u>and</u> be able to focus on individual students at other times. If there are more than two rooms (including the instructor's room) and a multipoint control unit, then the instructor may depend on voice-activated switching or may explicitly control the video viewed by the sites. In elaborate installations, extra communication and coding equipment is used to allow the sites to see multiple sites simultaneously.

  Within a given student site, the same technologies used to enable video tracking of the instructor can also be used for video location of the students.

- *Presentation material support.* Charts, slides, computer usage, videotapes, and other classroom material <u>must</u> be visible at all of the student sites. The technology we discussed in Chapters 3 and 4 is likely sufficient, except that we need physically larger devices. For example, we need the equivalent of a chalkboard. Several companies have developed remote marker board devices for use in distance learning environments. Figure 6.2 illustrates a marker board that provides for display on a remote computer or videoconferencing system.

  The presence of audio, video, and data communications equipment encourages usage that would not be contemplated in a single classroom. For example, with video facilities readily in place, an instructor can conduct a "virtual field trip." The class stays in the classroom but audio and video is transmitted from a manufacturing plant, or a museum, or other "field trip" sites.

- *Individual attention/communication facilities.* Student response terminals, based on a numeric keypad or computer keyboard, may be used for the distance equivalent of raising one's hand. These terminals can also be used to allow all the students to respond to questions, to be accumulated at the instructor's station, to give explicit feedback to the instructor and the class as a whole. The students can use computerized facilities to submit homework and take tests. An instructor may wish to give grades and other feedback privately on a student-by-student basis. With appropriate data security protocols, this individual communication can be included in the videoconference environment.

6.9 CLINICS

Computing and communications have changed phenomenally in the last few decades, in capabilities, in technology, in economics, and in interaction with society. Medicine is one of the few fields of endeavor that has changed as dramatically, if not more dramatically, in this same time. The visiting family physician has all but disappeared in the United States. In urban areas, independent medical practices are also disappearing rapidly, as health maintenance organizations and similar centralized enterprises have become the primary delivery vehicles for health care. Many rural areas have no health care providers outside of the nearest city. Medical technology has advanced at least comparably to computer technology (but without the cost drops!), including computerization of many medical instruments. Along with the rise of medical technology has been the rise of specialists with the insight and skills to use and advance the technology. These specialists are usually located at major medical centers, often some distance even from mid-sized urban areas. Last, but certainly not least, the cost of medical treatment has risen more rapidly than other costs of living. The dramatically enhanced capabilities of the medical profession substantially compound the costs. Many previously untreatable conditions are now treatable, albeit with extensive and expensive care.

Videoconferencing has the potential to help with both these distance and economic challenges. Much of the potential is independent of medical issues. Medical organizations operate like other businesses, so the use of videoconferencing for administrative purposes, and other general business purposes, can enhance the effectiveness of medical organizations. As medical practice advances, the need for continuing education of physicians grows, encouraging physicians to benefit from distance learning by videoconferencing.

Increasing use of computers and other digital technology in medicine provides for integration of medical usage with videoconferencing equipment. Radiology is gradually shifting from traditional photographic processes to digital representations. Without effective digital representation of images, electronic transmission is awkward, if not unacceptable. For example, the resolution of most typical video cameras is clearly inadequate for viewing a full X-ray film, but it is possible to focus a video camera on a small portion of the film and get better effective resolution. Digital radiology uses resolutions much higher than typical computer and video equipment, typically either 2560×2048 pixels or 4096×4096 pixels, with gray scales represented by 12 bits per pixel.

The same approaches used to transmit lower resolution still images in videoconferences can be used to transmit high-resolution medical images. Unless higher bandwidth communication circuits are used, the transmission delays will be longer than for lower resolution images. Just as diagnostic requirements call for higher resolution still images, diagnostic use of motion video calls for higher resolution than 352 × 288. If the equipment and/or communication circuits do not allow for higher resolution, then diagnosis may require zooming the camera in to focus on small areas of a patient.

Many medical instruments, even relatively simple ones such as a blood pressure cuff (sphygmomanometer), are available with interfaces to computer serial ports, allowing computer control and acquisition of data with the instrument. A videoconferencing system's serial ports can be used to control these devices remotely and acquire their data.

Figure 6.3 shows a videoconferencing system specifically designed for medical environments.

Figure 6.3 F.R.E.D. ("Friendly Roll-about Engineered for Doctors")

Beyond administration and continuing medical education by video conference, medical practice itself is being enhanced by videoconference. In lieu of the visiting family physician, video equipment, including medical instrumentation, is being placed in patients' homes while they are ill, and a physician can virtually visit the patient at home, take readings from the instruments, observe the patients' appearance and condition, and provide treatment. Though not the same as a face-to-face appointment, a physician's visit by videoconference can be much more effective than a simple telephone consultation, and, for those patients intimidated by medical facilities, having the appointment at home may be more comfortable.

There are many comparable situations where video, and remotely controlled medical instruments, enable medical practice at a distance. In the absence of visiting physicians, some communities have established visiting nurse organizations. With a nurse, or a paramedic, visiting the patient at home while a physician is present by video, the nurse can overcome limitations of the equipment, and the equipment can enable the physician to direct and observe the patient/nurse more effectively. In a rural environment, a paramedical facility equipped with videoconferencing can enable an urban physician to treat patients remotely.

Telemedicine by videoconference is not limited to patient/physician interaction. A general practitioner needs consultation from specialists. The right specialists may be unavailable locally, and may be very far away. In a time-critical situation, travel may not be possible. Consultation by videoconference, when effective, can not only save travel time of the general practitioner, it may be the only viable option when time is short.

All of these have the potential for cost savings, in saving the time and improving the effectiveness of the physicians, in avoiding hospitalization of the patients, and improving the effectiveness of the other medical personnel. However, one of the biggest inhibitions to such approaches is economic: Medical insurers have been slow to accept such approaches and reimburse the costs, so there is a significant financial disincentive for the patients. We hope this is a temporary phenomenon.

6.10 ENTERTAINMENT

In the production of movies and television shows, in advertising, in music recording and similar activities, working at remote locations and collaboration across distances is the norm. Though the primary activity is at a project-specific site, for example, a location for filming a movie, there are usually support and review activities that must be conducted elsewhere, at a sound studio, a producer's office, a client's premises, and so forth. The video and/or audio is likely to result in a commercial product. Thus it is critical that the visual quality and sound quality be representative of the product. The still image and motion video requirements of these activities are similar to those of telemedicine.

REFERENCE

STRA94   Strauss, P., "Beyond Talking Heads: Videoconferencing Makes Money," *Datamation 40,* 19 (October 1, 1994).

PART 2

Behind the Curtain

Chapter 7

Analog, Digital, and Television

Television began its life as an analog system and has been gradually converting to digital over time. Decades of optimization and high-volume production have given the analog systems price advantages that are only gradually eroding. A video camera, radio-frequency (RF) modulator, and a television receiver constitute the lowest cost videoconferencing terminal. However, two-way transmission of the RF analog signal to one or a few other terminals is expensive. TV transmission is cost effective only when one signal is broadcast to many receiving sets. Nevertheless, when RF analog transmission was the only choice, there were a few users who were willing to bear the expense of analog videoconferencing. For video communication within a campus, the situation has been somewhat different. In the recent past, cable TV and related technologies have allowed relatively low-cost, high-quality videophone networks within a building or campus. Digital systems now match or beat such local analog systems in price, with varying degrees of reduction in picture quality.

For some time, in most two-way long-distance communication situations, digital systems have had an overall cost advantage over analog. The expense of the massive computations necessary to compress video for transmission over digital circuits is more than overcome by the lower transmission costs. Both the cost of such compression and the cost of digital transmission have been diminishing rapidly. An acceptable videoconference can now be held for little more than twice the cost of a long-distance phone call, using a terminal that can be assembled for well under $2,500 (as of 1996).

7.1 ANALOG TO DIGITAL TO ANALOG

The analog audio and video signals from the outside world, into and out of a videoconferencing system, must be converted to and from digital representations. Although digital audio and video are handled somewhat differently, certain fundamental concepts are common to the conversions.

Consider a signal $S(t)$, that is, one that has an amplitude varying as a function of time. (See Figure 7.1.) As some readers know, $S(t)$ can be represented as the weighted sum of a series of sinusoidal basis functions. This set of functions spans a range from slowly varying in time, including a constant function, to varying successively more and more rapidly in time. If $S(t)$ does not change rapidly in time, then it can be generated or re-created from a fairly simple set of sinusoids. If $S(t)$ varies more rapidly, then more rapidly varying basis functions are required. The most rapidly varying basis function needed (the one with the highest frequency) determines the frequency of $S(t)$. That is, its frequency is $S(t)$'s frequency.

To digitize $S(t)$, we must sample the signal frequently enough to capture the highest frequency components that are present, and must quantize each sample to the desired numerical accuracy. Thus information can be lost in two ways, from using too large a sampling interval and from quantizing too coarsely. Fax machines are a familiar example of digitizing. (The sampling done by a fax is better thought of in terms of samples per unit distance across a page, rather than as per unit time.) Basic fax samples are taken at about 200 per inch, and are quantized to one of only two values, one representing white and the other black. This is adequate for most typewritten material, but not for color photographs or very small type fonts.

7.1.1 Sampling

Consider a signal that varies smoothly and periodically in time, like the sine wave, $\sin(2\pi t)$, of Figure 7.2, with a frequency of one cycle per second (1 Hz).

According to Nyquist's theorem [NET95], taking a sample every 0.5 second completely characterizes the signal. That is, it can be reconstructed from

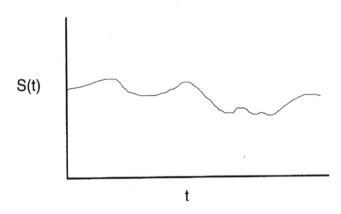

Figure 7.1   Time-varying signal

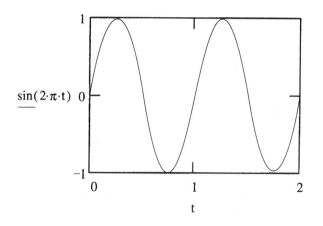

$\sin(2 \cdot \pi \cdot t)$

Figure 7.2 Sine wave at 1 Hz

the samples. Notice from Figure 7.3 that $\sin(6\pi t - \pi)$ varies three times as fast as $\sin(2\pi t)$. If both signals are sampled at 0.5-second intervals, beginning at $t = 0.25$, the samples are the same. We cannot distinguish between $\sin(2\pi t)$ and $\sin(6\pi t - \pi)$ from the samples. This phenomenon is called "aliasing." However, if we know that we will be encountering no signals with frequency components higher than 1 Hz, we know that this aliasing will not occur.

Nyquist's theorem actually assumes that the function being sampled is infinitely long in time, and states that it can be reconstructed by summing a weighted series of an infinite number of samples. What the theorem tells us practically is that we want to sample at somewhat greater than twice the frequency of the signal so that we can avoid aliasing. It is quite important to

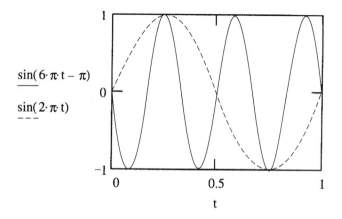

$\sin(6 \cdot \pi \cdot t - \pi)$

$\sin(2 \cdot \pi \cdot t)$

Figure 7.3 Sine waves at two different frequencies

avoid aliasing because of the way it can distort the signals in the frequency range of interest. Consider Figure 7.4, which shows the time-varying value of sin(2πt), and a second signal, which is the sum of sin(2πt) + sin(3πt). If we assume that the sin(3πt) component is not present and we sample at 0.5-second intervals, we get something quite different from sin(2πt). Sin(3πt) must be filtered out before we sample. It cannot be filtered after sampling because the total signal, and hence the sin(3πt) component, is not sampled finely enough. If we knew that sin(3πt) was the only signal present at greater than 1 Hz, we could subtract it out later, but in general we cannot know. Frequency components higher than we want to deal with must be filtered out. For traditional telephone circuits, the frequency range is 300 to 3,300 cycles per second. (For more modern equipment, with sharper filters, this is typically extended to a range of 200 to 3,500.) The standard sampling rate for digitizing analog telephone signals is 8 KHz. If, say, 7-KHz audio signals are digitized (sampled) at this rate, noticeable aliasing will occur. That is, samples from the higher frequency components will be heard as false lower frequency components. Like all practical filters, those in the telephone system cannot cut off sharply at 3.3 KHz. They roll off gradually above 3.3 KHz, but any signal components at 4 KHz or above are attenuated sufficiently to not be bothersome.

7.1.2 Quantizing

Samples are not taken and stored with infinite precision. Computers store only a finite subset of the rational numbers. This means that we frequently lose information when we store information from the real world into a computer system. The cost of analog-to-digital converters is also a factor in de-

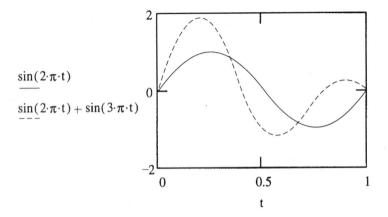

Figure 7.4 Composite signal with two sine wave components

termining with what precision to sample a value. Eight bits per sample are usually considered adequate for videoconferencing video and telephone quality audio. For color video, each of the three color components is usually sampled to 8 bits, giving a total of 24 bits per pixel. For higher fidelity audio, samples are digitized at 14 to 16 bits each.

7.1.3 Conversion Back to Analog

To be comprehended by human senses, digital signals must be converted back to analog form. Care and filtering is also necessary when going in this direction. No doubt most readers of this book will have experienced the "jaggies" when viewing lines and edges in computer-generated graphics. This is caused by displaying a "signal" at a higher bandwidth than is actually contained in the signal. The sharp pixel edges apparent in jaggies on a diagonal line represent high-frequency information not actually intended to be present. When a diagonal line in a video scene is digitized, information is lost, as we have seen. When the time comes to display it, this information is, in a sense, often treated as more accurate than it really is.

The false high-frequency information can be reduced by postfiltering, which will blur the sharp transitions between pixels. The computer graphics community has historically called this "antialiasing," since the only aliasing they had to worry about was in the display, and not in sampling input signals.

7.2 ANALOG: LOW-COST TERMINALS, HIGH-COST TRANSMISSION

In the early 1980s and before, TV satellite systems were used by a small number of people to do videoconferencing. There were even occasions of small organizations renting satellite transponder time and rooms in TV stations in two cities in order to hold conferences. The major components of an analog terminal do not have to be expensive. If standard TV RF modulation techniques are used, the receiver portion is essentially a TV set. The transmitting part needs a microphone, camera, and RF modulator. Low-power modulators are built into every VCR and many camcorders. The expense lies in transmitting the analog signal over distances. The bandwidth is high, approximately 6 MHz, and the only "long-distance" networks (the TV broadcasting system and cable TV networks in conjunction with satellites) are optimized for one-way transmission.

By the mid-1980s, conference room and desktop products were available that made use of LAN coaxial cable networks for the transmission medium. There are also methods for transmitting analog video over glass fiber and over twisted-pair LAN cabling. Such products have been only sporadically used, even when they were less expensive than similar digital products. To the extent that they have been used, it has usually been in hybrid networks. That is, the connections within a building or campus have been analog, but long-distance transmission has been digital, with the local/long-distance interface containing a video codec.

For the initial input and the final output, videoconferencing systems still depend heavily on (mostly analog) television technology and equipment. Video cameras capture the moving pictures that are to be transmitted, and television monitors usually are the final display device. Because of this dependence, a very short look at TV cameras and monitors is in order.

All systems for capturing and displaying moving picture information do so in terms of a series of still frames. The still frames are captured or created, and then displayed rapidly in order to fool the human visual system into perceiving motion. Movies are displayed at 24 frames per second, TV at 25 or 30, depending on which standard is used,[1] and flip books at a rate that varies with the skill and desire of the user. Each of these television still frames is made up of horizontal lines. That is, the image captured in the frame is sampled vertically as a sequence of horizontal lines. For traditional analog television, this allows a frame's image to be captured a line at a time, from top to bottom, so that a two-dimensional image can be transmitted as a one-dimensional signal, one line after another. For digital TV, and for related systems like videoconferencing, horizontal sampling and quantization must be added to capture a digital representation of an image into a frame. Digital systems almost always adhere to the traditional, top to bottom, left to right scanning of an image. This is called a "raster scan." Sometimes the digitized contents of a frame stored in a digital memory are called a raster.

We might be happier today if TV had been developed to use 60 or more frames per second, but engineering compromises are usually necessary. When TV was being brought to commercial realization in the 1940s, the trade-offs led to the use of 25 or 30 frames per second, with each frame being split into two fields, displayed one after the other, so that 60 (or 50) fields are displayed per second. The two fields that form a frame are interlaced, with the odd-numbered lines of the frame forming the odd field and the even-numbered lines forming the even field. Having new information displayed on a TV screen at 60 times per second reduces the apparent flicker of an image, though the interlace can cause a more local form of flicker, sometimes called "twitter," when there are sharp differences between adjacent lines in a frame. The most obvious example of twitter is when a scene contains a hori-

---

[1] In North America and Japan, 30 frames per second (actually 29.97) are used. In Europe, 25 are used.

zontal line that is captured as exactly one line in a frame, so that it is in, say, the odd field but not in the even field. Thus the line appears for 1/60 of a second and then disappears when the even field is displayed. If there is no movement in the scene being captured, then this line will flash on and off (it will twitter) at 1/60 of a second intervals. In actual practice, TV cameras do not capture details that are only one line high, partly to avoid twitter. However, it can be a problem with highly processed video or computer-generated images.

On the display side, color CRT TV monitors remain the display of choice for most videoconferencing rooms. Many readers will be at least somewhat familiar with how electron beams are swept line by line, top to bottom across the fine pattern of red, blue, and green phosphor dots inside the face of a CRT. The beam sweeping pattern matches the order in which each field of an image is captured. When the beam strikes a phosphor, it emits red, green, or blue light, depending on its type. Three beams are used, one for each of the primary colors, red, green, and blue. Depending on the exact design of the tube and the pattern of color phosphor deployment, either an aperture grille or a shadow mask is used to help ensure that each beam does not strike the wrong color phosphor. The amount of light emitted by each phosphor is a nonlinear function of the intensity of the beam striking it. It is nearly proportional to the input voltage raised to the power *gamma*. (See NET95 and POY93 for detailed explanations.) "Gamma correction" is applied to make sure that each color is emitted at the correct intensity. Camera and CRT designers must make sure that their signals match properly. In the television world, cameras have historically been far outnumbered by television receivers, so it is more economical overall to assign the job of gamma correction to the cameras. For most CRTs, *gamma* is approximately 2.5. Any CRT that differs too much from this value should supply a correction for pictures captured from TV cameras. This is frequently not done properly in the computer world, but gamma correction is not usually a concern for the designer of room videoconferencing systems, as long as the cameras and display devices adhere to normal television practice. For this reason, the ITU-T videoconferencing standards are not concerned with gamma correction.

7.3 COLOR REPRESENTATION

As alluded to in the previous section, CRTs depend on mixing different amounts of light from the red, green, and blue phosphors in order to present pictures with the correct colors. These are known as the "primary colors," and correspond to the three wavelengths of light at which the three types of cones in the eye's retina have their peak sensitivities. It is the existence of these three types of color receptors, the cones, in the eye that are the basis for the trichromatic theory of color vision. This leads to the principle, proven daily in television practice, that any perceived color can be approximated very well by a mixture of the proper amounts of the primary colors. Although such a mixture rarely matches the actual spectrum of the natural color being reproduced, the eye perceives the color of the appropriate RGB mixture as being the same as that of the natural color. Many measurements and experiments in the decades preceding the advent of color television led to a good understanding of the relative proportions of red, green, and blue that are needed, and of the best wavelengths of red, green, and blue to use. The proportions are also influenced by the properties of the materials used to form the phosphors on the face of the CRT.

In addition to color, there is intensity, or *luminance*. "Luminance is an objective measure of that aspect of visible radiant energy that produces the sensation of *brightness*" [NET95]. Suppose R, G, and B represent the amount of red, green, and blue light sensed by a camera at a small element of the image called a *pel* (*pic*ture *el*ement) or *pixel*. (The two terms are interchangeable, with pixel perhaps the more common.) The luminance,[2] Y, is a linear combination of the red, green, and blue values, and is found from the equation $Y = 0.299 \cdot R + 0.587 \cdot G + 0.114 \cdot B$. Y is what is displayed on a monochrome television set. These coefficients of R, G, and B, which sum to 1.0, work fairly well on gamma-corrected, normalized signals, which are usually limited to the range of 0 to 1 volt. Notice that a phosphor cannot emit, nor can a camera sense, a negative value of R, G, or B. (The presentation here is very simplified. The interested reader can find much greater detail about both the science and the engineering trade-offs in NET95 and POY93.)

Notice that if one knows Y, and the amount of any two colors, the third can be computed. We can take this concept a step further and compute color difference signals. Since the greatest luminance contribution comes from green, let us subtract Y from R and from B, and reduce the amplitudes by dividing by attenuation factors, to get

$$U = \frac{B-Y}{2.03} \quad and \quad V = \frac{R-Y}{1.14}.$$

Thus U and V are computed from R, G, and B according to

$$U = -0.147R - 0.289G + 0.436B$$
$$V = 0.615R - 0.515G - 0.100B.$$

---

[2] Here, as is commonly done, we use the term "luminance" and the symbol Y to indicate the video signal representative of luminance.

For NTSC, a further transformation is carried out, forming a different pair of chrominance signals, I and Q, from the relations

$$I = V \cdot \cos 33° - U \cdot \sin 33° \qquad \text{and} \qquad Q = V \cdot \sin 33° + U \cdot \cos 33°.$$

Thus I and Q are computed from R, G, and B according to

$$I = 0.596R - 0.274G - 0.322B$$
$$Q = 0.211R - 0.523G + 0.311B.$$

Since R, G, and B are gamma corrected before either Y, U, V or Y, I, Q is formed, the luminance and chrominance values are not the true gamma-corrected values. However, the effects of the errors are not usually large enough to be noticed.

On average, U and V (and therefore I and Q also) are smaller than the luminance. In both PAL and NTSC systems, these chrominance signals are transmitted at a lower bandwidth than Y. This provides a form of analog compression of the video. Digital video compression schemes take advantage of the lesser importance of chrominance by sampling chrominance more coarsely than luminance.

For traditional composite video, the luminance and chrominance analog signals are multiplexed together by using the chrominance signals to modulate a color subcarrier, and then adding this modulated signal to the luminance signal. PAL and NTSC use different techniques [see NET95 for details]. For television broadcasting and cable transmission, the composite signals are used to modulate a carrier with a frequency of above 40 MHz, and audio is added in also. The carrier frequency determines the channel used for transmission, with ranges of carrier frequencies allocated to groups of channels. For example, in the United States, the 6-MHz band between 54 and 60 MHz is designated as channel 2, the band between 60 and 66 MHz is designated channel 3, and so forth up through channel 6. Then there is gap for radio and other services, then channels 7 through 13, then another gap, and so on.

In practice, separation of the components by the receiver is done imperfectly. In particular, there is some crosstalk between luminance and chrominance. One way to avoid this is to never combine them. S-Video, introduced along with Super VHS, is a YUV interface standard for interconnecting video equipment with separate luminance and chrominance signals. Y is transmitted on one pair of wires, and U and V are multiplexed together on a second pair.

CCIR 601.[3]   The ITU has established a standard for component digital signals, designed to be compatible with NTSC, PAL, and SECAM. It comes in a 60 field per second, 525-line flavor like NTSC, and a 50 field per second, 625-line flavor for PAL and SECAM.[4] There are 720 visible luminance pixels per line, and 360 visible chrominance pixels.[5] NTSC has 486 visible lines, but digital video systems usually work with only 480. PAL and SECAM have 576 visible lines. The luminance and chrominance pixels are quantized to 8 bits, except that the minimum and maximum values (0 and 255) are reserved for synchronization, giving a range of 1 to 254 actually available. Further, some allowance is made for variations in equipment calibration and for rounding errors in coding and filtering, so the digital luminance range is 16 to 235. That is, a zero-volt luminance value is represented by 16, and one volt is represented by 235. Therefore, if R, G, and B are in the range of 0 to 1 volt, our digital luminance Y is computed from

$$Y = 219 \cdot (0.299R + 0.587G + 0.114B) + 16.$$

The standard color difference signals are defined by

$$C_B = \frac{112\,(B-Y)}{0.886} + 128$$

$$C_R = \frac{112\,(R-Y)}{0.701} + 128$$

rounded to the nearest integer. The color difference values are centered at 128 and range from 16 to 240.

The H.261 standard uses Y, C_B, C_R. In much of what is written about video coding in general and H.261 coding in particular, the explanations are in terms of Y, U, and V. In keeping with this convention, we ourselves did this in "The Big Picture" section. We may be overly pedantic in pointing this out, since the difference is largely a matter of how to convert to a good integer representation.

---

[3] Since the CCIR is now called the ITU-R, the proper name is now ITU-R Recommendation 601. However, it is as yet rarely seen written this way.

[4] SECAM (Sequential Couleur avec Memoire) was developed in France and is used primarily in France, countries of the former Soviet Union, and former French colonies. It differs from PAL in the modulation scheme used for Y, U, V transmission.

[5] Although a tentative provision is made for sampling luminance and chrominance at the same rate (designated as 4:4:4), the standard mode is 4:2:2 (half as many samples in the horizontal direction only). In H.261 and MPEG, 4:2:0 (half as many samples in the horizontal and vertical directions) is used.

7.4 VIDEO CAMERAS

"We live in wonderful times. The slow elimination of all evil analog circuitry is progressing nicely" [BLI92]. However, for the initial input and the final output, videoconferencing systems still depend heavily on (mostly analog) television technology and equipment. Video cameras capture the moving pictures that are to be transmitted, and television monitors usually are the final display device. Until the late 1980s, tube-type cameras prevailed, but cameras with semiconductor sensors are by far the more common now. Most cameras use charge-coupled device (CCD) sensors (see Figure 7.5). A CCD sensor can be thought of as an array of light-sensing cells, each of which is a capacitor that builds up charge as light strikes it. The brighter the light, the greater the charge. The charge buildup is a linear function of the light intensity and of exposure time (usually called "integration time"). After the array

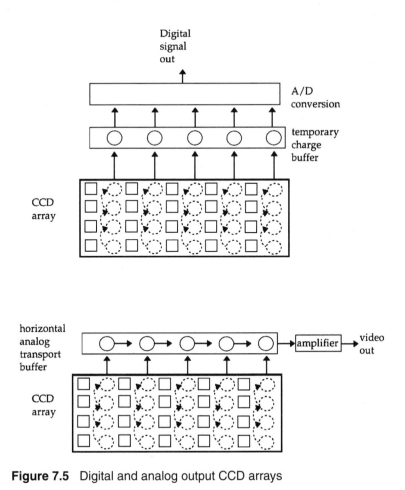

Figure 7.5 Digital and analog output CCD arrays

of cells is exposed to light, it generates signal output by shifting the charges along columns (or rows) until each value has been read. That is, at each pulse of a read clock, the charge in each capacitor is shifted to its neighbor. The charges must be protected from further light until they are shifted out and read. This can be done by a camera shutter, but is usually handled in the design of the CCD chip itself. "Interline transfer" is a common shielding technique. Each light-sensing column of cells is paired with a column covered by an opaque shield. After exposure, the charge from each sensing cell is shifted to its shielded neighbor. Then the charges are shifted up a row at a time as shown in Figure 7.5. Little lenses are often added over each sensing cell to gather more light.

The discrete cells of the CCD array inherently provide sampling. The charge in each cell, representing the intensity of the light that struck it during the charging, or exposure time, can then be quantized for digital representation.

The highest quality cameras use one CCD array for each of the primary colors, red, blue, and green (see Figure 7.6). Less expensive, lower quality cameras will use a single CCD array with each individual CCD cell covered by a red, green, or blue filter. The color filtering arrangement may be as simple as laying down alternating diagonal stripes of red, blue, and green filtering material, or a more complex mosaic may be constructed. Sometimes the filters are cyan, magenta, and yellow, which are the complements of R, G, and B. That is, cyan is $G+B$, magenta is $R+B$, and yellow is $R+G$. These filters pass more light, and YC_BC_R can also be calculated from these complement values. The most common output signals are composite video, either NTSC or PAL. RGB output is sometimes offered as an option, or offered as a choice within a specialty line of cameras. More recently, in anticipation of the growth of desktop videoconferencing, cameras have been offered with YUV output. This can improve quality by eliminating the composite video encoder step, which must then be immediately undone by the video codec, which needs

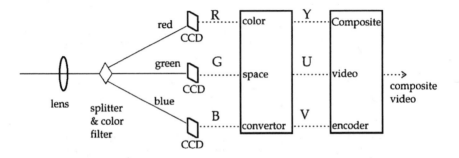

Figure 7.6 Block diagram of camera

the signal in its YUV form. We expect cameras that output digital YC_BC_R to become common in the near future.

REFERENCES

BLI92   Blinn, James, "The World of Digital Video," *IEEE Computer Graphics & Applications*, pp. 106–112 (September 1992).

NET95   Netravali, Arun H., and Haskell, Barry G., *Digital Pictures*, 2nd ed., Plenum Press, NY, 1995.

POY93   Poynton, Charles A., "'Gamma' and Its Disguises: The Nonlinear Mappings of Intensity in Perception, CRTs, Film and Video," *SMPTE Journal*, pp. 1099–1108 (December 1993).

Chapter 8

Communications Infrastructure

Connections are everything. There is no communication without them. Videoconferencing systems must be connected to communicate. The communications infrastructure is as important to videoconferencing as are the terminals themselves.

8.1 SWITCHED DIGITAL CONNECTIONS

Historically, videoconferencing systems have been used much more for long-distance communication than for local, so connections to long-distance networks have been of primary importance. Early buyers of systems usually bought them for internal communication within their own organizations, and often connected them over dedicated networks originally put in place for other reasons. In the late 1970s, long-distance telephone companies in the United States began to provide switched digital services and interest began to grow in using videoconferencing for communication among different organizations. Unfortunately, even after long-distance switched services became generally available, local switched services were difficult to obtain. There remained a significant "last mile" problem, because of this difficulty. Most early users of long-distance switched services had to lease dedicated lines from their local phone companies in order to get a connection to the long-distance carrier's nearest point of presence (POP). However, that situation has changed as ISDN has become more widely available from local telephone companies.

In most of the developed world, there is adequate infrastructure for conference room videoconferencing. In Japan and Western Europe, support for ISDN connections to the desktop is also fairly good. Basic rate ISDN (BRI) is readily available in Japan, Western Europe, Singapore, Australia, and Hong Kong. The United States is catching up, but ISDN connections to the desktop have frequently been difficult to arrange. Desktop connections need to be inexpensive and need to provide access to dial-up networks. This has not been as necessary for conference room videoconferencing. For the conference room, the classic way has been to use dedicated communication lines, leased from local telephone companies, to connect to a long-distance carrier. These leased lines have come in two sizes: 56 Kbps (DS0 speed) and 1.544 Mbps (DS1 speed, usually carried on a T1 line). Since 112 Kbps has been the recognized lower limit of bit rates for acceptable video quality, the 56-Kbps lines are leased in pairs (see Figure 8.1).

In many cases, especially in earlier days, a leased connection was used for the whole route, since videoconferencing was largely internal (intracompany or intra-agency). Organizations that had already leased T1 lines for voice or data traffic frequently had excess or backup capacity available for holding videoconferences.

8.2 PRACTICAL CONSIDERATIONS WITH SWITCHED DIGITAL CONNECTIONS

Voice services have been evolving toward fully digital for many years. Because we did not start clean with digital services, there is a patchwork of services, built up in *ad hoc* fashion over the years, in order to provide limited switched digital services.[1] These have been adaptations of things done for the voice world. Switched digital services are now of major interest. They are based on bearer channels, which take two forms, restricted or nonrestricted (clear channel). Restricted channels deliver 56 Kbps and clear channels run at 64 Kbps. The major difference is whether the channel uses in-band or out-of-band signaling.

Historically, the most basic switched service has been with 56-Kbps channels. This is frequently referred to as "Switched 56" service. In-band signaling limits its use for data traffic to 56 Kbps. Where no signaling is necessary, or where signaling is out-of-band (i.e., outside of the data channel), a full 64 Kbps can be made available. The term "bearer channel" usually refers to a channel of 56- or 64-Kbps capacity. In ISDN, "B channel" designates a 64-Kbps channel. One may also find the term occasionally used for 56 Kbps. Here we use "bearer channel" to refer to either a 56- or 64-Kbps channel, and will use "B channel" to refer only to an ISDN 64-Kbps channel.

Higher rate channels are desirable to many users. These are built up by combining bearer channels. Sometimes the bearer channels are combined by the network so as to be switched together and kept synchronized, for exam-

---

[1] Partly for these reasons, we can give no guarantees about the precision of use in the telecommunications world of the terms we use here.

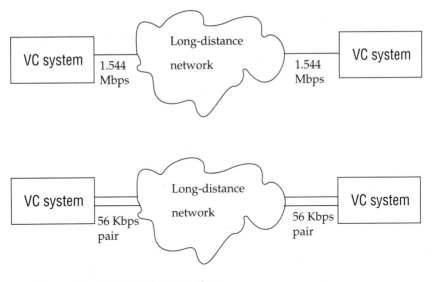

Figure 8.1 Dedicated connections

ple, to provide an H0 (384-Kbps) channel. Otherwise the terminal or external equipment such as an inverse multiplexer (IMUX) is responsible for checking and adjusting each channel for different delays and multiplexer time.

Around 1976, AT&T announced its first switched digital 56-Kbps service [DOL78]. In the mid-1980s, the service was expanded and named Accunet 56™. US Sprint and MCI later offered similar services. Unfortunately, a user of one long-distance carrier could not dial a user of another. This problem was eased somewhat when the regional Bell operating companies (RBOCs) followed with switched digital services of their own. These carried marketing names such as Microlink II[2] or Switchway,[3] for example, and allowed dial-up, switched access from a customer's premises. Users could now dial local calls or dial out long-distance through their long-distance carriers.

Suppose the user of terminal 1 in Figure 8.2 has selected long-distance carrier 1 as his default long-distance carrier, and user 2 has selected carrier 2. If the dashed line connections exist, then each user can call the other, even though they have selected different long-distance carriers. In other words, this means that the local exchange carriers must have access arrangements with both long-distance carriers. Several variations of the problem can occur. Figure 8.3 shows a case of one user with leased line local access and another with switched. User 1 cannot use his primary long-distance carrier to dial

[2] Southwestern Bell trademark.
[3] NYNEX trademark.

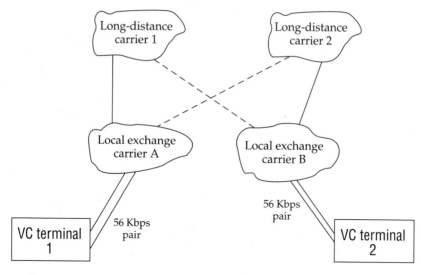

Figure 8.2   Long distance connections to different carriers

user 2. However, if local exchange carrier A has a connection (dashed line) to long distance carrier 2, user 1 can dial an access code to carrier 2 to call user 2. This problem is greatest in the United States, because of the structure of our phone system. Part of the importance of ISDN deployment in the United States is that the carriers are cooperating to solve this problem. Eventually,

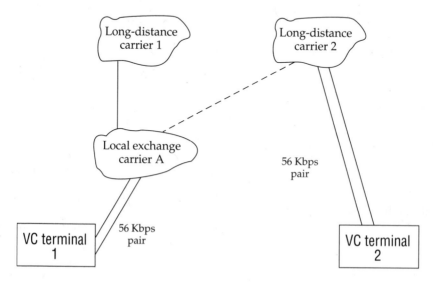

Figure 8.3   Variation on long distance dialing problem

these issues should be transparent to ISDN users, just as they (almost) are to telephone voice call users.

Other switched services were also available in the mid-1980s, such as AT&T's Accunet™ Reserved 1.5 Service [REY83] and US Sprint's Meeting Channel™. For example, US Sprint offered switched service at rates between 128 Kbps and full T1 (1.544 Mbps.) The catch was that users had to lease a T1 line to Sprint's nearest point of presence (POP), and had to reserve the bandwidth at least 30 minutes prior to the call. That is, a user had to call the operator and ask to be connected to the other party at a specified time, at a specified bandwidth, and for a specified duration. Sprint also offered international access, multiway calling services, and even a signal conversion service to allow linking selected models of different, proprietary terminals.

8.3 OTHER TYPES OF NETWORKS

Perhaps the most sweeping communications development during the second half of the 1980s was the rapid growth of local-area network (LAN) installations. A typical office now has both a LAN connection and a phone connection for communication, but the phone connection usually provides only a voice channel, sometimes with a modem used for transmitting data over the voice channel. Naturally, those installing desktop videoconferencing would like to make use of the existing data connection, the LAN port, for video telephony.

Virtually all LAN communication is packet based, definitely a challenge for carrying real-time, two-way video and audio. Existing international standards for video telephony were developed for switched circuits, and some of them, especially H.221 (the main communications protocol of H.320), do not adapt well to LANs.

In presenting the present and near future state of networks, we use three main categories: WANs (wide-area network), LANs, and asynchronous transfer mode (ATM). Here, LAN has its usual meaning. The term WAN is sometimes used in the computer communications field to refer to methods for linking LANs. We use the term here in a much broader sense, covering all terrestrial services outside the building or campus, plus all "telephone-like" services even within the building or campus.

ATM networks will eventually bridge this gap. There seems to be consensus in the telephony world that ATM will become the basic method for carrying all telephony services. There is disagreement about how soon. ATM LANs became available, but expensive, in 1994. ATM switch deployment began to show up in WANs at about the same time, but in ways hidden to the user. ATM's cell concepts based on rapid switching of small packets (53-byte "cells") allow packet networks to be built that provide virtual connections that behave well enough to carry voice and videotelephony as if they were carried on switched digital circuits. The ATM system architecture, with rapid switching of 53-byte cells, promises to offer the low delay and low delay variance transmission necessary for voice and video traffic, while offering the LAN-like advantage of transmitting information only when needed, rather than making a constant bit rate connection. New video telephony standards are being developed that will take advantage of ATM characteristics.

ISDN, Switched 56, T1, and fractional T1 are the most useful WAN services for videoconferencing, and are also used to link LANs (in the narrow sense of WAN that is sometimes used). We expect ISDN to increase in popularity and availability until the end of the century, when ATM-based services such as broadband ISDN (B-ISDN) will become common.

8.4 SPECIFICS OF WIDE-AREA NETWORKS

8.4.1 Switched 56

By the mid-1980s, a large part of the U.S. long-distance voice network was already fully digital. Voice calls were carried at 56 Kbps (8,000 samples per second at seven bits per sample). It was a fairly simple matter to offer 56-Kbps data traffic on the same facilities. Networks that carry 56 Kbps of information per "voice channel" are sometimes called "restricted networks." The actual channel bandwidth is 64 Kbps, but restricted networks use older transmission technology that requires some bandwidth for signaling, which is in-band. Also, a minimum density of "one" bits is required in order to maintain receiver synchronization with the network. In a restricted network, every eighth bit is subject to being robbed for signaling, so only seven bits out of eight can reliably carry actual data. Seven-eighths of 64 Kbps is 56 Kbps. This "robbed bit signaling" actually robs only one bit in every six octets (bytes). However, the terminal equipment does not know which ones might be robbed. For carrying digitized voice, some newer equipment uses eight bits per sample, letting these least significant bits get robbed, but gaining some improvement from the octets that aren't robbed. The use of out-of-band signaling, as in ISDN, makes this unnecessary. Such unrestricted networks are sometimes called "clear channel" networks. ISDN networks are intended to be clear channel, though hybrid situations occur in which a long-distance link between two ISDN sites might have restricted channels. These situations will become less frequent.

The initial problem with switched digital data transmission, as pointed out earlier, was in giving users digital access to the long-distance network. This has been solved for most potential customers, as shown in Table 8.1.

Table 8.1 Switched 56 Availability in 1994

- Monthly cost (per pair): $90–$250
- Usage at 112 Kbps: $6–$30/hr
- Availability

Ameritech	+90% of all customers
Bell Atlantic	+90%
BellSouth	+90%
NYNEX	+90%
Pacific Telesis	+90%
Southwestern Bell	+80%
US West	+65%
GTE	+25% (?)

Typical costs per line vary considerably from region to region, with $80 to $100 per month being typical, not including usage charges. The fixed costs are not prohibitive for conference room installations, but are too high for most desktop users. Local usage charges are usually around $0.05 per minute. Long-distance charges are usually at a slight premium over voice calls, but the local usage charges are usually absorbed. Since two lines are necessary for 112 Kbps, a typical long-distance call within the United States might cost about $30 per hour.

There are several ways to connect terminals to Switched 56 lines. Since 112 Kbps is desired, in most cases two interface boxes are required, usually called CSU/DSUs (channel service unit/data service unit). Less commonly, one might see them called TIEs (terminal interface equipment), or TAs (terminal adapters). The most common interface to such equipment is by V.35 for the data and RS-366, or less commonly, RS-232, for the signaling information.

The two 56-Kbps connections are not synchronized, and could be routed along different paths through the telephone network. The videoconferencing terminal must combine the two channels internally. (This is also true for the two 64-Kbps B-channels in basic ISDN service.) ITU-T Recommendation H.221 specifies techniques for synchronizing data on the two channels.

8.4.2 T1: Full and Fractional

In the Bell system (prior to 1984), several levels of digital communication service were defined, called digital signal levels, ranging from DS0 through DS4 [REY83] (Table 8.2). These services were defined separately from the actual, physical connections that carry them.

Table 8.2   Digital Signal Levels

Digital Signal Level	Bit Rate
DS4	274.176 Mbps
DS3	44.736 Mbps
DS2	6.312 Mbps
DS1C	3.152 Mbps
DS1	1.544 Mbps
DS0	64 Kbps

DS1 service to a customer's premises is usually carried on a T1 line, more formally called a T1 digital carrier, which was introduced in 1962 as the Bell system's initial short haul digital transmission line. T2 lines carry DS2. There is a certain amount of carelessness in the way these terms are used. One may hear someone speak of leasing a T1 line between two cities. What one has in this case is DS1 service, which may be carried to the nearest central office (CO) or POP on a T1 line, but is then multiplexed onto higher rate, long-distance services. T1 was designed for 50 miles or less, and T2 for 500 miles or less.

A T1 line may carry 24 DS0 channels or 1 DS1 channel. The DS0 channels are not guaranteed to stay synchronized with one another. Although, in a sense, DS1 is 24 DS0s, the DS1 components can be made to remain in synchronization for customers requiring it. The capacities in Table 8.2 are given according to usual telephone system practice. As stated earlier, the payload of a DS0 channel is often restricted to 56 Kbps. Further, the reader might notice that $64 \times 24 = 1{,}536$ and wonder why DS1 (and T1) has a 1.544-Mbps bandwidth. A T1 bit stream uses the format shown in Figure 8.4. Each group

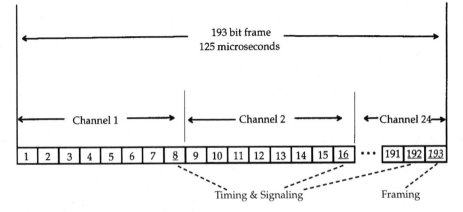

Figure 8.4   T1 frame structure

of eight bits from each of the DS0 channels is considered to be a frame. One bit is added per frame, giving 192+1 bits per frame. Eight thousand frames per second are transmitted, giving $8,000 \times 193 = 1.544$ Mbps.

Since 384 Kbps (and 768 Kbps, to a lesser extent) has become a popular bit rate for videoconferencing, there is demand for using only portions of DS1 service. Although this has been offered for some time by some of the long-distance carriers, the local exchange carriers have been slow to offer fractional T1 local connections. The usual connection is a leased T1 line. Customers may use a multiplexer as an interface between the videoconferencing system and the T1 line, where the multiplexer presents a 256-, 384-, 512-, or 768-Kbps connection to the videoconferencing system. The physical interface is typically RS-449. Such a multiplexer is frequently used to split T1 bandwidth among several devices. Figure 8.5 illustrates a traditional use for a multiplexer: share a leased DS1 link between two company sites, a PBX and a videoconferencing terminal. Traditional multiplexers have no dialing capability and are used for "nailed up" T1 lines, which maintain a fixed connection between two points. The configuration shown allows videoconferencing between the two sites at 336 Kbps (6×56 Kbps, synchronized), and leaves up to 18 voice channels available. Any other long-distance calls go out through the T1 line to the long-distance network.

Inverse multiplexing offers another way to get fractions of DS1 rates, by assembling multiple, unsynchronized DS0s from independent switched digital services (see Figure 8.6). Different models of inverse multiplexers (IMUXs) can assemble multiple channels from a T1 carrying 24 DS0s, from multiple BRIs, or from multiple switched 56 interfaces. IMUXs also offer dialing capability, since they are designed for switched circuits. A disadvantage is that bits must be robbed to provide interchannel synchronization.

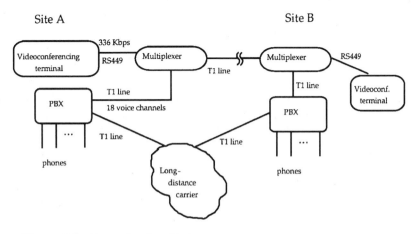

Figure 8.5 Example of multiplexer use

Figure 8.6 Videoconferencing terminals using inverse multiplexing

8.4.3 ISDN

ISDN (Integrated Services Digital Network) is the most recent practical advance in the natural evolution of voice telephony, and is a considerable improvement over Switched 56. Switched 56 provides a 56-Kbps payload on one or two voice-style telephone wire pairs into a home or business. It uses in-band, pulse signaling, much like rotary dial telephones. ISDN adds full digital specifications and out-of-band signaling to allow much greater flexibility in call management. The call management functions are useful in many situations but, for videoconferencing, the most important feature is that ISDN provides end-to-end digital connections in a sufficiently standard way. ISDN provides 128 Kbps of payload on a basic telephone wire pair, plus additional bandwidth for signaling, maintenance, and performance monitoring.

The basic building block for ISDN data transmission is the B-channel, or bearer channel, of 64 Kbps. Other data rates are formed from synchronized aggregations of B-channels. The most common access to ISDN is basic access, provided by the basic rate interface, which gives two B-channels and one D-channel for signaling. This is sometimes designated "2B+D" and provides two unsynchronized 64-Kbps B-channels and one 16-Kbps D-channel. One may see claims of 144-Kbps total bandwidth, since there are schemes for packet data transmission on the D-channels. The H.320 videoconferencing standards make no use of the D-channel for data transmission. From a practical, videoconferencing point of view, only 128 Kbps are available, split into two unsynchronized channels.

ISDN as currently offered is sometimes called narrowband ISDN, and ranges in bandwidth up to nearly 2 Mbps. Broadband ISDN, using ATM technology, is anticipated but not yet generally offered. Current ISDN bandwidth is delivered as B-, D-, or H-channels. H0-, H11-, and H12-channels are provided by synchronizing and aggregating B channels (see Table 8.3). The H0 channel is of particular interest because 384 Kbps is a popular speed for conference room videoconferencing, and is also used for high-quality video for desktop connections.

Table 8.3 ISDN channels

Channel	Bandwidth (Data Rate)
B	64 Kbps
H0	384 Kbps
H11	1.536 Mbps
H12	1.920 Mbps
D (basic access)	16 Kbps
D (primary access)	64 Kbps

Separate from the channel definitions are the actual, physical data lines, or interfaces, to which one can connect. For ISDN, there are two: basic rate ISDN (BRI) and primary rate ISDN (PRI). These are also called basic access and primary access. As stated earlier, BRI provides two 64-Kbps data channels and one 16-Kbps signaling channel.[4] [See HAR89 for more details on ISDN.] A PRI can be configured in several ways. Any combination of B and H0 channels that adds up to 1,472 Kbps (or 1856 Kbps in Europe) is possible. One 64-Kbps D-channel must be included, except in special configurations for using a full PRI for H11 (H12 in Europe) and having a companion PRI with a D-channel. In the United States, PRI is delivered to the customer premises on a clear channel T1 line (E1 in Europe).

ISDN growth has been hampered by several things. The local exchange carriers and long-distance carriers have been reluctant to make the necessary investment, sometimes claiming there was no demand. Potential users didn't order what they couldn't get, so no demand was being demonstrated. ISDN was not sufficiently standardized, so one maker's equipment might not talk to that of another. These difficulties led to a certain amount of cynical joking among those disappointed about "ISDN"—I Still Don't kNow, or It Still Doesn't Network. Bellcore's National ISDN-1[5] initiative (NI-1) has helped greatly. TRIP 92[6] was a kickoff demonstration in late 1992 that demonstrated that NI-1 was practical, and availability has improved rapidly since. Three important uses driving the deployment of ISDN are access to the Internet (Metcalfe has said that ISDN means "Information Superhighway Delivered Now"), videoconferencing, and remote LAN connections for telecommuters.

---

[4] The physical layer actually has up to 192 Kbps when framing and maintenance bits are included.

[5] Along with *The National ISDN User's Forum* and vendors.

[6] Transcontinental ISDN Project.

Table 8.4   Overall ISDN Availability in the United States

	YE92	YE93	YE94 (est.)	YE95 (est.)	YE96 (est.)
Ameritech	26%	70%	80%	80%	80%
Bell Atlantic	47%	59%	87%	90%	90%
BellSouth	30%	46%	53%	64%	77%
NYNEX	15%	31%	55%	76%	83%
Pacific Telesis	43%	60%	78%	87%	90%
Southwestern Bell	17%	54%	60%	66%	75%
US West	38%	42%	57%	59%	65%
GTE	9%	14%	16%	18%	25%
Totals	28%	47%	61%	68%	75%

Note: Not all BRI lines can make LD data calls. Also, many LD calls are limited to 2 × 56 Kbps.

Table 8.4 shows overall ISDN availability in the United States and Table 8.5 shows National ISDN-1 availability. NI-1 makes things easier for terminal manufacturers, because it defines a limited set of interfaces. However, it should be understood that once a terminal is properly installed on any flavor of ISDN, it can call an NI-1 terminal, if the long-distance connection is available.

In most cases, ISDN can be offered less expensively than Switched 56. Typical monthly charges range from about $25 to $75. Usually the lower monthly cost is paired with usage charges so that the metered charge on each B-channel is equivalent to that for one voice call. Thus a local 128-Kbps video

Table 8.5   National ISDN-1 Availability

	YE92	YE93	YE94 (est.)	YE95 (est.)	YE96 (est.)
Ameritech	3%	64%	79%	79%	80%
Bell Atlantic	15%	55%	87%	90%	90%
BellSouth	0%	13%	29%	64%	77%
NYNEX	11%	26%	55%	76%	83%
Pacific Telesis	0%	25%	49%	73%	85%
Southwestern Bell	1%	9%	14%	50%	60%
US West	0%	3%	49%	59%	65%
GTE	0%	0%	0%	0%	10%
Totals	4%	26%	46%	62%	70%

Note: Not all BRI lines can make LD data calls. Also, many LD calls are limited to 2 × 56 Kbps.

Table 8.6 Estimated Percent of BRI Lines (Any Flavor) That Can Make Long-Distance Data Calls

At 56 Kbps per channel	*YE92*	*YE93*	*YE94*	*YE95*	*YE96*
U.S. average (est.)	15%	33%	75%	90%	95%
At 64 Kbps per channel	*YE92*	*YE93*	*YE94*	*YE95*	*YE96*
U.S. average (est.)	1%	10%	25%	50%	60%

call will be billed at approximately twice the voice rate, if metered. As with Switched 56, the local charges are usually absorbed into the long-distance rate for long-distance calls. ISDN long-distance rates are similar to those for Switched 56, and range up to $30 per hour for 128-Kbps calls within the continental United States. As of this writing, ISDN long-distance calls are often restricted to 56 Kbps per channel in the United States. This situation is expected to improve rapidly, as shown in Table 8.6.

8.4.4 Connecting to BRI

Figure 8.7 shows examples of how a terminal might be connected to BRI. Most terminals have the S/T interface built in, and connect directly to the NT1 (network termination 1) box, which connects to the U interface supplied by the local exchange carrier from its central office. A terminal without a built-in ISDN interface can connect through terminal adapters (TAs), which are available with X.21 or V.35/RS-366 interfaces. In the United States,

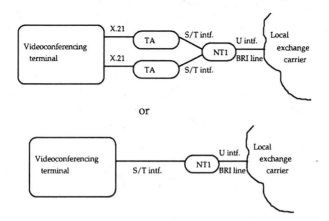

Figure 8.7 Connecting to BRI

customers purchase the NT1 unless it is built in to the TA or the terminal. In Europe, they are supplied by the telephone company as part of the service.

8.4.5 Primary Rate Interface

Users who need more bandwidth, and those who cannot get BRI, may find PRI useful. PRI is often available from a long-distance carrier even when the local exchange carrier offers neither BRI nor PRI. In the United States, PRI is provided to customers over a T1 line. A T1 for PRI can provide clear channel (or unrestricted) 64-Kbps B-channels, because signaling information is never carried in the data channels. One of the T1s 24 channels is designated as the D-channel, for signaling. In the case of multiple associated PRI/T1s, all of the signaling may be carried on a D-channel on just one of the T1 lines. This allows the full bandwidth of an associated T1 to be used for carrying an H11 channel or four H0 channels. Figure 8.8 illustrates the use of PRI to provide one H0 channel for 384-Kbps videoconferencing, plus the equivalent of eight BRIs. In most such installations, more than 11 terminals can be connected with 128 Kbps, but only 11 at a time can simultaneously use the PRI line for video calls. More complex situations are also possible. Figure 8.9 shows the use of two ISDN-capable digital switches with multiple T1 and PRI lines from carriers and the ability to switch an entire PRI line to a conference room.

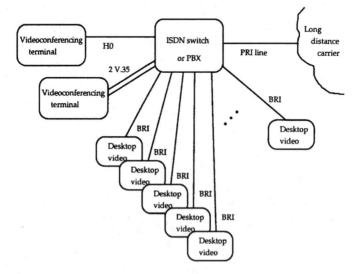

Figure 8.8 Example of use of single PRI

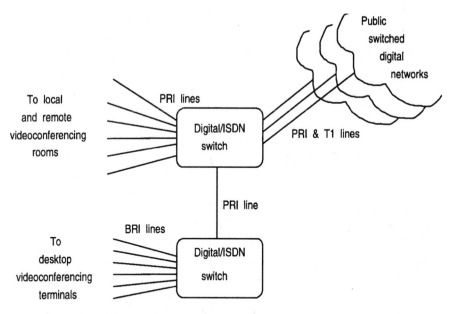

Figure 8.9 Multiple PRI and T1 use

8.4.6 Inverse Multiplexing

Even though there are defined switched digital offerings for communication channels that provide higher bit rates than 56 or 64 Kbps, such offerings are often unavailable. For this or other reasons, a user may want to aggregate multiple channels together to get higher digital bandwidth. Somewhere in the system, these channels need to be aligned and synchronized together. ITU-T Recommendation H.221 (part of the H.320 suite) spells out how multiple B-channels are aligned and synchronized. Frame alignment signals, called FAS codes, are embedded in each B-channel. Once the FAS code position in the bit stream is detected, the locations of all other information carried in the channel are known. If a channel slip occurs during a call, the FAS will be lost. When it is found again, the information carried in the channel can be again synchronized and aligned with other channels.

The bonding standard (in ISO Committee Draft form in mid-1994), developed by the Bandwidth ON Demand Interoperability Group, also provides methods to aggregate channels and detect loss of synchronization. The BONDING document describes four modes of operation:

Mode 0   Initial parameter negotiation and parameter exchange. No delay equalization.

Mode 1   Provides a single channel with a rate of $n \times 56$ or $n \times 64$. Sets up synchronization and then removes the overhead bits from the stream after setup. There is no checking for the occurrence of a slip.

Mode 2   Provides a single channel with a rate of $(63/64)$ of $n \times 56$ or $n \times 64$. One bit from each 64 is used to monitor synchronization.

Mode 3   Does not rob bits from the "single channel" presented to the user. Extra bandwidth, usually another bearer channel, is added to make room for adding monitoring bits.

Mode 1 is the required minimum implementation. True statistics are hard to come by, but it is speculated that a slip may occur once every half hour or so.

Most videoconferencing terminals that are designed to operate at 112 or 128 Kbps have built-in inverse multiplexing capability for two bearer channels of 56 or 64 Kbps. H.221 channel aggregation is the most common, but one will find proprietary schemes as well. Although H.221 also defines how to aggregate six B-channels, most terminals that operate at higher bit rates expect a single, higher rate channel, such as H0. This is usually presented to the terminal on a V.35[7] or RS-449 port, providing what looks to the terminal to be a single, higher bit rate connection.

H.221 and BONDING do not mix well. The synchronization techniques and call setup are different, so a terminal with a BONDING IMUX cannot call an H.221 terminal.[8] The BONDING bit robbing causes other problems for H.221 terminals. Suppose mode 2 is used to aggregate 6 B-channels, as shown in Figure 8.10. Only 378 Kbps will be presented to the terminal. An H0 connection must be at exactly 384. Mode 3 would add a seventh channel to make up the missing bandwidth, adding extra cost. Mode 1 would drop the monitoring after call setup, giving a full 384 on six channels, but if one of the channels slips, the call must be torn down and placed again.

8.5 SPECIFICS OF LOCAL-AREA NETWORKS

There is a strong and natural desire to put videoconferencing on LANs in order to take advantage of the large digital communication infrastructure that LANs provide. We must, however, face two conflicting realities. The domi-

---

[7] V.35 was developed for 56 Kbps, but is often used at higher bit rates.

[8] The relevant standards bodies are looking at easing this problem, but it is not likely to go away totally.

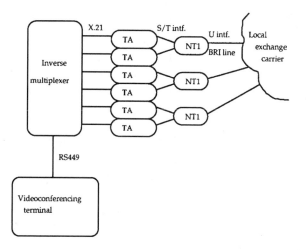

Figure 8.10 Inverse multiplexer with external TAs

nant international standard for videoconferencing, H.320, is designed for *isochronous* circuits, synchronous circuits with guaranteed delivery characteristics, such as a fixed amount of delay. The most common digital connection available in the office, the LAN, is very much *not* isochronous.[9] This can be fixed by developing a new standard, developing techniques to adapt H.320 and LANs to each other, or developing improved LANs. In fact, all three directions are being pursued. The ITU-T is developing the H.323 family of standards for videoconferencing on both packet and switched circuit networks, including gateway capabilities to H.320 systems. Switching hub and higher bandwidth technology helps mask the lack of isochronous characteristics. New LAN approaches with isochronous capability include ATM and IsoEthernet. In the following sections, and in Table 8.7, we summarize the more likely near future possibilities for improved LAN technology and infrastructure for handling two-way video.

8.5.1 H.320 Encapsulated on Legacy LANs

The most commonly installed LANs, 10-Mbps Ethernet and 16-Mbps token ring, are not designed for bidirectional, real-time video transmission. Packet delays are unpredictable, and packets can be lost in congested networks. The typical legacy LAN controller in a desktop computer is half duplex, as is the typical interface in a 10BaseT Ethernet hub. These characteristics are

---

[9] LAN packet arrival times are highly variable, and packets can be lost.

Table 8.7 Comparison of "Ethernet Replacement" LAN Technologies

LAN Technology	Requires New LAN Network Interface Card for Desktop Video PCs?	Estimated LAN Card Cost and Hub Cost (per desktop video station)	Cabling Requirements	Probability of Needing New Cabling
Switched Hub 10BaseT; half duplex Ethernet	No	$0*/$150 (3Q96)	2-pair UTP; category 3	Low
Switched Hub 10BaseT; full duplex Ethernet	Yes	$100/$250 (3Q96)	2-pair UTP; category 3	Low
Fast Ethernet	Yes	$100/$150 (3Q96)	2-pair UTP; category 5 4-pair UTP; category 3	Moderate
100BaseVG	Yes	$300/$400 (3Q96)	4-pair UTP; category 3	Moderate
IsoEthernet	Yes	$400/$500 (3Q96)	2-pair UTP; category 3	Low

* Assuming existing Ethernet card is used.

troublesome for transmitting H.320 standard video, because the H.221 multiplexing design depends strongly on bit synchronous transmission. Some of the specific dependencies are discussed in Chapter 9. However, companies such as RADVision have demonstrated success with equipment for encapsulating H.221 (H.320) bit streams on standard Ethernet.

8.5.2 H.323 LAN Conferencing and Gateway

Alternate approaches, for example, those used in some InSoft and Intel products, demonstrated that protocols designed to cope with asynchronous networks can be made to work well. Experience with the Internet multicast backbone (the MBone, [MACE94]) also encouraged the leap of faith that videoconferencing can work well on legacy networks. The Internet Engineering Task Force (IETF) has proposed RTP standards based on the MBone, and ITU-T Study Group 15 has incorporated RTP into the H.323 draft standards. H.323 avoids use of the H.221 bit synchronous protocols on the LAN. Instead, audio, video, and data are transmitted in separate packets, allowing the LAN to provide the multiplexing. H.323 uses the same H.261 video standard, G.7XX audio standards and T.120 data standards as are used in H.320.

H.323 also defines a gateway capability for interoperation of H.323 LAN-based systems and H.320 systems. The gateway uses the H.323 native packet protocols on the LAN side and H.221 on the H.320 side. The gateway is responsible for multiplexing the audio, video, and data packets into an H.221-compliant, bit synchronous stream and demultiplexing H.221 into independent audio, video, and data packets.

8.5.3 Full Duplex and Switched Hub Ethernet

Traditional Ethernet shares the coaxial cable with all of the attached systems. Since there is a single signal conductor, operation is inherently half duplex. Ethernet with typical 10BaseT hubs has very similar characteristics. However, 10BaseT wiring has separate conductors for transmitting and receiving, so full duplex implementation is possible and supported in some products. A so-called "switching hub" can support simultaneous traffic between different pairs of stations, without changing the stations or the wiring. This is much preferable for audio and video. In typical operation, the switching hub provides isochronous communication for the attached stations.

Figure 8.11 shows a possible network for connecting existing H.320 video-conferencing terminals to a long-distance network. The NIUs (network interface units) convert the constant bit rate data stream of H.320 to and from the LAN packet protocols. An external NIU, as shown in Figure 8.11, has the advantage that it should work with nearly all existing H.320 systems, both desktop and group systems. However, an external NIU could be a significant portion of the cost of a desktop system, and thus may be too expensive for common use. Depending on the architecture of the H.320 system, it may be possible to perform the equivalent of the NIU with no added hardware, beyond the LAN interface, or with minimal additional internal hardware.

Suppose that a video terminal is connected through an Ethernet switch so that it sends and receives packets only from servers and the gateway device, as shown in Figure 8.12. The terminal's video packets will be interfered with only by packets sent to and from the servers. Users want to be able to use any software applications. The main system design issue is to keep small the probability of having packets lost or delayed long enough to interrupt H.221 synchronization. The main difficulty in analyzing the concept may be in determining the probability of packet loss due to interference from server

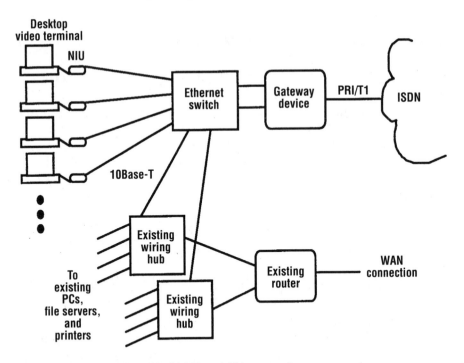

Figure 8.11   Possible H.320 to LAN connection

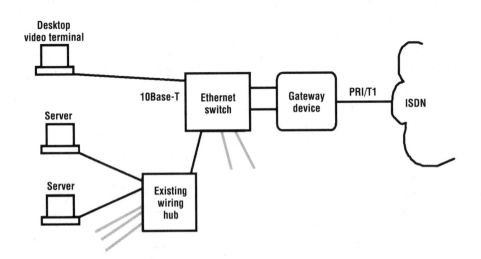

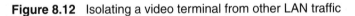

Figure 8.12   Isolating a video terminal from other LAN traffic

packet traffic. Making full duplex connections among the video terminal, Ethernet switch, and gateway will improve the odds significantly.

If the terminal is connected to a BRI call through the gateway, it needs to transmit and receive at an aggregate rate of 256 Kbps, plus the overhead of the packets containing the H.320 data. Packet overhead will consist of LAN header and check sum bits, plus whatever else is needed for the higher level protocols. Even if one chooses to use small data packets to reduce latency, LAN utilization for encapsulated H.320 is likely to be under 300 Kbps, so no significant transmission delays due to collisions should be encountered.

8.5.4 IsoEthernet™ (ISLAN16-T)

IsoEthernet is well suited for isochronous data, as implied by the name, but it has not yet gained popularity. IsoEthernet offers each port the usual 10-Mbps Ethernet connection, along with 96 switched B-channels. IsoEthernet uses the same wiring as 10BaseT, a major advantage. Both the interface card and the hub must support the IsoEthernet to gain the 96 B-channels, but the interface cards are designed to default to normal 10BaseT if it is connected to a standard hub. IsoEthernet has been standardized by the IEEE 802.9a specifications.

8.5.5 Asynchronous Transfer Mode

ATM offers the hope of a seamless bridging of the gap between WANs and LANs. Early in its development, ATM was referred to as the "fast packet" network. Telephone people and computer communication people from many countries worked, studied, experimented, and compromised to achieve it. The cell size and protocols were designed to allow rapid switching of packets through the networks, so that short, predictable, bounded delays could be provided.

ATM advocates intend that ATM connections will offer 25 to 155 Mbps to each desk. If they prevail, ATM may be more or less standard across both LANs and WANs. Or it may be that ATM will be used for backbone and wide area, with other technologies, new and old, used for LANs. At this writing, ATM equipment for LANs continues to drop in price, but remains several times more expensive than competing technologies such as 100BaseT.

8.5.6 100Base VG / Any LAN

100BaseVG is one of two competing proposals for 100-megabit "Ethernet-like" networks. The 100BaseVG design is substantially different from Ethernet at the physical layer. This allows 100BaseVG to work with lower grade wiring and allows for prioritization of traffic at the media access control layer. However, the difference in physical layer makes it more difficult to gradually upgrade a local network from 10BaseT.

IEEE 802.12 is the standard for this approach. In spite of the advantages of 100BaseVG, it appears to be losing the competition to 100BaseT, "Fast Ethernet." Hewlett-Packard and IBM have been two of the strongest advocates of 100BaseVG. In early 1996 Hewlett-Packard announced that it would provide products for 100BaseT, apparently recognizing the momentum toward 100BaseT.

8.5.7 Fast Ethernet

100BaseT is very similar to 10BaseT, with changes at the physical layer to support the faster transmission rate. These changes require either "Category 5" level wiring, the *de facto* standard for new installations for several years, or extra pairs of "Category 3" wiring. Interface card products are often designed to support both 10BaseT and 100BaseT, and 100BaseT interface cards usually are offered for less than $100 premium over 10BaseT, so it is practical to convert a network gradually from 10BaseT to 100BaseT by incrementally changing interface cards and hubs.

8.6 SATELLITE

Using a geosynchronous satellite adds approximately 300 milliseconds of delay to the signal. This is acceptable in broadcast situations, but is very undesirable in interactive conversations. Some videoconferencing situations are enough like broadcast to benefit from satellite use, and sometimes satellite transmission is the only available method.

Educational video networks have traditionally been one-way video with limited two-way audio. In many cases, the video and audio are broadcast, and students reply by telephone. Traditional analog broadcast TV uses 6 MHz of bandwidth per channel. Modern modulation methods can put well over 20 Mbps into a 6-MHz TV band, so video compression greatly reduces the portion of satellite signal bandwidth needed. Conversion to the use of compressed video and audio can save on communication costs and at the same time add some measure of interactivity. For example, a teacher can lecture from one site, and view any student site that has backchannel video capability. If all student sites are so equipped, then any selected site can transmit back to the teacher.

In much of the world, there is no suitable terrestrial communication infrastructure, so satellite transmission is the only choice. Low earth orbit (LEO) satellite systems may become available in a few years, reducing delay to nearly that present in terrestrial systems.

8.7 U.S. REGULATORY ISSUES

U.S. readers will be well aware that their phone system is more fragmented than that of any other major country. In most countries, there is a single telephone company, often government owned and perhaps combined with the postal service.[10] The breakup of "the bell system," with the breakup of AT&T, has offered an unprecedented combination of opportunity and confusion. No doubt the breakup has greatly aided the public in some ways and hurt it in others. We will try to convey no judgment on the issue, but will give a brief description.

The court-ordered divestiture in 1984 led to the formation of seven Regional Holding Companies, which in turn own Bell Operating Companies (BOCs), which are often called Regional Bell Operating Companies (RBOCs). GTE and many smaller companies also supply local phone service.[11] The term "local exchange carrier" (LEC) can be used to cover all local phone companies. The RBOCs have not been allowed to manufacture equipment, offer "content services," or offer long-distance service outside of a LATA (local access and transport area). Similarly, long-distance companies, known as interexchange carriers (IXCs), have not been allowed to offer local service. As part of the AT&T breakup, portions of AT&T Bell Labs were spun off into Bellcore (Bell Communications Research), to give the BOCs a research consortium. Bellcore sometimes refers to its owners as Bellcore Client Companies (BCCs).

In February 1996, the United States enacted the Telecommunications Act of 1996, which to a large extent deregulates the BOCs, IXCs, and cable providers. As a result, there will be significantly more competition for local and long-distance telecommunications services. New alliances and mergers among these companies are likely. One of the BOCs, U S West, announced later in February 1996 that it had acquired Continental Cablevision. Two of the BOC parent companies, SBC Communications and Pacific Telesis Group, announced in April 1996 their intent to merge, and two other BOCs, Bell Atlantic and NYNEX, also announced intention to merge later that same month. Change will continue.

---

[10] A few other countries, most notably the United Kingdom, are allowing some telephone company competition.

[11] There are some "in between" situations, like Southern New England Telephone Company, which we will not try to explain.

REFERENCES

DOL78   Doll, Dixon R., *Data Communications*, John Wiley & Sons, NY, 1978.

HAR89   Hardwick, Steve, *ISDN Design; A Practical Approach*, Academic Press, San Diego, 1989.

MACE94   Macedonia, M. R., and Brutzman, D. P., "Mbone Provides Audio and Video Across the Internet," *IEEE Computer 27*, pp. 30–34 (April 1994).

PLAT96   Platt, Richard, "Why IsoEthernet Will Change the Voice and Video Worlds," *IEEE Communications Magazine*, pp. 55–59 (April 1996).

REY83   Rey, R. F., Ed. *Engineering & Operations in the Bell System*, 2nd ed., AT&T Bell Laboratories, Murray Hill, NJ, 1983.

Chapter 9

Video

Video processing is the most computationally intensive part of videoconferencing. Video signals require a large bandwidth (around 90 Mbps), but usually contain a great deal of redundancy. The bit rate for representing the signal can be reduced by removing redundancy, and if some degradation is acceptable, the bit rate can be greatly reduced. Transmission bit rates available for videoconferencing most commonly range from 112 Kbps to 2 Mbps. These bit rates must also include audio and control signals, and frequently carry other data. Thus the original, raw video content of 90 Mbps is sometimes reduced, or compressed, by a factor of as much as 1,000.

The terms "compression" and "coding" are used almost interchangeably in referring to processes for reducing the bit rate. Compression (or coding) is one of several video processing steps necessary for video telephony. The compression/coding step requires the most computation, but others are important, as well. Digital video input processing, before compression, may include color space conversion, de-interlacing, scan conversion, anti-aliasing filtering, and noise reduction filtering. Digital video output processing may include scan conversion, windowing, resizing, aspect ratio changes, and various post filters to reduce the objectionable appearance of certain compression artifacts. Motion video coding itself usually includes selection of picture regions to code, motion vector search, and coding of the motion-compensated differences between transmitted frames.

At each of the preceding steps, trade-offs are required among picture quality, product cost, and development cost. Some steps can be left out altogether. The importance of these processing steps is covered in a later section of this chapter, in the context of an exposition of the overall processing done in a moderately high-quality H.320 video codec. However, since video compression is the heart of the processing problem, we begin with it.

9.1 COMPRESSION

The purpose of video coding/compression, as applied to videoconferencing, is to reduce the data rate for video transmission and storage by compressing the digitized video signal so that it is represented by fewer bits. In Chapter 7, we looked at how analog signals could be captured in digital form. The most common video compression techniques, sometimes called "waveform" coding, take advantage of the fact that the video signal is organized as an ordered scanning of lines in successive frames, but use little other information. In contrast, "model-based" coding tries to make use of knowledge of the scenes being pictured. Most model-based efforts so far have concentrated on modeling human heads and faces.

Waveform coding techniques produce a coded bit stream that contains no semantic structure related to scene content. There are no sequences of bits designated as "head," "chair," "eyes," "bed," "car," or "couch." However, semantic information from the scene being coded can be used to assist or direct waveform coding techniques. For example, in a system optimized for "talking heads," a search algorithm for finding the pixels representing the eyes and mouth can be used to inform the waveform coder to increase its allocation of bits to blocks of pixels containing these regions [BAD90].

9.1.1 Waveform Coding

The four steps in basic waveform coding for motion video are (1) reduce temporal redundancy, (2) reduce spatial redundancy, (3) discard information, and (4) statistically code the remaining bit stream (see Table 9.1).

Table 9.1 Basic Steps in Waveform Coding

Coding Action	H.261 Method	Other Choices
Reduce temporal redundancy	Calculate motion-compensated frame difference	Calculate frame difference
Reduce spatial redundancy	Apply DCT to difference	Wavelet or other transforms, fractal coding
Discard information	Scalar quantization	Vector quantization
Apply statistical coding	Huffman coding	Arithmetic coding

9.1.1.1 *Reduce Temporal Redundancy*

Television sets display 30 frames per second (25 where PAL is used). Matters can be complicated by the fact that each frame is halved into two fields, but let us ignore that for now. Most of the time, the latest frame contains a picture that is very much like the one just before it. For instance, if the scene is of actors on a stage, the set is the same from one frame to the next. The actors may change position slightly, a new one may carry something in or out of the field of vision, or there may be (much less often) an entire scene change. In any case, most frames contain much of what was in previous frames. Conventional analog television simply transmits all of the information in each frame, with no knowledge or use made of previously transmitted information. While this may be acceptable for most broadcast situations, it is too wasteful of bandwidth for most videoconferencing applications. The obvious thing to do is to send only the changes that have occurred with the new frame. Both sender and receiver keep a copy of a "reference frame." The sender computes the difference between the new frame and the reference frame, and sends that difference. (In practice, this is done after other coding steps are applied.) Both sides then use the same information to update the reference frame, which the receiver then displays.

Even where frame-to-frame differences occur, the differences may be produced in different ways. Suppose an actor is removing a box from a bag. Successive frames will show more and more of the box as it appears. New information is introduced to each frame. The actor's arm also moves as the box is withdrawn, so in successive frames the arm appears in slightly different positions. When some of the difference between successive frames is because of the change in position of something that was already there, it may be possible to tell the receiver how to move picture parts it already has. That is, telling the receiver to take the set of pixels showing the arm and move it slightly may require fewer bits than sending the new set of pixels showing the new view of the arm. This technique is called "motion compensation," and is usually used in conjunction with frame differences. Conceptually, what is desired is to have the transmitter search its reference memory for the set of pixels showing the arm. This set of pixels is then moved to match the new location of the arm in the new frame. The difference between the new frame and the modified reference memory is now less than if there had been no motion compensation. (Even in the arm region, there will usually be some difference, because of slight changes due to lighting, some rotation of the arm, or some uncovering of other picture detail.) This "motion-compensated difference" can now be sent to the receiver, along with instructions about how to move the pixel regions in the reference memory before adding the frame difference to it.

9.1.1.2 Reduce Spatial Redundancy

Even within a single frame, there is usually a great deal of redundancy in that many pixels are much like the ones next to them. Consider a portion of a scene containing a painted wall. Adjacent pixels representing the wall are likely to have values that differ only slightly. The pixels representing an actor's blue jacket are likewise similar in value, although lighting effects and camera noise will cause some differences. One of the simplest ways to take advantage of this is to code each pixel in terms of the one before it in the raster scan of the frame. That is, the transmitter sends the change, or difference, between the new pixel and the one to the left of it on the scan line.

Another way to take advantage of likely redundancy is to look at blocks of adjacent pixels. One can compute the average value of a pixel in a block, and then compute how each pixel in the block differs from that average. If all of the pixels in the block have the same value, then only the average value needs to be transmitted. If the other pixels differ only slightly, and one can accept some loss of detail, then, again, only the average value need be transmitted. One of the most sophisticated and efficient ways of doing this (from a bit rate point of view) is to employ the discrete cosine transform (DCT). The ISO JPEG standard, the ITU H.261 recommendation, and ISO's MPEG 1 and MPEG 2 all use the DCT. Each of the four standards prescribes that the DCT be applied to blocks of 64 pixels that are eight rows high and 8 pixels wide. The transformation produces 64 values, called "coefficients," which describe how a particular set of basis functions[1] can be combined in order to produce the original set of pixel values. The reason that the set of coefficients is more useful (for coding) than the original set of pixels is that the coefficients are ordered according to the fineness of detail contributed by their corresponding basis functions.

$P_{0,0}$	$P_{0,1}$	$P_{0,2}$	$P_{0,3}$	$P_{0,4}$	$P_{0,5}$	$P_{0,6}$	$P_{0,7}$
$P_{1,0}$	$P_{1,1}$	$P_{1,2}$	$P_{1,3}$	$P_{1,4}$	$P_{1,5}$	$P_{1,6}$	$P_{1,7}$
$P_{2,0}$	$P_{2,1}$	$P_{2,2}$	$P_{2,3}$	$P_{2,4}$	$P_{2,5}$	$P_{2,6}$	$P_{2,7}$
$P_{3,0}$	$P_{3,1}$	$P_{3,2}$	$P_{3,3}$	$P_{3,4}$	$P_{3,5}$	$P_{3,6}$	$P_{3,7}$
$P_{4,0}$	$P_{4,1}$	$P_{4,2}$	$P_{4,3}$	$P_{4,4}$	$P_{4,5}$	$P_{4,6}$	$P_{4,7}$

[1] The set of basis functions can be thought of as a set of predetermined patterns of values. By taking the proper percentage of each pattern, and adding them, one can reproduce any actual set of 64 pixel values. The coefficients tell what percentage of each pattern needs to be added in order to reproduce the block being coded. If a particular pattern is not needed, its coefficient is zero. If only a little bit of a pattern is needed, its coefficient is small and can be approximated by zero. The DCT is important because frequently only a few of its patterns are needed to construct a good approximation to the original 64 pixel values. For most actual scene content, the patterns corresponding to fine detail have smaller percentage contributions.

$P_{5,0}$	$P_{5,1}$	$P_{5,2}$	$P_{5,3}$	$P_{5,4}$	$P_{5,5}$	$P_{5,6}$	$P_{5,7}$
$P_{6,0}$	$P_{6,1}$	$P_{6,2}$	$P_{6,3}$	$P_{6,4}$	$P_{6,5}$	$P_{6,6}$	$P_{6,7}$
$P_{7,0}$	$P_{7,1}$	$P_{7,2}$	$P_{7,3}$	$P_{7,4}$	$P_{7,5}$	$P_{7,6}$	$P_{7,7}$

is transformed into

$C_{0,0}$	$C_{0,1}$	$C_{0,2}$	$C_{0,3}$	$C_{0,4}$	$C_{0,5}$	$C_{0,6}$	$C_{0,7}$
$C_{1,0}$	$C_{1,1}$	$C_{1,2}$	$C_{1,3}$	$C_{1,4}$	$C_{1,5}$	$C_{1,6}$	$C_{1,7}$
$C_{2,0}$	$C_{2,1}$	$C_{2,2}$	$C_{2,3}$	$C_{2,4}$	$C_{2,5}$	$C_{2,6}$	$C_{2,7}$
$C_{3,0}$	$C_{3,1}$	$C_{3,2}$	$C_{3,3}$	$C_{3,4}$	$C_{3,5}$	$C_{3,6}$	$C_{3,7}$
$C_{4,0}$	$C_{4,1}$	$C_{4,2}$	$C_{4,3}$	$C_{4,4}$	$C_{4,5}$	$C_{4,6}$	$C_{4,7}$
$C_{5,0}$	$C_{5,1}$	$C_{5,2}$	$C_{5,3}$	$C_{5,4}$	$C_{5,5}$	$C_{5,6}$	$C_{5,7}$
$C_{6,0}$	$C_{6,1}$	$C_{6,2}$	$C_{6,3}$	$C_{6,4}$	$C_{6,5}$	$C_{6,6}$	$C_{6,7}$
$C_{7,0}$	$C_{7,1}$	$C_{7,2}$	$C_{7,3}$	$C_{7,4}$	$C_{7,5}$	$C_{7,6}$	$C_{7,7}$

The relationship between the pixel values and the coefficients is expressed by the equation,

$$C_{i,j} = \frac{1}{4} K_i K_j \sum_{m=0}^{7} \sum_{n=0}^{7} P_{m,n} \cos\left[\frac{\pi}{8} \cdot i \cdot \left(m + \frac{1}{2}\right)\right] \cos\left[\frac{\pi}{8} \cdot j \cdot \left(n + \frac{1}{2}\right)\right], \quad (9.1)$$

where $K_i = \dfrac{1}{\sqrt{2}}$, for $i = 0$ and $K_i = 1$, for $i \neq 0$.

Given the set of coefficient values $\{C_{i,j}\}$, the pixel values can be recon structed using

$$p_{i,j} = \frac{1}{4} \sum_{m=0}^{7} \sum_{n=0}^{7} K_m K_n \cdot C_{m,n} \cos\left[\frac{\pi}{8} \cdot m\left(i + \frac{1}{2}\right)\right] \cos\left[\frac{\pi}{8} \cdot n\left(j + \frac{1}{2}\right)\right], \quad (9.2$$

where $C_{0,0}$ provides the "coarsest" information about the pixels in the block, being in fact eight times the average pixel value of the entire block. That is, $C_{0,0} = \dfrac{1}{8} \sum_{m=0}^{7} \sum_{n=0}^{7} P_{m,n}$. If all of the pixels in the block have the same value, then each of the other $C_{i,j}$ values is zero, and need not be transmitted. $C_{0,1}$ and $C_{1,0}$ provide the next coarsest information, up to $C_{7,7}$, which provides the finest. In picture areas with no fine detail, "higher order" coefficients such as $C_{7,7}$ will be zero, or nearly so. Having all of the pixel values in a block being exactly the same is rare except in computer-generated graphics, but having them close in value is not so rare. In this case, most or all of the coefficients other than $C_{0,0}$ will have small values.

In most cases, using Eqs. (9.1) and (9.2) will be far too inefficient. The DCT has become important enough that a great deal of work has been done to find fast ways to compute it and its inverse (IDCT). The most common methods are "butterfly" techniques, such as those used for fast Fourier transforms (FFT). Figure 9.1 shows a butterfly flowgraph for computing a 4×4 DCT. (The 8×8 is too large to show here. See KAM82 for a derivation of both the 4×4 and an 8×8.) The p_i are the input pixel values, the $C(j)$ are the coefficient values, and $cnm = \cos(n\pi/8)\cos(m\pi/8)$. In the 4×4 case as shown, the algorithm requires 66 additions and 28 multiplications. The 8×8 version requires 430 additions and 128 multiplications. Research still continues on better techniques, some minimizing total operations, others minimizing multiplications, and yet others minimizing the complexity of DCT chip designs.

Fractal coding and wavelet transforms are other ways of removing spatial redundancy, but are much less widely used. Wavelet coding may offer some advantages, but has not yet been developed well enough to begin displacement of the DCT. [See RIO91 for a review and tutorial on wavelet theory.]

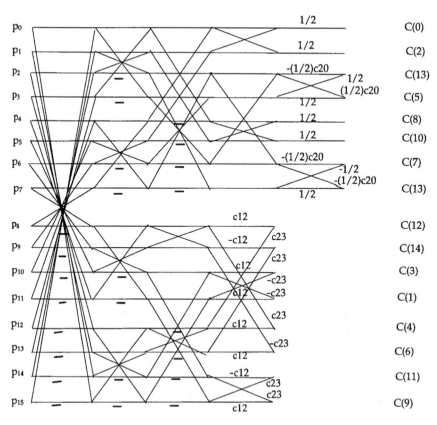

Figure 9.1   DCT butterfly flowgraph

9.1.1.3 Discard Information

Scalar Quantization. The DCT can be used even when lossless coding is required, because, if no coefficient bits are discarded, the original block of pixel values can be reconstructed. In a motion videoconference, large compression ratios are usually required, and lossless coding is rarely done, though it can be required in certain medical still image situations. Some of the necessary compression can be achieved by discarding the highest order coefficients and by quantizing the remaining coefficients to fewer bits.

In a sense, quantizing is like rounding. For example, in financial reporting, in order to save space, numerical entries in tables often represent thousands or millions of dollars. For example, the entry $187,310 might represent $187,310,000. The corresponding actual value might be $187,310,387 or perhaps $186,309,987. This is done in situations when the differences are not important to the reader. The idea is to convey the essential information with fewer numerals. Thus it can be conveyed with fewer bits.

Looking more closely at rounding, one can see that it can be considered to be a two-part operation. First, the entire range of input values to be considered is partitioned into a finite set of subranges. Second, a representative value is chosen to represent each subset. For example, if one were rounding financial figures to the nearest dollar, as is often done on tax returns, the set of subranges of values is {...,[−$2.5,−$1.5),[−$1.5,−$0.5),[−$0.5,$0.5), [$0.5,$1.5),[$1.5,$2.5),...}.[2] The set of representative values chosen is {..., −$2, −$1, $0, $1, $2, ...}. The representative value for a subrange need not be its midpoint. If there is compelling evidence that values in a subrange tend to cluster toward some value that is more probable than the midpoint, it might be decided to use this *most probable value* instead. This is sometimes done in video compression.

If some representative values are more common than others, further compression can be achieved by using a variable length code to transmit them. In the preceding example on financial figures, suppose that −$1, $0, and $1 occur much more frequently than, say, $20, $21, ... On average, then, one can represent a string of actually occurring representative values with fewer total bits by using short bit patterns for −$1, 0, $1 and longer patterns for less frequently occurring values like $20, $21, ... This is covered in the section on variable length coding.

Vector Quantizing. In the previous section, the examples were of quantizing one value at a time. There are advantages to collecting sets of values

---

[2] [a,b) indicates a half-open interval, a $\leq x <$ b.

together into vectors and assigning a single value to the set. This "vector quantizing" actually compresses data in two ways—it at once reduces redundancy and discards information [NET95, OHT94]. Although VQ has had some very successful applications in videoconferencing and computer video games, it is not used in the recognized standards. Major manufacturers who have used it have either replaced their products with DCT-based systems or have added the DCT-based H.320 standard to their product line. VQ can be applied in place of scalar quantization even after using the DCT, but the authors are not aware of any actual products that do this.

In vector quantization, n values are grouped together as an n-dimensional vector in an n-dimensional signal space. The vector space is divided into nonoverlapping regions, analogous to the subranges of scalar quantization. An input vector will lie in one of the regions, for which there must have been chosen a representative vector, analogous to the representative value used for a subrange in scalar quantization. It is easiest to visualize this in two dimensions. Figure 9.2 illustrates both scalar and vector quantization. The input vector (x_i, y_i) would be represented by the vector (x_2, y_2). The hard part is in determining the best boundaries and representative value for each region.

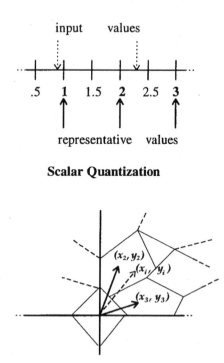

Figure 9.2   Quantization illustration

Computationally it is probably best to determine which representative value is the closest to an input vector (x_i, y_i), so in practice the regions will be shaped differently from the illustration of Figure 9.2. The measure of closeness should be reasonably easy to calculate and also be a good measure of how the human eye would view the difference between the representative value and the actual input vector. Mean square error (MSE) is the measure usually used, though the mean absolute difference (MAD) is sometimes tried in order to reduce the computational requirements.

For two vectors, x and y of dimension n, these are computed according to

$$\text{MSE} = \frac{1}{n}\sum_{i=1}^{n}(x_i - y_i)^2 \quad \text{and} \quad \text{MAD} = \frac{1}{n}\sum_{i=1}^{n}|x_i - y_i|.$$

In many processors, MAD is significantly cheaper to compute than MSE, so it may be used even in applications where MSE would otherwise be preferred.

The most straightforward way to use VQ in image coding is to group pixels into square blocks (usually 4×4) and treat the block as a vector. Blocks of 16 pixels (4×4) are typical because they are big enough to do some good and not too big to handle. The next convenient block size is 8×8. Such 64-element vectors have been considered too large to be practical. In encoding, one begins with a table of representative, 16-element vector values, called the *codebook*. To code a block of pixels, one finds the codebook entry with, say, the least MSE value with respect to the input block. The codebook index is sent to the decoder, which then looks up the representative value in its copy of the codebook. This is one of the main advantages of VQ; the simplicity of the decoder. Its chief structure is a look-up table, the codebook of representative values. If a codebook is created that closely matches the actual input vectors, then the visual performance will be good. The LBG algorithm is perhaps the best known for creating codebooks. The LBG method requires an initial codebook, and then improves it as it operates on a *training set* of input vectors.

As described in NET95, the LBG algorithm proceeds as follows:

1. Map the training set into the code words with least MSE (or other preferred distance measure). If the overall error measure of the mapping is low enough, stop.

2. For each representative value *r*, determine the subset of training vectors that was mapped into it. Replace *r* by a new representative value that reduces the overall error measure computed in Step 1. Go back to Step 1.

This method does not guarantee convergence to a globally optimal codebook, so it is important to choose a good starting codebook. One plausible choice is to pick a reasonable looking subset of the training vectors themselves.

The visual performance of VQ depends on how well the codebook matches the scenes being coded and how many entries are in the codebook. The more entries, the less the compression. A codebook with 2^N entries requires that an N-bit index value be transmitted for each coded input vector. If one wished to allocate 1 bit per pixel for coding 4×4 pixel blocks, then 2^{16} codebook entries are needed. Hierarchical or other multistage variations of VQ can be used to make practical VQ codecs. VQ can also be applied to motion-compensated frame differences.

9.1.1.4 Statistical Coding

Variable length coding (VLC) techniques achieve compression by transmitting more probable symbols in fewer bits than less probable ones. Since it depends on there being differences in such probabilities, it is also called "statistical coding." In video coding, even after the other techniques are performed, some of the remaining, quantized values will occur more frequently than others. Two basic techniques are in regular use, Huffman coding and arithmetic coding. Huffman coding is the more common, but arithmetic coding can provide better compression, because it does not require that each symbol to be transmitted be coded into an integral number of bits.

Huffman Coding. Simple examples can serve to illustrate the value of VLC, although they do not directly show the amount of bit savings that can be realized in an actual system. Consider an imaginary language with a four-symbol alphabet {A,B,C,D}. Messages will consist of strings of these symbols. A straightforward binary encoding of a four-character alphabet would assign a unique two-bit (fixed length) code to each character. This is what is done in ASCII for a 256-character alphabet with eight-bit codes. A VLC assignment gives the shortest code to the most probable symbol, that is, the symbol that has been found to occur most frequently over the history of many messages. Table 9.2 shows, for our imaginary language, the probabilities of occurrence of each symbol within a message, and the codes assigned

Table 9.2 Probability of Symbol Occurrence

Symbol	Probability	VLC Code	Fixed Length Code
A	1/2	0	00
B	1/4	10	01
C	1/8	110	10
D	1/8	111	11

to each. The VLC codes are assigned so that they can be uniquely decoded. For example, we could not use "1" for B and "10" for C, because the decoder wouldn't know whether "10" meant "C" or "BA".

Now, suppose one wishes to send the message "BAAC." Using the fixed codes, the binary coded representation of the message would be the eight-bit string "01000010". If we concatenate the VLC codes, we get the seven-bit string "1000110", so our message is one bit shorter. Let us now look at decoding it using the binary decision tree of Figure 9.3. We start with the first bit of the string to be decoded and take the 0 or 1 branch as indicated by the value of the first bit. We then discard the bit and look at the next one. When we reach an A, B, C, or D, we write it down and go back to first node of the tree. Using our example string, the decoder starts at node α. The first string bit is "1", which takes the decoder to node β. The next bit is 0, which takes the decoder to the leaf node "B". The encoder writes out a "B", and begins again at node α with the third bit in the input string, "0". This causes the decoder to write out "A", and then go back to node with the fourth bit, and so on until it finishes writing out "BAAC".

Arithmetic Coding.   The preceding example was a simple one used to illustrate Huffman coding, which has long been considered the best technique for VLC. However, arithmetic coding has the advantage of not requiring that each symbol be coded with an integral number of bits. The idea of arithmetic coding is that the message is represented by an interval of real numbers between 0 and 1 [WIT87]. The longer the message, the smaller the interval, and the greater the number of bits required to specify it. In fact, the decoder can work from a single number within the interval. Table 9.3 shows the same character set used earlier in Table 9.2, with the same occurrence probabilities, but with the addition of an interval range of a size corresponding to the symbol's probability. (Recall that the notation [0,1) indicates a half open interval, $0 \le x < 1$.)

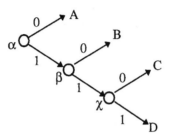

Figure 9.3   Decision tree

Table 9.3 Probability Table with Corresponding Interval Ranges

Symbol	Probability	Range
A	1/2	$[0, 1/2)$
B	1/4	$[1/2, 3/4)$
C	1/8	$[3/4, 7/8)$
D	1/8	$[7/8, 1)$

The ranges shown in Table 9.3 can be used successively to specify the interval "containing" the message string. Consider again the message "BAAC". The encoder starts with range $[0,1)$, and, when it sees the "B", narrows the range to $[1/2, 3/4]$. The next symbol will narrow the range to the appropriately positioned and sized subrange within this narrowed range. In our example, the encoder will next see an "A", and will narrow the range to $[1/2, 5/8)$. With the next symbol, "A", the encoder will narrow the range to $[8/16, 9/16)$, and with the fourth symbol, "C", the range becomes $[70/128, 71/128)$. The encoder can transmit the message by transmitting $70/128$, or $35/64$, to the decoder. As a binary fraction, $35/64$ is 0.100011, so the encoder must transmit the bit string "100011".

The decoder can determine that the first symbol is a "B", because $35/64$ is in the range $[1/2, 3/4)$. The decoder must then determine what symbol would narrow $[1/2, 3/4)$ and still contain $35/64$. A "B" would narrow the range to $[3/4, 7/8)$, which is $[48/64, 56/64)$, and "C" or "D" would cause intervals starting at $56/64$ or above, so only "A" could be the next character. An "A" narrows the interval to $[32/64, 40/64)$. The decoder can next determine that only "A" could have produced the next narrowed interval enclosing $35/64$, and so on until "BAAC" is reconstructed.

This particular example message required eight bits for fixed length coding, seven bits for Huffman, and six for arithmetic coding. However, we have left out such details as when to stop decoding, the effects of transmission errors, and how to adapt to varying symbol probabilities for different messages. For fixed length codes, having bit values inverted in transmission causes incorrect decoding only for the symbols whose codes are wrong. For VLC, the whole sequence is thrown out of synchronization. Error correction and recovery techniques must be used in conjunction with VLC. If the probabilities used by the encoder are too far wrong, inflation rather than compression could take place. Practical details for VLC, including various methods for combating problems, are discussed in [WIT87] for arithmetic coding and [HEL91] for Huffman. [WIT87 also presents encoding and decoding programs written in C.]

9.1.2 Model-Based Coding

Model-based coding makes use of information about the expected content of the video sequences to be coded. For example, a coder optimized for video phone "talking heads" can use a model of the human head to assist in compression. At call setup, specific information about the visual appearance of the participants in the call can be exchanged. Individual features are then overlaid onto the human head model. The coding of the heads' actions during the call can be done by sending the changes in value of a set of parameters that describes mouth movement, eye movement, facial expressions, etc. A good example of work in this area is the Candide model, developed at Sweden's Linköping University [LI93]. The Candide model is a parameterized, wireframe model containing both facial shape and expression information.

In a more limited form, model-based techniques are used to enhance waveform techniques. Background compensation is a good example [see MUK85]. The coder and the decoder, over time, build up a "background frame" that contains a picture of the static components of a scene. The coder works only from information available in the coded bit stream; that is, information available to the decoder. People who walk around a videoconferencing room are continually covering and uncovering parts of the room behind them as they move. The coder can then gain extra compression by signaling the decoder when to display stored background picture segments that correspond to those segments newly uncovered at the coder's site. For the other parts of the picture, normal waveform coding is done.

9.2 VIDEO PROCESSING IN AN H.320 CODEC

Let us consider a codec that adheres to ITU H.320, is designed for NTSC input and output,[3] and strives to attain moderately high quality, but without excessive costs. Using readily available chip sets, such a codec would capture composite or S-Video input at 30 frames per second, and transmit 15 to 30 frames per second of compressed video. Each frame is made up of two

---

[3] Since the number of lines of resolution in H.320 is based on the number of visible lines in the PAL format, designing a codec to accept PAL is easier.

interlaced fields of 240 active lines each, so each frame has 480 active lines. Figure 9.4 shows the basic processing blocks.

9.2.1 Capture at 720 × 480   4:2:2

There will be some degree of analog filtering, partly for noise reduction and partly for anti-aliasing. Off-the-shelf chip sets are available that will convert from NTSC composite to digital *YUV*. Typically the components are subsampled in CCIR 601 4:2:2 format. That is, for every four *Y* values captured on a line, only two *U* and two *V* values are captured. The pattern looks as shown in Figure 9.5, where there are 480 lines with 720 pixels per line.

For H.320, the video must be converted to the 4:1:1 format specified by H.261 (the video compression part of H.320). Each frame has 288 lines of *Y* (luminance) pixels, with 352 pixels in each line. For every four *Y* pixel values, there is one pair of chrominance values (*U* and one *V*). This is the Common Interchange Format (CIF). The relative pixel positions are illustrated in

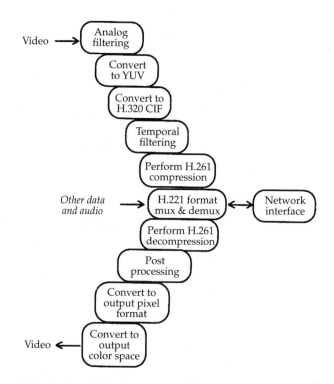

Figure 9.4   Basic video processing blocks

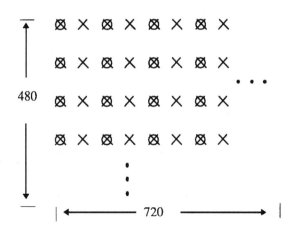

X–Represents luminance pixels
O–Represents chrominance pixels

Figure 9.5 The position of luminance and chrominance samples in CCIR 601

Figure 9.6. In this arrangement, there are 144 lines of U,V pairs, with 176 pairs per line.

For a slightly lower quality system, a CIF frame is formed from a single field, converting 240 lines into 288. Higher quality systems start with the full 480-line frame (two fields) and scale it down to 288 lines for Y (luminance) and 144 lines for U and V (chrominance). The number of pixels on each line is halved,

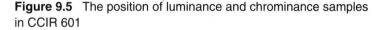

X–Represents luminance pixels
O–Represents chrominance pixels

Figure 9.6 The position of luminance and chrominance samples in H.261 CIF

and 8 pixels per line are dropped, giving 352 pixels for *Y*. A similar process gives 176 pixels each for *U* and *V*. These resolution and scan conversion processes are important enough to picture quality to warrant a closer look.

The pixel luminance and chrominance values are stored as eight-bit values. The values 0 and 255 are reserved for synchronization. The remaining range, 1 to 254, is limited further in order to reduce the odds that even after digitization, coding, decoding, and color space conversions, the various numerical inaccuracies introduced do not cause underflow or overflow, and do not cause the synchronization values 0 and 255 to be accidentally produced. However, to completely ensure that this does not happen, a codec must check the values and adjust them if necessary. The following range of values is prescribed in CCIR Recommendation 601:

Black	16
White	235
Zero color difference	128
Peak color difference	16 and 240

9.2.2 Input Resolution Conversion

In a higher quality codec, a full input frame, with both odd and even fields, will be used to create the 352 × 288 CIF frame. (We will discuss only luminance here. Chrominance is treated similarly.) In starting with a full frame, we have two problems to deal with: removing interlace effects and reducing the number of pixels per frame. If 480 lines are captured, that number of lines must be converted to 288. The horizontal capture resolution can be 352 pixels per line. This requires that the input be filtered adequately in the analog domain to prevent aliasing. It is more common, however, because of standard video capture chip sets designed for digital TV, to capture 720 pixels per line. It makes sense to first reduce the horizontal resolution to 352, since it can be done in conjunction with the capture step and since doing it reduces the computation and frame store requirements of later steps. As the 720 pixels are being captured, they are digitally filtered down to 360 pixels, and the four leftmost and four rightmost pixels are discarded to get to 352. Simpler, inexpensive codecs might just average adjacent pixels to step down from 720 to 360. A moderate- to high-quality codec might use a "seven-tap" filter to do this, with each pixel value calculated from

$$p_i = \frac{-2}{32} \cdot p_{i-3} + \frac{1}{32} p_{i-2} + \frac{9}{32} \cdot p_{i-1} + \frac{16}{32} p_i + \frac{9}{32} \cdot p_{i+1} + \frac{1}{32} \cdot p_{i+2} + \frac{-2}{32} \cdot p_{i+3}$$

or a similar equation. It is called a "seven-tap" filter because seven original pixels are used to determine the new pixel.

Next we face the problem of converting from 480 lines to 288. First, let us look at how we get 480 lines. Suppose both fields of a frame are captured and stored as shown in Figure 9.7. Lines 1,3, ..., 479 come from field 1, often called the odd field and lines 2,4, ..., 480 come from field 2, the even field. Since each line in the even field is captured 1/60 of a second later than its corresponding line in the odd field, an object in motion will be displaced in field 2 with respect to field 1. The most noticeable effect is that the object's edges will look serrated. This effect can be reduced by filtering.

One simple filtering scheme for reducing interlace effects is to combine adjacent lines in the frame with a 1/3, 2/3 weighting. That is, line 1 in the filtered frame will be 2/3 of the original line 1 plus 1/3 of the original line 2. Line 2 will be 2/3 of the original line 2 plus 1/3 of the original line 3, and so on, as shown in Figure 9.8. This scheme preserves resolution in nonmoving areas somewhat better than a straight average of the lines from the two fields. It would be even better if the filtering were done only on moving areas, but this is too costly at present for most implementations.

When we begin with a frame captured from NTSC, we have 480 lines, but must get to the 288 lines of CIF. This process is often called "scan conversion." Logically, de-interlacing and scan conversion are separate steps, but since good scan conversion requires filtering also, they can be combined. We must convert 480 lines to 288, which is 60% of 480, so we must produce three CIF lines for every five original input lines. The filtering scheme shown in Figure 9.9 is a reasonable cost/visual quality trade-off. It uses up to four input lines to produce one output line, so it is called a "four-tap" filter. Notice

```
line 1 x x x x x x x x x x x ... x
line 2 x x x x x x x x x x x ... x
line 3 x x x x x x x x x x x ... x
line 4 x x x x x x x x x x x ... x
line 5 x x x x x x x x x x x ... x
line 6 x x x x x x x x x x x ... x
line 7 x x x x x x x x x x x ... x
line 8 x x x x x x x x x x x ... x

                 .
                 .
                 .

line 480 x x . . .                     x
```

Figure 9.7 480 line captured frame (2 fields)

Captured frame   Filtered frame

line 1 x x x x x x x x x x x ... x   <2/3 line 1 + 1/3 line 2>
line 2 x x x x x x x x x x x ... x   <2/3 line 2 + 1/3 line 3>
line 3 x x x x x x x x x x x ... x   <2/3 line 3 + 1/3 line 4>
line 4 x x x x x x x x x x x ... x   <2/3 line 4 + 1/3 line 5>
line 5 x x x x x x x x x x x ... x   <2/3 line 5 + 1/3 line 6>
line 6 x x x x x x x x x x x ... x   <2/3 line 6 + 1/3 line 7>
line 7 x x x x x x x x x x x ... x   <2/3 line 7 + 1/3 line 8>
line 8 x x x x x x x x x x x ... x   <2/3 line 8 + 1/3 line 9>

.   .
.   .
.   .

line 480 x x . . . x   <line 480>

Figure 9.8   A simple filter for an interlaced frame

Captured frame   CIF frame

line 1 x x x x x ... x

line 2 x x x x x ... x <0.25 line 1 + 0.5 line 2 + 0.25 line 3>   (*line 1*)

line 3 x x x x x ... x

                    <0.09 line 2 + 0.34 line 3 + 0.41 line 4 + 0.16 line 5>(*line 2*)

line 4 x x x x x ... x

line 5 x x x x x ... x

                    <0.16 line 4 + 0.41 line 5 + 0.34 line 6 + 0.09 line 7>(*line 3*)

line 6 x x x x x ... x

line 7 x x x x x ... x <0.25 line 6 + 0.5 line 7 + 0.25 line 8>   (*line 4*)

line 8 x x x x x ... x

.
.
.

line 480 x x ... x

Figure 9.9   Four-tap filter for conversion to CIF

that the weights are scaled so that, for each resulting CIF line, half the contribution is from the even field and half is from the odd field. If higher visual quality is desired, filters with more taps can be used. Visual quality increases remain quite noticeable up to about seven taps.

9.2.3 Temporal Filtering

Filtering in the temporal domain is also valuable, and can help in at least three ways. Temporal filtering removes camera noise, performs temporal anti-aliasing, and blurs the edges of moving objects. Edge blurring reduces the fine detail, which reduces the need for the higher order DCT basis functions, increasing the likelihood that higher order coefficients will have small or zero values and need not be transmitted.

At transmission data rates of 384 Kbps or below, the most pleasing results are usually obtained by transmitting at 15 frames per second or less. Temporal filtering is best carried out before the frame rate reduction, though doing it in this order will usually cost more to implement than if the frame rate is reduced first [see CHE87].

The essence of the filtering process is that as each new frame is captured, a portion of each old pixel is added to a portion of each corresponding new pixel in order to produce the new filtered pixel value. This filtering is sometimes called recursive, because the "old pixel" value was itself previously filtered, and thus contains contributions from pixel values in previous frames.

Consider a given pixel position in a sequence of frames. Let u_n be the unfiltered pixel in the incoming frame n. Let p_{n-1} be the corresponding filtered pixel from frame n-1. Let p_n be the filtered pixel in the new frame n. Let α be the filtering coefficient, where $0 \leq \alpha \leq 1$. The new, filtered pixel value for frame n is given by

$$p_n = \alpha \cdot u_n + (1-\alpha) \cdot p_{n-1}. \tag{9.3}$$

Consider a picture region that is unchanging; u_n will differ from the previous pixel value only if noise is introduced. That is, $u_n = p_{n-1} + e$, where e is the added noise amount. From Eq. (9.3), p_n then becomes $p_n = p_{n-1} + \alpha \cdot e$. If $\alpha = 1/2$, then the noise is reduced by $1/2$. In practice, this causes more blurring in moving areas than one would like, so a larger value of α may be preferred. Using $\alpha = 0.9$ means that 90% of the newly acquired, unfiltered pixel value is retained, and 90% of any noise remains also. Still, even using $\alpha = 0.9$ will fairly quickly damp out a random noise impulse. Let *old* represent the correct pixel value, and let *old* + *e* represent the noisy value. Three frames later, successive applications of the filtering of Eq. (9.3) give us a filtered pixel value of *old* + *e* · (α − 2α^2 + α^3). For α = 0.9, the pixel value will be *old* + 0.009*e*, leaving no visible error. Some designers choose to perform temporal filtering only in areas of no motion. A simple way to approximate this is to apply Eq. (9.3) only when the new and old pixel differences are small. If the difference is above some threshold, then it is assumed that there is motion or a scene change, and no filtering should be carried out. This allows an α of around 0.5 to be used, filtering out noise more quickly in motionless areas, without blurring an object in significant motion.

9.2.4 Compress the Video

An H.320 codec compresses and decompresses video according to ITU-T Recommendation[4] H.261. The 1993 revision of H.261 is 28 pages, and we do not attempt to reproduce it here. (As of this writing, ITU document and availability information is posted on the Internet at the URL address http://www.itu.ch.) The standard is weighted toward specifying the decoding process without constraining the encoding process any more than necessary. The aim is to allow some freedom in the development of encoder capability, but in a way that leaves all H.261 standard codecs able to decode each other's bit stream.

H.261 was developed by Working Party XV/4 (Specialists Group on Coding for Visual Telephony) of Study Group XV of the ITU. In the course of its work, the group developed several codec system designs, the last of which was Reference Model 8 (RM8). RM8 is described in the unpublished Working Party Document #525 (1989). Since it describes an actual codec, RM8 gives details of motion search, quantization decisions, etc., that are beyond what is necessary for guaranteeing interoperability, so the details are not present in H.261.

9.2.4.1 Overall H.261 Coding Process

The overall block diagram of the H.261 processing within an H.320 codec is shown in Figure 9.10. The transform and quantization are carried out in the source coder block. Once bits are passed to the video multiplexer coder, no more information is discarded. The multiplexer coder assembles the bits representing the quantized, transformed values, together with control and the motion vector information, and performs the statistical (VLC) coding. It then feeds the bit stream into the output buffer. The transmission coder adds error correction and associated framing.

---

[4] ITU standards are formally titled "Recommendations" by the ITU.

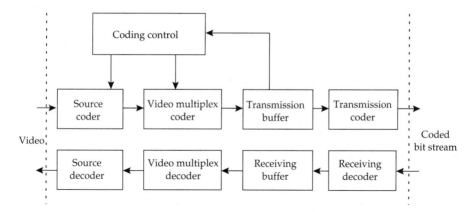

Figure 9.10 H.261 block diagram
(Reprinted with the permission of ITU, from Recommendation H.261 (3/93) figure 1.)

H.261 divides a CIF frame[5] into luminance blocks that are eight pixels wide and eight pixels high. Recall from Figure 9.6 that each luminance block has with it two 4 × 4 blocks for the color difference values. A set of four of these 64-pixel luminance blocks, with associated chrominance blocks, is called a "macroblock." That is, a macroblock is a region two luminance blocks wide and two blocks high. The block arrangement is shown in Figure 9.11. Each of the blocks, 1 through 6, is an 8 × 8 block, since each of the chrominance blocks is an aggregation of four blocks that are each four pixels wide and four high.

Macroblocks are aggregated into Groups of Blocks (GOBs). Each GOB contains 33 macroblocks, arranged as shown in Figure 9.12a, so a GOB is 1/12 of the area of a CIF frame, and 1/3 that of a QCIF frame. Spatially, a GOB represents 176 pixels by 48 lines of luminance. A GOB is half a CIF frame wide. GOBs are ordered within a CIF frame as shown in Figure 9.12b. The source coder portion of a codec that takes full advantage of what is

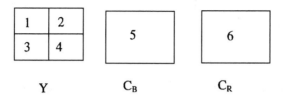

Figure 9.11 A macroblock
(Reprinted with the permission of ITU, from Recommendation H.261 (3/93) figure 3.)

[5] H.261 allows a codec to code pictures at quarter resolution (QCIF), in which luminance resolution is 176 × 144 and the color components are at 88 × 72. QCIF was included to allow lower performance, less expensive implementations of video telephones.

1	2	3	4	5	6	7	8	9	10	11
12	13	14	15	16	17	18	19	20	21	22
23	24	25	26	27	28	29	30	31	32	33

(a) Macroblocks within a GOB

1	2
3	4
5	6
7	8
9	10
11	12

(b) GOBs within a frame

Figure 9.12   GOB arrangement
(Reprinted with permission of ITU, from Recommendation H.261 (3/93) figures 6 and 9.)

allowed in H.261 will have a form similar to that shown in Figure 9.13. A copy of the previously transmitted frame is reconstructed and stored in reference memory RM. When a new frame in the video sequence has been captured and is ready to be coded, each macroblock is compared to its counterpart stored in RM. In motion video sequences, most of the time the new frame, or at least most of its macroblocks, is very much like the preceding frame. If not, then the frame, or some macroblocks within it, can be directly coded in INTRA (indicating "intraframe") mode. If a macroblock has changed very little, then the coder may decide not to code and send it, so that the receiver will redisplay the old macroblock.[6] When a macroblock has changed enough to warrant being coded, but not enough to trigger INTRA mode, it will be coded in INTER (interframe) mode. The best matching "old" macroblock, found through motion search, will be subtracted from the new before the DCT is applied. This "old" macroblock can be thought of as lying in the center of a 31 × 31 pixel region. If full motion search is being carried out,[7] the new macroblock is also compared to every 16 × 16 pixel subregion

---

[6] The traditional term for this is "conditional replenishment."

[7] Full search has been used in at least one product, but this brute force approach is expensive. Most codecs use some form of ordered seach or a "hill climbing" approach.

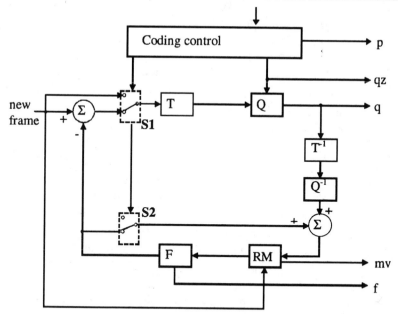

Transmission buffer fullness feedback

T, T⁻¹ DCT transform and its inverse
Q, Q⁻¹ Quantization and reconstruction
F Loop filter
RM Reference memory for reconstructed frame, as sent to a receiver
S1 Switch for intraframe or differential coding
S2 Switch for loop filter on or off
p Flag to indicate differential coding
qz Quantizer information
q Quantized values
mv Motion vector code
f Loop filter switch

Figure 9.13 Coder block diagram
(Reprinted with permission of ITU, from Recommendation H.261 (3/93) figure 10.)

within the 31×31 region. The search is for the subregion with the best match. This can be thought of as the "motion-compensated old macroblock" (MCM). The MCM is subtracted from the new macroblock, and the motion vector is saved for transmission to a decoder. A decoder uses the motion vector to calculate the location of its copy of the MCM. The motion vector components will have values in the range of –15 to +15, inclusive.[8] The measure

---

[8] RM8 and some commercial products limit the range to ±7. H.261 allows the encoder to restrict itself in this way, but the decoder must handle ±15.

usually used for determining the best match is mean absolute difference (MAD), though mean square error (MSE), or something else, could also be used. H.261 does not specify how an encoder is to determine the motion vectors. In fact, H.261 does not require the encoder to do motion search, but the decoder must be capable of decoding motion-compensated transmissions.

In addition to the four luminance blocks, each macroblock has four color difference (chrominance) blocks. The motion vector computed for the luminance is also used for the color. That is, one motion vector is used for all of the blocks in a macroblock. The vector components are halved and truncated toward zero in order to apply them to the color difference blocks. The ITU specialists group considered using separate motion vectors for each 8×8 luminance block. Using the 16×16 macroblocks reduces the number of bits taken up in transmitting motion vector values, and was found to be a better compromise.

The average bit rate of the coded video bit stream is determined by the communication channel. If an H0 channel is used, a steady 384 Kbps is provided—no more, no less—for the multiplexed video, audio, data, and control bit streams. The coder has an output buffer, and the decoder an input buffer to allow some temporary variation, but the average bit rate is fixed. A large buffer would allow more temporary variation, which lets a properly designed codec pair maintain a better picture, but a larger buffer adds more delay, which users do not like.[9] A coder can vary several parameters to control the bit rate. If the buffer is filling too fast, then the coder can choose to code fewer blocks, or quantize them more coarsely, or retain fewer coefficients per block. The coder can even choose to skip an entire frame, though this usually makes the next one more difficult to code. H.261 does not specify how these choices are to be made. It is up to the designers to decide the trade-offs.

Once the transformed values are quantized, they are statistically coded (see Section 9.1.1.4), and then multiplexed together with all of the side information, such as motion vector values and the various flags and indicators shown in Figure 9.13. That is, all data streams indicated by the arrows on the right-hand side of Figure 9.13 are multiplexed according to the specifications of H.261.

9.2.4.2 Motion Search Techniques

Some expensive codecs do full search. That is, all possible motion vectors are tried, and the one producing the best match is picked. Most codecs use techniques to reduce the search effort. The goal is to reduce the number of com-

---

[9] Old ITU (then CCITT) audio testing indicated that a 400-msec delay is approaching the tolerance limit for telephone calls. Many videoconferencing users seem willing to accept a bit more, if necessary.

putations without reducing the picture quality. One may attempt this by reducing the number of error evaluations (i.e., reduce the number of candidate
macroblocks looked at) or by reducing the number of operations required for
each error computation. RM8 used what was called a "three-step algorithm."
The evaluation function used to determine the error between the new macroblock and the candidate motion-compensated old macroblock is the sum of
the absolute difference between each old and new pixel. (This is equivalent
to using MAD, the mean absolute difference.) RM8 also limited its search to
the ±7 range.

Step 1: Compute the error between the new macroblock and the candidate
blocks at the following relative positions in reference memory, where (0,0) is
the center of the nonshifted macroblock; that is, the one whose position in
reference memory corresponds exactly to the position of the new macroblock
being processed for coding.

$$(-4,4) \qquad (0,4) \qquad (4,4)$$

$$(-4,0) \qquad (0,0) \qquad (4,0)$$

$$(-4,-4) \qquad (0,-4) \qquad (4,-4)$$

Pick the candidate with the lowest error. If no other position has a lower error than (0,0), keep (0,0).

Step 2: Use the best match from Step 1 as the center of the new search pattern shown here:

$$(-2,2) \qquad (0,2) \qquad (2,2)$$
$$(-2,0) \qquad (0,0) \qquad (2,0)$$
$$(-2,-2) \qquad (0,-2) \qquad (2,-2)$$

Step 3: Use the best match in Step 2 as the center of the new search pattern
shown here:

$$(-1,1) \quad (0,1) \quad (1,1)$$
$$(-1,0) \quad (0,0) \quad (1,0)$$
$$(-1,-1) \quad (0,-1) \quad (1,-1)$$

The best match here is selected as the matching, motion-compensated old
macroblock.

For RM8, the sum of absolute pixel differences was used because it was
considered "cheaper" than using MSE. In some DSP-based systems [see
DUR89, for example] computing MSE may actually cost less, while giving a
slightly better result.

The three-step approach of RM8 is a particular example of what are sometimes called "coarse/fine" search strategies. The idea is to calculate the error at each of a set of sample locations within the allowed 31×31 pixel region, then search more carefully around the location of the best match from the coarse search. Such techniques may or may not be combined with schemes that reduce the number of pixels used in calculating the error. For instance, one may compute the MAD or MSE using every other pixel, thereby operating on only 128 pixels per macroblock. Another interesting scheme for a lower cost solution [see KUM88] uses a fixed but random-looking pattern of 31 pixels scattered throughout the macroblock. The experimental results looked promising, but the authors are not aware of any current commercial product that uses this method.[10]

9.2.4.3 Loop Filter

A low-pass filter is employed in the coding loop to reduce quantization noise and to reduce high-frequency artifacts introduced by motion compensation. As shown in Figure 9.11, the filter, F, is applied to blocks from the reference memory RM before they are subtracted from the corresponding blocks in the new frame being coded, and before they are added to the reconstructed block differences at point "A" in Figure 9.11. In RM8, the filter is controlled by the motion vector, in that it is always applied when a nonzero motion vector is used and transmitted. In H.261, the coder can choose to do motion compensation with or without employing the loop filter. Side information, as indicated by the loop filter switch in Figure 9.11, tells the decoder when to apply the filter.

The filter operates on pixels within blocks (not macroblocks) from the reference memory RM. When it is time to subtract a particular pixel from the corresponding new pixel in the input frame, a filtered pixel value is constructed from a weighted sum of its value and those of four neighboring pixels. The values used here are the motion-compensated values. That is, they are retrieved from locations displaced according to the motion vectors. The filter pattern and weights are as follows:

$$\begin{array}{ccc} 1/16 & 1/8 & 1/16 \\ 1/8 & 1/4 & 1/8 \; . \\ 1/16 & 1/8 & 1/16 \end{array}$$

Filtering does not cross block boundaries. For a pixel at a block top or edge, the pattern used will be:

---

[10] The reader will appreciate that such details may be closely guarded trade secrets, since motion search techniques are not specified in H.261.

$$
\begin{array}{ccccc}
 & & & & 1/4 \\
1/4 & 1/2 & 1/4 & \text{or} & 1/2 \\
 & & & & 1/4.
\end{array}
$$

9.2.4.4 DCT Computation

Once the block differences are calculated, the DCT is applied, using some suitable fast technique. There is no specification on the accuracy of the forward transform, but H.261 does specify the accuracy of the inverse DCT (IDCT). Annex A of H.261 describes a procedure for testing IDCT accuracy with 10,000 blocks of random pixel data. The maximum allowed error in any pixel value is 1 (out of 256), except that zeros in must always produce zeros out. Other limits are given for error patterns at any pixel position within a block. Over time, the error differences between coder IDCT and decoder IDCT will cause the reference memory values to drift apart. At least once every 132 times that a macroblock is coded and transmitted, it must be forcibly updated in INTRA mode. That is, each block's pixel values will be transformed directly, rather than pixel difference values.

9.2.4.5 Quantization

In INTRA mode, the DCT is applied to the 64-pixel values of a block. In INTER mode, the DCT is applied to the 64-pixel difference values. In either case, the resulting 8×8 array of coefficients is "zigzag scanned," as shown in Figure 9.14, in order to form a linear set of coefficients. The coefficients are calculated as 12-bit values and, until quantization, are treated as signed integers ranging from -2048 to $+2047$.

Recall that $C_{0,0}$ is proportional to the average pixel value of the block. It thus carries no information about how the pixel values vary. Since it contains no spatial frequency information, it is often referred to as the "DC term." $C_{0,0}$ is linearly quantized, with a single, fixed stepsize. All of the other $C_{i,j}$ are quantized with 1 of 31 different stepsizes (also called levels), depending on buffer fullness. The quantizing is linear, except around zero, where there is a "dead zone." The quantizer form is shown in Figure 9.15. In Figure 9.15(a), the quantizer stepsize is 2. A coefficient value between -2 and 2 will be quantized to "level 0." A value between 2 and 4 is quantized to "level 1", and so on. Of course, "level 0" or "level 3" are not directly transmitted values. The quantized values are statistically coded, and the decoder has tables for decoding to the correct value. The decoder is sent a new stepsize value whenever the encoder wants to change it. For example, with a quantizer stepsize of 4, as shown in Figure 9.15(b), a coefficient value of 4 would quantize to

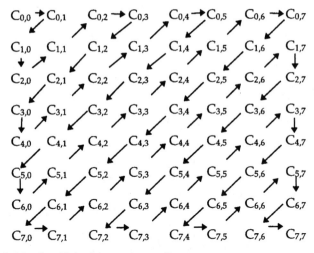

Figure 9.14   Coefficient scanning pattern

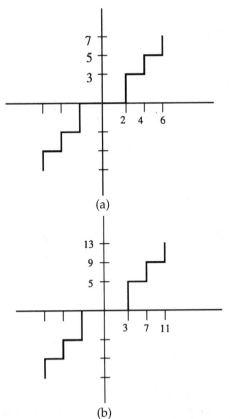

Figure 9.15   (a) Quantization stepsize = 2 and (b) quantization stepsize = 4

"level 1", which in this case would be reconstructed as a "5." Such quantizer stepsize changes are usually based on buffer fullness feedback.

Only the decoding method is defined in H.261. The encoder is not constrained to make the decisions indicated in Figure 9.15. For instance, with a quantizer stepsize of 4, the encoder could choose to code a coefficient value of 3 (or even 4) as "level 0", causing it to be reconstructed as a "0". This can actually be desirable at times. The statistical coder codes more than just individual values. Certain of the more common patterns of runs of zeros followed by small level values are represented by a single VLC symbol. Therefore it can be costly to break a run. For instance, a run of five "level 0" values followed by a "level 1" is coded as the VLC symbol "0001110". Suppose this were followed by a sequence of two "level 0" values followed by a "level –1". This would be coded as "01011". Concatenating these two strings gives the 12-bit string "000111001011". However, if the "level 1" value at the end of the first sequence were set to "level 0", the sequence would become that of eight "level 0" values followed by a "level –1". The VLC symbol representing this case is "00001111". Thus four bits are saved. If the coefficient that was originally quantized to "level 1" was only just over the threshold, it might be better to call it "level 0" and spend the four bits elsewhere. The encoder is free to make such choices.

9.2.4.6 Video Multiplexer

As we have seen, blocks are grouped together as macroblocks, which themselves are grouped together as groups of blocks (GOBs). In H.261, a CIF frame is referred to as a "picture," with each GOB covering one-twelfth of the picture area. Each picture (or frame) begins with a picture start code of 20 bits. Picture header information also includes the frame number, CIF/QCIF indicator, and various other flags. Each GOB begins with a 16-bit start code, followed by its group number and by quantizer level information. Each macroblock then has its own header and identifier information, which can contain a quantizer level value that overrides that of the GOB header. The encoder need not transmit macroblocks that do not contain picture update information. However, each GOB must be transmitted, even if none of its macroblocks is chosen for transmission. The details are specified in Section 4 of H.261.

9.2.4.7 Forward Error Correction

In an uncompressed video bit stream, an error disappears by the next field, as long as synchronization is not affected. Similarly, in a compressed bit stream with intraframe coding, an error disappears within a single frame period. With interframe coding, the effects of an error can last much longer. The sender's copy of reference memory may disagree with that of the receiver. The periodic forced update of macroblocks described in Section 9.2.4.1 would eventually correct this, but the error would linger far too long. Errors affecting synchronization can have much more serious effects. A single bit error can cause a VLC decoder not only to decode to the wrong symbol, but to use too few or too many bits while doing so, totally confusing the decoder. The resynchronization mechanisms specified in H.261 correct such difficulties, but the effects are likely to be too visible for too long. Therefore H.261 includes a BCH[11] (511,493) forward error correction (FEC) mechanism. [See RHE89 for a presentation of the theory and algorithms.] An error correction frame consists of 492 bits of coded data, 18 parity bits, 1 fill indicator bit, and 1 framing bit. Errors in 1 or 2 bits of the sequence can be corrected. The framing bit holds a frame alignment pattern that repeats every eight frames. That is, there is an 8-bit pattern (00011011), the bits of which are distributed over eight frames.

The use of FEC is optional in the decoder but required for the encoder. There are differences of opinion about the value of being able to correct two random bit errors, and some decoders do not do it. There is anecdotal evidence, at least in U.S. long-distance networks, that random bit errors are less common than burst errors of more than two bits.

9.2.4.8 Block Picking (What to Work On)

Near the end of the coding process for a frame, the codec will discard the less important blocks, the ones with the least change from the previous frame, and send no update information. Typically this is done by raising the quantizer levels, based on output buffer fullness, so that the coefficient values quantize to zero. The encoder is also free to decide not to send any macroblock that it determines contains too little information to be worth the overhead. If it can be determined in advance which ones will be discarded, much unnecessary computation can be saved. This is usually done by checking block differences at the start, and then ignoring those that have changes below a certain threshold. The encoder can adjust the threshold at the start of each frame.

9.2.5. Multiplex According to H.221

ITU Recommendation H.221 is entitled "Frame Structure for a 64 to 1920 Kbit/s Channel in Audiovisual Teleservices." (A 56-Kbps channel, and multiples thereof, is also allowed, being treated as a restricted 64-Kbps channel,

---

[11] This stands for Bose, Chaudhuri, and Hocquengham, developers of the technique.

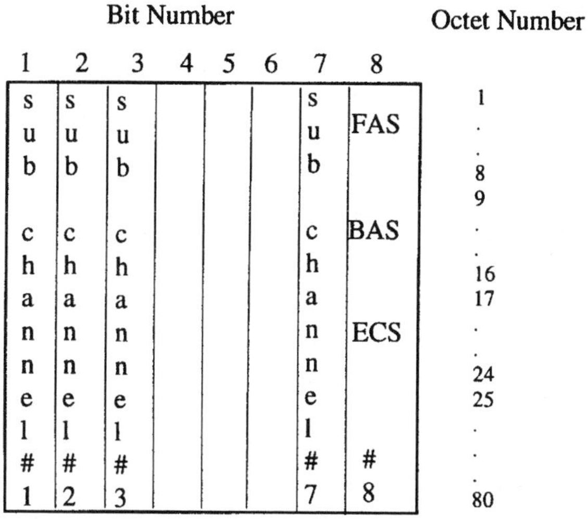

Figure 9.16 Frame structure of a single B-channel
(Reprinted with permission of ITU, from Recommendation H.221 (3/93) figure 1.)

as discussed in Chapter 8.) H.221 defines how the H.261 bit stream, the audio bit stream, the data streams, control signals, and synchronization codes are all multiplexed together. It also defines how the resulting multiplexed stream is transmitted using multiple B channels or multiple H0 channels, or on single B, H0, H11, or H12 channels.

As mentioned in Chapter 8, the bit stream in a channel is broken into octets.[12] Each bit in the octet is thought of as being in one of eight subchannels within a 64-Kbps channel. Figure 9.16 illustrates how the subchannels are organized when a single B-channel is used, and shows where certain control signals are placed. Eighty octets form a frame, hence each subchannel carries 80 bits per frame. A synchronization signal called the frame alignment signal (FAS) is used by the receiver to determine frame alignment, as the name implies. The FAS allows the receiver to determine the transmitter's octet alignment (i.e., which is the most significant bit) without reference to a network clock signal, which is not always available. (For instance, the terminal adapter might not pass the information through to a codec.) H.221 specifies where FAS should be put with respect to the network clock signal, if it is available to the transmitter. The receiver should search for FAS in all bit positions, since the transmitter may not have used network timing. This means that the received FAS position may be "in the wrong place," but, if so, the actual FAS position takes precedence. (If one wants the videoconferencing

---

[12] In telephony, the term "octet" is used instead of "byte."

system to be able to make ISDN calls to regular telephones, the system must use network timing.) In the case of multiple B or H0 channels, FAS helps the receiver to synchronize the multiple channels and allows it to detect any slips in synchronization that might occur after the video call is set up.[13]

The FAS code resides in what can be thought of as an 8-Kbps service subchannel of whatever communication channel is present. The other two signals carried in this channel are the bit rate allocation signal (BAS) and the encryption control signal (ECS). An eight-bit BAS code is sent in an even-numbered frame, followed by eight error correction bits in the corresponding bit positions in the following odd-numbered frame, allowing double error correction. During the development and subsequent revisions of H.221 and related recommendations, the set of BAS codes has grown beyond the original concept of just being used to indicate bit allocations in the multiplexed bit stream. BAS codes are used to indicate what audio compression is desired,[14] to indicate the desired transfer rates and number of channels to be used, to request various maintenance modes, and to carry other signals and requests. Recommendation H.230, entitled "Frame Synchronous Control and Indication Signals for Audiovisual Signals," has additional definitions of control and indication BAS codes, some of which require more than eight bits. This is handled by procedures for using single and multibyte extensions. Some of the control and indication signals used for multiparty conferences are specified in H.230.

9.2.6 Decoding the Received Bit Stream

Most of the decoding process has already been described in earlier sections on encoding. The reader will recall that the encoder must keep a copy in reference memory of the frame that the receiver will decode from the bit stream it receives. The decoding is essentially the inverse of the encoding process. The receiver must demultiplex the bit stream into its audio, video, control, and data components. The video bit stream component is directed to a video decoder, which must reconstruct the quantized values from the Huffman coded symbols. For each block whose differences are received, the reconstructed coefficients are transformed, using the inverse DCT, into pixel differences, which are then added to the corresponding motion-compensated block to form an updated block of the new frame. The inverse transform calculations are carried out via a butterfly algorithm similar to that shown in Figure 9.1.

---

[13] The authors have not found any reliable statistics, but folklore has it that such a slip might occur as often as once per hour.

[14] All calls start with G.711 audio, and then changes are negotiated according to the capabilities of the video terminals being connected.

9.2.7 Postprocessing

Various kinds of filtering have been experimented with to enhance the appearance of the decoded video [see LIM90]. Two well-known facets of the H.261 coding/decoding process are "blocking artifacts" and the "mosquito effect." The motion compensation on 16×16 pixel macroblocks and the DCT on 8×8 pixel blocks can both produce visible blocks in the picture. Block edge filtering can reduce the effect, at the expense of producing a slightly fuzzier picture under many conditions. The concept is to blend the block edges together, so naturally some sharpness is lost. For example, one might replace each pixel that lies on an edge by a weighted sum of half its own value and a quarter of the value of the pixel on either side along the perpendicular to the block edge. That is, a pixel $p_{i,j}$ on a vertical boundary would be replaced by the sum

$$0.25p_{i,j-1} + 0.5p_{i,j} + 0.25p_{i,j+1}.$$

Graininess and mosquito noise are introduced by quantizing the DCT coefficients. Mosquito noise is so called because it tends to be noticeable around the shoulders of persons in videoconferencing test scenes with sharp changes between a person's shoulders and the background. Median filters are useful in reducing random noise while preserving edges, and so can be useful with graininess. In median filters, each pixel value is replaced by the median value of the pixels surrounding it. Adaptive variations may be applied.

Once the postprocessing is completed, various conversions are usually needed to fit the display circumstances. On the output side, there is usually a need to convert from CIF frames back to NTSC fields for interlaced display. Figure 9.17 illustrates a two-tap scheme for doing so.

Alternatively, one may want to view the output on a noninterlaced computer monitor. If it is to be windowed, one could put the 288 lines directly into the output frame buffer. However, the 352 pixels for each line are too few to give the correct aspect ratio on most computer monitors, which have "square pixels." To get square pixels on a 4:3 aspect ratio screen, the ratio of pixels to number of lines must be 4/3. CIF gives only $352/288 = 11/9$, so the number of pixels per line must be slightly increased through interpolation. Further, one may want to provide the user the ability to select arbitrary video window sizing on the computer monitor. The number of lines, and of pixels per lines, will have to be changed as required. Any such implementation should use at least a two-tap filter (simple interpolation).

Another type of "conversion" is also frequently necessary, that of frame rate. It is typical to receive CIF frames at the rate of 15 per second, or even 10 for basic rate ISDN connections. Frame repeat is the best technique.

CIF frame	odd field	even field	line #
line 1 x x x x x … x	<line 1>		1
		<0.4 line 1 + 0.6 line 2>	2
line 2 x x x x x … x			
	<0.8 line 2 + 0.2 line 3>		3
		<0.2 line 2 + 0.8 line 3>	4
line 3 x x x x x … x			
	<0.6 line 3 + 0.4 line 4>		5
line 4 x x x x x … x		<line 4>	6
	<0.4 line 4 + 0.6 line 5>		7
line 5 x x x x x … x			
		<0.8 line 5 + 0.2 line 6>	8
	<0.2 line 5 + 0.8 line 6>		9
line 6 x x x x x … x			
		<0.6 line 6 + 0.4 line 7>	10
line 7 x x x x x … x	<line 7>		11

.
.
.

Figure 9.17   Conversion from 288-line CIF to 480-line interlaced frame

Temporal interpolation is not cost effective, especially since little or no temporal anti-aliasing may have been done at the transmit side.

9.2.8 H.263, Video Coding for Low-Bit-Rate Communication

The ITU has developed a new video coding standard aimed at very low bit rate communication. In particular, the main target was for a video bit rate of approximately 15 to 20 Kbps, so that it could be used with high-speed modems on traditional, analog phone lines. High-speed modems, adhering to the ITU V.34 standard, can connect, full duplex, at up to 28.8 Kbps, though 19.2 to 24 Kbps is more commonly achieved in practice. Approved in the spring of 1996, H.263 is beginning to appear in products as of this writing.

H.263 has been shown in simulations to be superior to H.261 at low bit rates. In May 1996, Recommendation H.320 was modified to allow H.263 use to be negotiated at call setup. We expect that H.263 will eventually be commonly employed in H.320 conferencing systems that use ISDN BRI connections.

Essentially, H.263 results from further development and refinement of H.261. Arithmetic coding is used for the VLC, which gives a gain of perhaps 3% to 5% in statistical coding efficiency. Most of the improvement may come from the use of subpixel motion compensation, where motion search and compensation is done more finely, being carried out at half-pixel intervals. Since this reduces the introduction of high-frequency artifacts, the loop filter of H.261 is not used. To reduce blocking artifacts, H.263 offers the option of using overlapped motion compensation. Each block uses its own motion vector, plus vectors from the blocks above, below, to the left, and to the right. The final displayed block has pixels that are weighted averages of the pixels created from three motion vector applications. Each pixel is created using the vector from its own block, plus the motion vectors of the blocks at the two nearest block borders. Another option is the use of bidirectionally predicted frames, called B-frames. A frame predicted from the previous frame in the manner described for H.261 is called a P-frame. A B-frame is computed by motion-compensated interpolation from both the P-frame preceding it in time and the P-frame following it. This introduces additional coding latency.

9.2.9 Still Frame Processing

Annex D.   Annex D of H.261 specifies a still image transmission protocol for transmitting images at four times the moving video rate. That is, if CIF is being used, the still frame resolution will be 576 lines of 704 pixels. If the call is set up for QCIF, the still frame is specified to be CIF resolution, since it is four times QCIF. Annex D also states that Recommendation T.81, which is equivalent to ISO JPEG, is preferred "when the procedures for using T.81 within audiovisual systems are standardized." The ITU T.126 series standard subsequently added the necessary procedures (see Chapter 12). The Annex D technique consists of dividing the still frame into four, interleaved, quarter-resolution subpictures, then using the normal H.261 motion coding scheme to transmit each subpicture in turn. The subpictures are formed by subsampling 2:1 horizontally and 2:1 vertically, with the first subpicture beginning with $p_{0,0}$, the second with $p_{0,1}$, the third with $p_{1,0}$, and the fourth with $p_{1,1}$. (Notice that this technique means that a codec that does not provide Annex D still frame decoding will display a quarter-resolution version during the time of still image transmission.) Once the image is received, it is held uncompressed in a display buffer, and is not available in a good form for storage. JPEG compression (in its baseline mode of operation) is similar to H.261 INTRA coding, and is useful for both storage and transmission.

JPEG.   JPEG's baseline coding method is to apply the DCT to 8×8 blocks, quantize the coefficients, and then apply statistical coding. As in H.261, $C_{0,0}$ is treated differently from the other 63 coefficients in the block, in that it is encoded as the difference between its value and that of the $C_{0,0}$ term in the previous block. The baseline VLC method is Huffman coding, but arithmetic coding is an option. [See WAL91 for a tutorial on JPEG. See also PENN93.] However, the JPEG (Joint Photographic Experts Group) committee didn't specify such details as the actual Huffman code tables to be used,[15] or how to transmit side information about the actual resolution of the picture being sent, or what color space is being used.[16] These details, among others, are provided in the T.126 recommendation.

9.3   VIDEO QUALITY METRICS

Codec performance is judged by the relation between bit rate and distortion (that is, how much the decoded picture is changed from the original). Signal-to-noise ratio (SNR) or mean square error (MSE) are common measures of distortion. However, it is well known that some codec techniques can produce a better looking picture while causing a higher SNR and MSE. To think about how this could be true, consider a "head and shoulders" picture that is a faithful reproduction of the original, except for badly miscoding the eyes. This will be perceived as a worse picture than one that does a good job on the eyes (and other features), but has a little overall grain or snow, causing a worse overall SNR and MSE. For this reason, video quality metrics that include factors such as peak local SNR and retention of edge sharpness are being studied. However, to date, the authors are aware of no generally accepted quality metrics proven to be superior to SNR/MSE in how they correlate with measured mean opinion scores.

REFERENCES

BAD90   Badiqué, Eric, "Knowledge-Based Facial Area Recognition and Improved Coding in a CCITT-Compatible Low-Bitrate Video-Codec," Picture Coding Symposium, Cambridge, MA, March 1990.

CHE87   Chen, W.-H., and D. Hein, "Recursive Temporal Filtering and Frame Rate

---

[15] The protocol with which the encoder transmits the table to the decoder is specified, and an example set of tables is given.

[16] The coding could be Y only, *RGB*, *YUV*, or *YIQ*.

Reduction for Image Coding," *IEEE Journal on Selected Areas in Communications SAC-5*, 7, pp. 1155–1165 (August 1987).

DUR89   Duran, Joe W., and Kenoyer, Michael L., "A PC-Compatible, Multiprocessor Workstation for Video, Data, and Voice Communication," in *Visual Communication and Image Processing IV*, SPIE Proc. 1199, pp. 232–236 (1989).

HEL91   Held, Gilbert, *Data Compression*, John Wiley & Sons, Chichester, UK, 1991.

KAM82   Kamangar, F. A., and Rao, K. R., "Fast Algorithms for the 2-D Discrete Cosine Transform," *IEEE Transactions on Computers C-31*, 9, pp. 899–906 (1982).

KUM88   Kummerfeldt, Georg, May, Franz, and Wolf, Winfrid, "Fast Algorithms of a Full Motion 64 kbit/s Video Codec," Picture Coding Symposium, Torino, Italy, September 1988.

LI93   Li, Haibo, Roivainen, Pertti, and Forcheimer, Robert, "3-D Motion Estimation in Model-Based Facial Image Coding," *IEEE Transactions on Pattern Analysis and Machine Intelligence 15*, 6, pp. 545–555 (June 1993).

LIM90   Lim, Jae S., *Two-Dimensional Signal and Image Processing*, Prentice Hall, Englewood Cliffs, NJ, 1990.

MUK85   Mukawa, Naoka, and Kuroda, Hideo, "Uncovered Background Prediction in Interframe Coding," *IEEE Transactions on Communications COM-33*, 11, pp. 1227–1231 (November 1985).

NET95   Netravali, Arun H., and Haskell, Barry G., *Digital Pictures*, 2nd ed., Plenum Press, NY, 1995.

OHT94   Ohta, Naohisa, *Packet Video: Modeling and Signal Processing*, Artech House, Norwood, MA, 1994.

PENN93 Pennebaker, William B., and Mitchell, Joan L., *JPEG Still Image Data Compression Standard*, Van Nostrand Reinhold, NY, 1993.

RHE89   Rhee, M. Y., *Error-Correcting Coding Theory*, McGraw-Hill, NY, 1989.

RIO91   Rioul, Olivier, and Vetterli, Martin, "Wavelets and Signal Processing," *IEEE Signal Processing Magazine*, pp. 14–38 (October 1991).

WAL91   Wallace, Gregory K., "The JPEG Still Picture Compression Standard," *Communications of the ACM 34*, 4, pp. 30–58 (April 1991).

WIT87   Witten, Ian H., Neal, Radford M., and Cleary, John G., "Arithmetic Coding for Data Compression," *Communications of the ACM 30*, 6, pp. 520–540 (June 1987).

Chapter 10

Audio

It may be called "videoconferencing," but audio is the most important ingredient. "If the video fails you talk, if the audio fails you walk." In general, one wants the audio quality to be at least equal to "toll quality" telephone audio and to have it delivered in a full duplex, "hands free" mode. Of the established, standard compression methods, the most useful in videoconferencing are G.728, for compressing 3.3-KHz audio to 16 Kbps, and G.722, for compressing 7-KHz audio to 64 Kbps. In time, there will be standards for compressing 7-KHz audio to 16 Kbps, and for improving the frequency response of audio compressed to 64 Kbps.

Good echo canceling is just as critical as good compression. To have natural conferencing, the microphones and speakers must be "open" at all times, unless deliberately muted, so that each participant can continuously hear the sounds from the other locations, even when speaking. This requires acoustic processing to eliminate feedback and echoes.

Although the basic needs are the same, the conference room and the desktop present somewhat different challenges. Microphones strewn along the table in a conference room can present both aesthetic and practical clutter. Users may block them with papers, coffee cups, and briefcases. At the desk, a microphone in the monitor can be close without clutter, but open microphones and speakers at a desktop in an open office area may not be desirable.

Additional acoustic processing can aid some situations. For instance, phased microphone arrays in a conference room can be electronically steered to take the place of table microphones (see SIL92). De-reverberation processing and noise canceling can also be useful.

10.1 COMPRESSION

10.1.1 PCM coding (G.711)

The three audio algorithms most used in videoconferencing, based on the ITU H.320 suite of standards, are shown in Table 10.1. G.711 is the basic, default audio coding method for video telephony and for regular telephone

169

Table 10.1 Common Videoconferencing
Audio Algorithm

Standard	Audio Bandwidth (KHz)	Bit Rate (Kbps)
G.711	3.3	48–64
G.722	7	48–64
G.728	3.3	16

calls. Even though it requires from 48 to 64 Kbps in digital bandwidth, it will remain important for a time for two reasons. Sometimes called pulse code modulation (PCM), it is the basic, fall-back, default standard used when two videoconferencing systems have no other common audio standard between them. It also requires the least computation to implement, and therefore is particularly interesting when processor power is scarce or prioritized for other purposes, such as video coding. As mentioned in Chapter 7, the sampling rate for telephone bandwidth audio (with a maximum frequency of approximately 3.3 to 3.5 KHz) is 8,000 samples per second. Eight bits per sample (or seven, in the case of restricted networks) are transmitted.[1] However, uniform quantization using eight bits leaves the lower amplitude signals too coarsely quantized for the best perceived audio quality. Nonuniform quantization methods that have a stepsize that increases with amplitude sound better to the ear. The A-law and μ-law schemes specified in G.711 give almost the same performance to the ear as a 12-bit uniform quantizer. These methods operate by uniformly quantizing the logarithm of the input signal [see PAP87 and DUN94]. This is sometimes called COMPANDING (for COMPressing and EXPANDing).

A-law compression actually has a linear region for small amplitudes, and then a region where the uniform quantization is carried out on the logarithm of the signal. For an input signal level normalized so that its amplitude ranges from 0 to 1, the equations for the two regions can be expressed as

$$\text{level} = \frac{A \cdot \text{input}}{1 + \ln A} \qquad \text{for } 0 \leq |\text{input}| \leq \frac{1}{A} \qquad \text{and}$$

$$\text{level} = \frac{1 + \ln (A \cdot \text{input})}{1 + \ln A} \qquad \text{for } \frac{1}{A} \leq |\text{input}| \leq 1$$

---

[1] G.711 states that "eight binary bits per sample should be used for international circuits."

The ITU recommended value for *A* is 87.6.

Similarly, μ-law compression is carried out according to

$$\text{level} = \ln(1 + \mu \cdot \text{input}), \qquad \text{for } 0 < |\text{input}| < 1,$$

where μ is usually 255. In practice, the equations are not used during actual compression. Instead, the equations are used to compute quantization boundaries and levels to construct a nonuniform quantizer table.

10.1.2 ADPCM

Just as a pixel's value is likely to be close to that of its neighbors, so does an audio sample have considerable correlation with the one preceding it. One can take advantage of this by coding each sample in terms of its difference from the preceding sample. That is, the previous sample is subtracted from the current sample, with the difference being quantized and transmitted. One might call such techniques differential pulse code modulation (DPCM). There is even more coding efficiency to be gained if differential techniques are adapted according to behavior of the input audio signal, as in adaptive differential pulse code modulation (ADPCM). In telephony, ADPCM is used to convert a PCM eight-bit code word into a four-bit code, halving the data rate. The technique is outlined in Figure 10.1.

For PCM, a sample's predicted value is the value of the preceding sample, after reconstruction. For ADPCM, the predicted value can be different, depending on the recent history of the input. That is, the predicted value is "adaptive," as is the stepsize. The predicted value is subtracted from the input sample, and the difference is sent to the quantizer, which puts out a

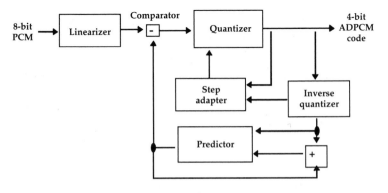

Figure 10.1 ADPCM block diagram

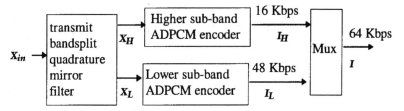

Figure 10.2 Sub-band ADPCM encoder
(Reprinted with permission of ITU, from Recommendation G.722 (3/87), figure 3.)

four-bit "sign-magnitude" code in which one bit is used for the sign and the other three designate one of seven quantizer levels.[2] Different ADPCM methods vary in terms of how the adaptation decisions are done. ITU G.721 is perhaps the best known example of an ADPCM audio coder. It compresses 3.3-KHz audio into 32 Kbps. However, G.721 is *not* one of the specified audio compression standards for H.320 videoconferencing systems. The general technique, modified for 7-KHz input, and specified in ITU Recommendation G.722, is used in H.320 systems.

10.1.3 G.722 Sub-band ADPCM

Basically, a G.722 coder splits the 7-KHz signal into two frequency bands and applies ADPCM to each band, with more bits allocated to the lower band, as shown in Figure 10.2. The input signal, x_{in}, is digitized from an input signal that should be prefiltered to 7 KHz. The sampling is at 16 KHz, with 14 bits per sample. The bands are split so that the lower band covers 0 to 4,000 Hz and the higher covers 4,000 to 8,000 Hz.[3] Because of the lower bandwidth, x_H and x_L have a "sample rate" of 8 KHz.

Sub-band coding requires sharp cutoff filters. Quadrature mirror filters work as high-pass/low-pass pairs and perform well enough for sub-band splitting. G.722 specifies a particular quadrature mirror filter. At sample time n, x_H and x_L are computed according to Eqs. (10.1) through (10.4). Here the index n represents a sample at 8-KHz intervals, and j represents samples from 16-KHz intervals. Thus j-1 indicates the 16-KHz sampling interval just previous to the sample at j.

---

[2] The four-bit string "0000" was not allowed, so that the ADPCM would never violate the "one's density" requirements of older network transmission equipment.

[3] This gives a little headroom above the nominal 7-KHz input, and reduces the need for rapid roll-off of the input filter to prevent aliasing.

$$x_L(n) = x_A + x_B, \tag{10.1}$$

$$x_H(n) = x_A - x_B, \tag{10.2}$$

$$x_A = \sum_{i=0}^{11} h_{2i} \cdot x_{in}(j - 2i), \tag{10.3}$$

$$x_B = \sum_{i=0}^{11} h_{2i+1} \cdot x_{in}(j - 2i - 1). \tag{10.4}$$

The values of the coefficients h_i are given in Table 4 of G.722.

The operation of the lower sub-band ADPCM encoder, which is the more complex, is outlined in the block diagram of Figure 10.3. G.722 also has modes for coding at 56 and 48 Kbps. This is to allow a "data insertion device" to open an 8- or 16-Kbps data channel, using the one or two least significant bits (LSBs) of the 60-level quantizer output. In the worst case, the effect is that of a 15-level quantizer, so that is what is used in the feedback loop of the encoder, since the encoder is not expected to "know" whether any LSBs are removed in the downstream path. A "data extraction device" at the receiver extracts the data stream and indicates to the audio decoder whether the LSBs have been used for data. Even if the decoder does not receive the correct mode indicator, the system will not fail, but degradation will occur.

As G.722 is used within the H.320 suite of recommendations, there is no "data insertion" into the G.722 bit stream, but any of the three coding modes may still occur. The multiplexing recommendation, H.221, specifies how a 48-, 56-, or 64-Kbps G.722 audio bit stream is multiplexed together with the video, control, and data streams. This means that when a videoconferencing system is demultiplexing the received bit stream, it "knows," from H.221 BAS codes, what mode of G.722 is being received.

As indicated in Figure 10.3, the quantizer adapts according to the size of the signal being transmitted. The prediction signal is a function of both the difference signal and the signal as reconstructed from the truncated code word. The coefficients of the predictor function are themselves functions of their past values and the new d_{LT} and r_{LT} values. That is, the prediction function is a linear combination of past samples, where the coefficients of the linear combination are also time dependent.

The lower sub-band decoder operation is outlined in Figure 10.4.

As outlined in Figure 10.5, after the lower and higher sub-bands have been decoded, the two resulting 8-KHz sample rate signals must be combined into

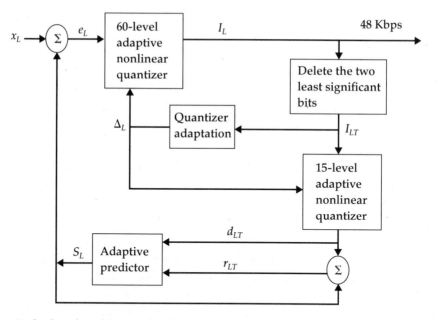

x_L is the low-band input signal
e_L is the low-band difference signal
Δ_L is the low-band quantizer scale factor
I_L is the low-band code word
I_{LT} is truncated code word
d_{LT} is the truncated, reconstructed difference signal
S_L is the low-band predictor output signal
r_{LT} is the truncated, reconstructed signal

Figure 10.3 Low-band encoder quantizer loop
(Reprinted with permission of ITU, from Recommendation G.722 (3/87) figure 4.)

one 16-KHz sample rate output signal. They are combined through filters similar to those used for splitting the original input signal.

Recall that the index n represents a sample at 8-KHz intervals, and j represents samples from 16-KHz intervals. The output signal x_{out} is computed using Eqs. (10.5) and (10.6), alternating between them at successive 16-KHz sample times. In other words, each of the following equations is used once for each value of n:

$$x_{\text{out}}(j) = 2\sum_{i=0}^{11} h_{2i} \cdot x_d(i), \qquad (10.5)$$

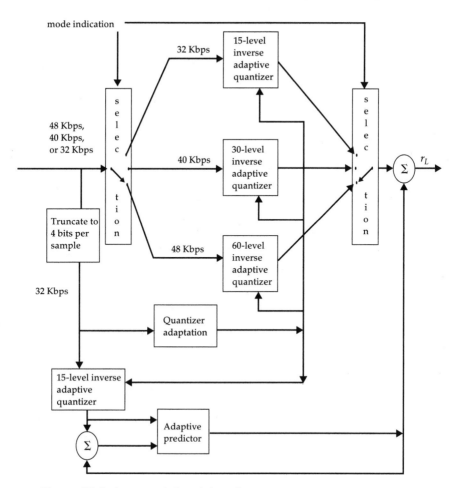

Figure 10.4 Lower sub-band decoder
(Reprinted with permission of ITU from Recommendation G.722 (3/87) figure 6.)

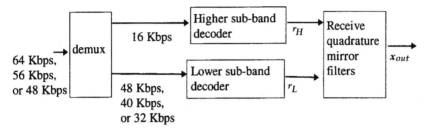

Figure 10.5 Sub-band ADPCM decoder
(Reprinted with permission of ITU from Recommendation G.722 (3/87) figure 7.)

$$x_{out}(j+1) = 2\sum_{i=0}^{11} h_{2i+1} \cdot x_s(i), \tag{10.6}$$

where

$$x_d(i) = r_L(n-i) - r_H(n-1)$$
$$x_s(i) = r_L(n-i) + r_H(n-1).$$

The values of the coefficients, h_i, are the same as those used in Eqs. (10.3) and (10.4), as given in Table 4 of G.722.

Although G.722 was primarily designed for speech, it performs reasonably well on music, and sounds somewhat comparable to basic AM radio. G.722 sounds noticeably better than G.711, and is certainly to be preferred when network connections of 384 Kbps or greater are available. Some users also prefer using 48-Kbps G.722 rather than 16-Kbps G.728 for 128-Kbps or even 112-Kbps connections, feeling that the greater audio bandwidth is worth the loss of 32 Kbps from the video bit stream. However, using G.722 requires a higher bandwidth echo canceler, requiring more computing power.

10.1.4 G.728 CELP (Codebook Excited Linear Prediction)

G.728 provides good quality speech coding at 16 Kbps. Among the ITU audio choices for H.320, it is the most practical audio compression method for use with network connection rates of 64 or 56 Kbps—anything else but G.723, just now beginning to appear in H.324 systems, would not leave enough bits for useful video. Whereas ADPCM is waveform coding, CELP methods are a move in the direction of model-based coding, in the sense of using properties of human speech and hearing mechanisms. It might be more accurate to say that CELP is a waveform coder, the design of which was strongly guided by considering speech and hearing properties.

G.728 uses vector quantization to code the waveform samples. The encoder block diagram is shown in Figure 10.6, and the decoder black diagram is shown in Figure 10.7. Five samples at a time are grouped as a vector, and the codebook index of the best match to the vector is transmitted. Since G.728 is a 3.3-KHz technique, it uses a sample rate of 8,000 Hz. If an A-law or μ-law PCM codec is used to capture the samples, the samples must be converted to uniform quantization.[4] The codebook has 1,024 entries, requiring a 10-bit

---

[4] ITU recommendations for 3.3 KHz audio compression standards typically assume that a G.711-style PCM codec chip is used for the input, since they are common and cheap. For ADPCM or G.728, the A-law or μ-law output must be converted to linear quantization before further processing.

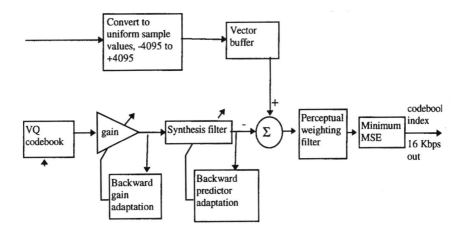

Figure 10.6 G.728 encoder
(Reprinted with permission of ITU, from Recommendation G.728 (9/92) figure 1A.)

index value to specify a selected vector.[5] Since the sample rate is 8,000 Hz, and five samples per vector are aggregated, 1,600 indices per second are generated. In basic VQ, the codebook entry would be the output of the decoder. Here, however, the entry is modified by an adaptive gain function and by adaptive filtering. In fact, the modifications are done as part of the codebook search. That is, each codebook entry goes through the gain and filtering blocks shown in Figure 10.6. As discussed in the vector quantization section of Chapter 9, the best match is determined by using MSE. Here, however, the MSE calculation is frequency weighted. Both the encoder and decoder base the adaptation only on the history of the transmitted codebook indices, hence only the indices are transmitted. At 1,600 indices per second and 10 bits per in-

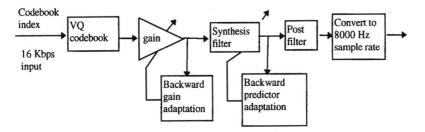

Figure 10.7 G.728 decoder
(Reprinted with permission of ITU, from Recommendation G.728 (9/92) figure 1B.)

---

[5] Actually, to reduce the complexity of searching the codebook, the codebook is split into two components; one, called the "shape codebook," with 128 entries, and another, called the "gain codebook," with 8 entries.

dex, a bit rate of 16 Kbps is generated. The adaptive synthesis filter is designed to improve the output signal by modifying the selected vector from the codebook to restore key spectral components normally present in speech [see WAD94]. The perceptual weighting filter is designed to minimize perceived distortion by allowing more quantization noise into the frequency regions of greater speech energy, and reducing it elsewhere. The coefficients for both filters are updated once every four vectors. The gain is updated once per vector.

The perceptual weighting filter is applied only in the encoder. Together with the frequency-weighted MSE calculation, it helps pick a codebook entry that, after synthesis, better "hides" the quantization noise in the frequency regions that hold more speech energy. For nonspeech audio coding, Recommendation G.728 hints that the perceptual weighting filter should be disabled. The decoder does have a postfilter that acts somewhat like the perceptual weighting filter. Recommendation G.728 states that ". . . for some nonspeech signals, the performance of the coder is improved when the adaptive postfilter is turned off." In the authors' listening experience, even speech often sounds better with the postfilter turned off.

G.728 was first developed in a floating-point arithmetic version. A new Annex G to Recommendation G.728 describes the fixed-point implementation.

10.1.5 Other Audio Coding

Attempts to find better audio coding methods continue as does development of tailoring the trade-offs better for specific situations. More efficient techniques are of particular importance to POTS videoconferencing and to digital cellular phone systems. H.263 video falls off rapidly in quality below 20 Kbps, so it is very important to use less than 6 Kbps or so for audio, if possible. For cell phone systems, service providers want to use 8 Kbps (and lower) algorithms to pack as many calls as possible into their licensed portions of the radio spectrum. G.723 goes even lower. It has been developed for H.324 POTS videophones, and can be less concerned with delay than if it were used for cell phones.

CELP codecs like G.728 are members of a class of techniques sometimes called analysis-by-synthesis LPC (linear predictive coding). G.728 is a CELP variant sometimes called low-delay CELP (LD-CELP). Its small, five sample per vector buffer size and other efficiencies allow a total one-way delay of less than 2 msec. Typical CELP codecs have been designed for bit rates lower than 16 Kbps and have more samples per vector, perhaps 40 or more. G.723 goes far beyond this, using a 30-millisecond sampling window, with 240 samples per block. The total algorithmic delay approaches 40 milliseconds, with actual implementations likely to add more, but this is no handicap in a point-to-point videophone application, being much lower than the video

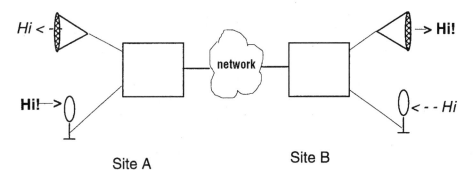

Figure 10.8 Simple audio conference connection

coding delay. As with G.728, G.723 is optimized for speech. It has two bit rates, 5.3 and 6.3 Kbps. It offers much greater compression than G.728, and at least for the 6.3-Kbps option, is said to be near G.728 in voice compression quality. See SCHA96 for further discussion of G.723.

10.2 ECHO CANCELING

10.2.1 The Mechanics of Echo Canceling

Consider a simple, two-room conference connection such as the one illustrated in Figure 10.8. Suppose someone at site A speaks while site B is silent. Sound input to the microphone at site A is digitized, compressed, and sent over the network to site B, where it is reconstructed, amplified, and output through the speaker at site B. At site B, if nothing is done to counteract it, this reconstructed sound is both transmitted directly and reflected from walls and other objects at site B so that it becomes input to the microphone at site B, where it is digitized, compressed, and sent back to site A. There, it is reconstructed and heard as echo. In videoconferencing, the audio signal is often delayed by its own processing, and then additionally delayed to match the usually greater delay of video processing. This makes the echo easier to perceive and more annoying.

Several things can be done to reduce or eliminate the echo. The acoustic path between speaker and microphone can be attenuated (or eliminated), and the echoes can be canceled to various degrees by digital signal processing. Replacing the microphone and speaker arrangement with a telephone handset or headset essentially eliminates the acoustic feedback paths. Acoustic tiles or other sound absorption treatment in a room will attenuate many of the paths. Positioning the microphone far from the speaker and/or using a directional microphone also helps. The paths may be eliminated by turning off the microphone whenever a signal above some threshold is received from site A and output through site B's speaker. This is sometimes called "echo suppression" and is the familiar "half duplex" speakerphone technique used (and disliked) in traditional and inexpensive speakerphones.

Echo canceling works by "remembering" at site B what signal has been put through its speaker, and then subtracting it, appropriately attenuated and delayed, from the signal entering site B's microphone. The difficulty is in attenuating and delaying the correct amount. This is further complicated by the need to vary the attenuation with frequency, since the echo paths are frequency dependent, and the need to allow for multiple echo paths. In some cases these multiple paths are strong enough in echo and delayed differently enough to be perceived separately by listeners. This means that the subtraction must be done more than once, and with different attenuation patterns. Fortunately, there are digital filtering techniques that yield very tractable solutions.

Properly done, echo canceling allows natural, full duplex communication. Participants will hear no echoes, and will still be able to hear voices from other sites even while they themselves are speaking. Echo canceling is made easier if the conference system and the room in which it is installed are designed to reduce echoes. However, this must often be balanced against users' desires to have simple, portable systems that can be used in a wide range of environments, and may even interfere with users' aesthetics. Anything that attenuates the "connection," often called the "return path," between speaker and microphone makes echo canceling easier (and potentially cheaper) to carry out. Techniques include keeping microphones far from speakers and close to persons speaking, keeping microphones away from ambient noise sources, and using directional microphones oriented away from speakers. Unfortunately for system designers, this puts more burden on users, requiring more complex installation and less flexibility in use. The ideal system would be self-contained, portable, and contain enough sophisticated, but inexpensive, signal processing to cancel echoes in all reasonable environments.

10.2.2 The Mathematics of Echo Canceling

In normal videoconferencing applications, the audio signals are digitized, and usually compressed, for transmission. Echo canceling is performed in the digital domain. The echo canceler attempts to remove echoes by subtracting a digital representation of the predicted echo from the digital representation of the actual signal. A model of the "echo response" of the room is needed. In

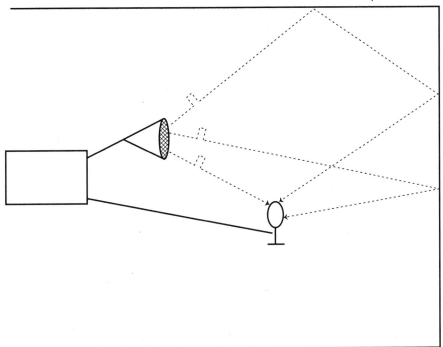

Figure 10.9 Multiple sound paths

concept, this can be determined by introducing a discrete noise pulse into the room from the speaker and measuring the response (the signals that travel from the speaker to the microphone, either indirectly or reflected).

Let us use Figure 10.9 to illustrate a thought experiment. The figure shows three of the many sound paths in the room between the microphone and speaker. Suppose a sound pulse is transmitted from the speaker to the air in the room and sampling is begun. The sound pressure level at the microphone is measured at every Δt until N samples are measured. A typical Δt might be about 62.5 microseconds for 7-KHz audio systems. If $N = 256$, then the measurement takes place over a 16-millisecond interval. This will measure echo paths up to about 18 feet long. More samples are needed for larger rooms. Let the set of samples be designated as $\{h_i\}$. Thus h_0 represents the sound pressure level at the microphone initially, h_1 is the level at Δt, h_2 the level at $2\Delta t$, and so on. This set of measured values would be an excellent characterization of the room response, because, properly scaled, each $\{h_i\}$ is in fact the set of coefficients that tells us what portions of sounds that passed through the speaker earlier are now contributing to echo at the microphone. Let $y(i)$ represent the signal transmitted to the speaker during a conference; h_1 tells us what portion of $y(i)$ will come back to the microphone after one time interval has elapsed; $y(i-1)$ is the amount of sound that was transmitted to the speaker one Δt interval into the past from time i; and $h_1{}^*y(i-1)$ is the amount of that sound now reaching the microphone. The total echo reaching the microphone includes contributions from $2\Delta t$ in the past, from $3\Delta t$, and so on. Thus the discrete reflected echo signal $r(i)$ can be represented by

$$r(i) = \sum_{k=0}^{N-1} h_k y(i-k)$$

over a period of N samples. Suppose now that someone is talking at site B while sound from site A is being put through site B's speaker and then reflected to site B's microphone. Let $p(i)$ represent the local signal at site B as picked up by the microphone at site B, where $p(i)$ is the sum of any speech generated at site B, the echo signals, $r(i)$, and any other noise generated at site B. At any discrete time point i, the actual transmitted signal, $u(i)$, desired to be transmitted back to site A, is $p(i) - r(i)$. Thus,

$$u(i) = p(i) - \sum_{k=0}^{N-1} h_k y(i-k).$$

The practical problems are in finding $\{h_i\}$ and making sure N is large enough to cover all of the important echoes in the room. (The larger the room, the longer it takes for an echo from the far wall to be reflected back to the microphone.) The value of N must be large enough so that $|h_i|$ is small for $i > N$. One might attempt to measure $\{h_i\}$ during a calibration phase. Actually transmitting a pulse as described above is not practical. The perfect pulse generation and ideal sampling described in the "thought experiment" above cannot actually be carried out. Even if it were possible, it would be undesirable to the user. Users don't want to hear calibration tones, noises, or pulses, and the acoustics change over time as people move about, bring in equipment, move furniture, etc. The solution is to guess at $\{h_i\}$ and improve the guess during operation. Let $\{a_i\}$ represent the "guessed at" impulse response set. The calculated room response is then

$$\hat{r}(i) = \sum_{k=0}^{N-1} a_k y(i-k),$$

and the transmitted signal is obtained from

$$u(i) = p(i) - \sum_{k=0}^{N-1} a_k y(i-k).$$

There is always error in calculating $u(i)$. The set of coefficients $\{a_i\}$ is not the correct one, and there is also residual echo due to echo signals that arrive at the microphone after the N'th sample time. There are efficient adaptation schemes to move the $\{a_i\}$ toward the correct set of values. If no sound is generated locally at site B, then all sound entering the site B microphone must be "echo," so $u(i)$ would be 0 if the echo were perfectly canceled. If $u(i)$ is not 0 when site B is quiet, we have information to help correct $\{a_i\}$, since we can adjust $\{a_i\}$ to move $u(i)$ closer to 0. Ignoring the effects of residual echo and noise, the error is

$$e(i) = \sum_{k=0}^{N-1} (h_k - a_k) \cdot y(i-k).$$

When there is no locally generated sound, $p(i)$ is just $r(i)$, so

$$u(i) = r(i) - \sum_{k=0}^{N-1} a_k \cdot y(i-k) = \sum_{k=0}^{N-1} (h_k - a_k) \cdot y(i-k).$$

Thus $e(i) = u(i)$ when there is no locally generated sound.

We would like to correct the entire set $\{a_i\}$ at each time point, before a new $u(i)$ is calculated and sent back to site A. The stochastic gradient algorithm, also called the LMS (least mean squares) algorithm, uses the following correction formula,

$$a_k(i+1) = a_k(i) + 2\beta \cdot e(i) \cdot y(i-k), \qquad k = 0, \dots, N-1.$$

It is called stochastic because we don't know the actual gradient along which to correct, so we use the best estimate we have. [See MES84 for further explanation.]

Recall that $e(i)$ is the actual, echo-canceled sound pressure level when there is no locally generated sound at site B. In practice, there will usually be locally generated sound. If such locally generated sound is not too loud and is uncorrelated with the sound from site A (which is normally true), and if β is small, the LMS technique will converge anyway. It goes faster if there is no local sound. A common technique is to use "near-end speech detection" to determine when to temporarily stop updating $\{a_i\}$. The desire is to correct only when there is far end sound, not locally generated sound. (Again, such detection does not have to be perfect to succeed.)

When sound is generated at both sides, this is sometimes called "double talk." (Although the terms "speech" and "talk" are historically used, it is the sound levels, not the kind of sound, that are important.) A common method is to compare the sound levels being received through the speaker and at the microphone to try to determine when this is happening. For example, one might stop updating whenever

$$|p(i)| \geq 1/2 \max\{|y(i)|, |y(i-1)|, \ldots, |y(i-N)|\}.$$

The comparison must look at $y(i)$ values from the recent past, because these are the signals that are being reflected into the microphone to become part of $p(i)$.

The usual starting guess for $\{a_i\}$ is to set them all to zero. The value of β should be set by experiment after system prototypes are constructed. There are too many variables in terms of speaker and microphone efficiencies, amplifier gains, A/D converter outputs, and scaling of values for a β value to be suggested here. In one example, in a system that uses 16-bit integers to represent the sound pressure levels, a β of 0.02 was picked. The factor of 1/2 in the "double talk" test actually comes from telephone line echo cancelers used to cancel echoes from telephone hybrids. It is not an unreasonable value to use in a room echo canceler, but the actual value should be picked after experimentation with the particular system being designed. Double talk detection can be confused by local conditions of microphone placement, soft spoken talkers, and ambient noise, but β and "double talk" detection factor values can usually be chosen so that echo canceling works quite well.

There is always some residual echo after echo cancellation is performed. Its sound is frequently masked by other talkers and noise sources. When it is not, it can be "suppressed," in the traditional sense, by not transmitting any of the microphone signal back to the other site. Users may then notice that minor background noises cut in and out as the microphone signal is turned on and off. This can be alleviated by transmitting a little white noise, or other approximation of the background noise, whenever the microphone signal is turned off.

Some improvements to the preceding technique are coming into use, such as bandsplitting. In bandsplitting, the audio signals are separated into a number of sub-bands (32 is typical) and the echo canceling is applied separately to each sub-band. Since high-frequency echoes die out faster, fewer filter coefficients are needed, and more computational effort is put into lower frequencies.

10.3 SOME PRACTICAL CONSIDERATIONS

Digital signal processing can eliminate most echoes and generally provide a satisfactory full duplex audio communication path, even for roll-about videoconferencing systems located in rooms with little or no regard for acoustics, though some attention may have to be applied to microphone placement. However, acoustic treatment of the room will almost always add some noticeable improvement. Whenever it is practical, it should be done. Echo canceling always has at least a trace of effect on the transmitted signal, whereas acoustic treatment has no such negative effect, and can have the further benefit of reducing reverberation and ambient noise. This will generally make the transmitted audio signal more pleasing.

Rules of thumb for microphone placement are to keep the microphone as far from the speaker as possible, as far from ambient noise sources as possible, and as close to the person(s) speaking as possible. This last rule sometimes requires multiple microphones. Acoustically, placing microphones on a table at which users are seated usually works fairly well, but users must be cautioned not to put briefcases in front of a microphone, not to shuffle papers on top of them, or to tap them with pencils. Some users also find table microphones aesthetically unpleasant, and may request ceiling microphones. These usually perform the worst. They frequently pick up unpleasant noise from the air conditioning system, and tend to be too far from persons talking. This lowers the ratio of primary sound pressure level to reverberation sound pressure level entering the microphones, and can give too much of the classic speakerphone "barrel effect." Techniques similar to echo canceling are being developed for de-reverberation, and should eventually be in common use.

Multiple microphones are often needed to keep microphones in proximity to persons speaking. If more than three or so microphones are used, simply mixing their signals may "raise the noise floor" too much. Each microphone is constantly transmitting ambient noise, whether or not it is near a person speaking. To get around this, gated mixers are sometimes used, which transmit sound from a microphone only if it is above a certain threshold. The idea is to gate it on only when someone is speaking into it. When one microphone switches on and another switches off, the echo response of the microphone/room system changes. New filter coefficient values are needed to subtract away the echo properly. If the effect is too pronounced, the echo canceler will not adapt fast enough to prevent audible echoes. The worst case is probably when sound received through the speaker suddenly gates a microphone on. Gated mixers are more likely to be used in permanent videoconferencing installations, where some care can be taken with speaker placement and acoustic treatment to make this worst case unlikely. Some gated mixers can be adjusted so the microphone is attenuated rather than gated completely off. This reduces its contribution to ambient noise without changing echo characteristics so abruptly as it gates in and out.

Sophisticated auditorium sound systems that dynamically change the echo characteristics of the total room/electronics system can cause problems. Dynamic equalizers and AGC (automatic gain control) microphones fall in this category. AGC is best applied after the echo signal is subtracted.

For the desktop, a camera/microphone housing is often placed on the computer monitor. A speaker may also be in the housing, but a separate speaker is preferred. If the microphone and speaker are in the same housing, the designer must keep them as isolated (acoustically) as possible. Although desktop designs usually have the speaker and microphone closer together than is acoustically desirable, echo canceling remains feasible.

REFERENCES

DUN94   Dunlop J., and Smith, D. G., *Telecommunications Engineering*, 3rd ed., Chapman and Hall, London, UK, 1994.

MES84   Messerschmitt, David G., "Echo Cancellation in Speech and Data Transmission," *IEEE Journal on Selected Areas in Communications SAC-2*, 2, pp. 283–297 (March 1984).

PAP87   Papamichalis, Panos E., *Practical Approaches to Speech Coding*, Prentice Hall, Englewood Cliffs, NJ, 1987.

SCHA96   Schaphorst, Richard, *Videoconferencing and Videotelephony: Technology and Standards*, Artech House, Norwood, MA, 1996.

SIL92   Silverman, Harvey F., and Kirtman, Stuart E., "A Two-Stage Algorithm for Determining Talker Location from Linear Microphone Array Data," *Computer Speech and Language 6*, pp. 129–152 (1992).

WAD94   Wade, Graham, *Signal Coding and Processing*, 2nd ed., Cambridge University Press, Cambridge, 1994.

Chapter 11

Putting It Together with Multipoint

In the early days of videoconferencing, point-to-point calls were often achievement enough, but interest in multipoint connections grew quickly. AT&T was working on multipoint techniques as it experimented with the PicturePhone service in the 1960s. Nearly all serious users of videoconferencing have realized the necessity of multiple-site videoconferencing. VTEL introduced a LAN-based desktop videoconferencing system in 1986 that had multiway capability. Some early installations of videoconferencing used fully connected sites as mentioned in Chapter 5 (Figure 5.1). Other early users built expensive networks in which codecs at a central site decoded the video and audio streams to analog signals, sent the audio to a mixer and the video to a switch, then re-encoded the mixed audio and the selected video for transmission back to the conference participants (see Figure 11.1).

The most practical way to enable multiway video conferencing is to use a multipoint control unit (MCU) as discussed in Chapter 5. Such bridging equipment for allowing three or more sites to conference together has been available since the late 1980s. ITU Recommendation H.140 for MCUs was approved in 1988.[1] Recommendations H.243 and H.231, approved in 1993, are companion documents that specify MCUs for H.320 terminals. H.243 and H.231 are concerned mostly with handling multiway audio and video. Most data issues, such as sharing and annotating documents, are specified by the T.120 series of recommendations, discussed in the following chapter. H.243 and H.231, together with T.122/125 (the multipoint communication service portion of the T.120 series) and T.124 (generic conference control), provide a standard for multiple-site videoconferencing with data sharing capabilities.

---

[1] H.140 was for codecs that adhered to the H.120 video coding standard. H.120 products did not perform as well as many proprietary codecs that were available in the mid- to late 1980s, and were not widely used except in Europe.

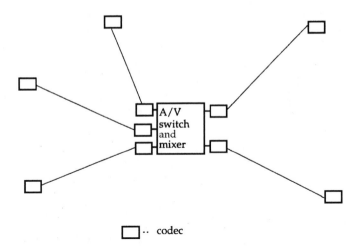

Figure 11.1   Multipoint conference using codec pairs and analog switching

11.1 GENERAL DESIGN CONSIDERATIONS

First, let us review the general components of a videoconferencing system, since part of an MCUs job is to tie everything together. Figure 11.2, from H.320, is commonly used to show how the parts are related. The functional units in Figure 11.2 are shown according to various ITU recommendations. The video and audio I/O equipment, such as microphones, monitors,

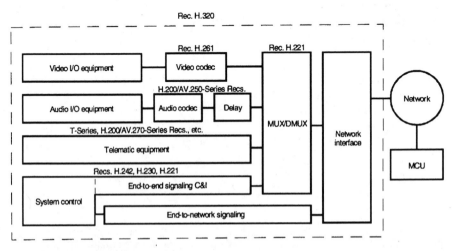

Figure 11.2   Videoconferencing system
(Reprinted with permission of ITU, from Recommendation H.320 (3/96) figure 1.)

cameras, speakers, and even echo cancelers, is not specified. Telematic equipment provides meeting aids such as electronic whiteboards and still image capture and annotation. This is covered mostly by the T.120 series. System control and end-to-end signaling is for such things as call setup, negotiating which audio compression standard to use, or opening a data channel during a call, for example. The video and audio codecs carry out signal coding and decoding as presented earlier. Delay is added in the audio path to compensate for the greater delay of video codecs, allowing lip synchronization to be maintained. The MUX/DMUX section combines the transmitted video, audio, data, and control signals into a single bit stream, as prescribed by H.221 and discussed in Chapter 9, and demultiplexes the received bit stream correspondingly. The network interfaces have varied from leased lines to switched 56 to ISDN, with the historical preponderance of leased line installations giving way to ISDN (PRI or BRI). The ITU I.400 series covers the user network interface specifications.

What does one want in an MCU? Where should it be located? How many ports should it have? Should the video be switched or mixed together (via multiple windows)? Should the audio be mixed or switched? These are just a few, though among the most important, of the questions that MCU and videoconferencing systems designers face.

Within a reasonable limit, for a given number of ports, the lowest cost per port is achieved by putting all of the ports that a customer wants onto a single MCU. What is the maximum number needed in an MCU? Is 20 enough? It is hard to imagine having a useful, interactive videoconference with more than, say, 20 active sites. However, there are certainly situations where one might want to address more than 20 sites simultaneously. If interaction is not required, then two-way communication is not required, and an MCU is not required. ITU Recommendation H.331 specifies how videoconferencing equipment should behave during such a broadcast in order to allow the audiovisual signal from a transmitting terminal to be distributed to multiple receiving terminals by using the signal distribution function of ISDN switches. Since, in this situation, terminals cannot exchange messages related to call setup, including exchanging information on their capabilities, H.331 specifies certain defaults and describes what information should be known about the participating terminals before such a broadcast service is set up.

Aside from broadcasting, there will certainly be useful situations in which more than 20 sites will want to participate, interactively, in multiway calls. Should, then, 20 or more ports be built into a single MCU? One 20-port MCU shares a power supply, chassis, and overall system control circuitry among 20 ports, whereas two 10-port MCUs must each have their own, and thus will cost more. However, a user with multiple sites in Asia and the United States

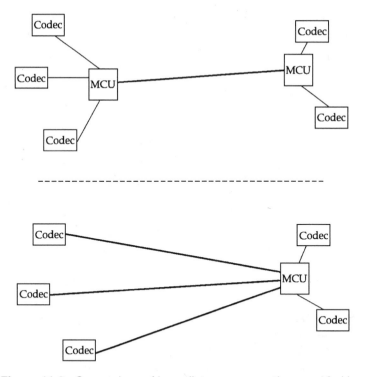

Figure 11.3 Comparison of long-distance connections needed in one and two MCU configurations

may find it more economical to buy two 10-port MCUs and install one in each region. Figure 11.3 illustrates why. This configuration requires only one trans-Pacific long-distance connection (of whatever desired bandwidth). For this and reasons of design, manufacturing, and purchasing flexibility, MCUs are frequently built with 20 or fewer ports,[2] and are designed to be cascaded. Figure 11.4, taken from H.231, illustrates the cascade structure. A performance cost is exacted when two MCUs are cascaded. An extra audio decoding/encoding sequence is added, which results in more delay and creates more degradation of the audio fidelity. For this reason cascading is usually limited to one level, so that a signal traverses at most three MCUs. The ITU recommendations allow more layers of cascading, but we have not person-

---

[2] Historically, most MCUs have been purchased by end users. It is more natural for the MCU to be part of the network. As network providers install a greater proportion of MCUs, there may be a growing market for "megaport" MCUs. There is at least one MCU product with more than 100 ports.

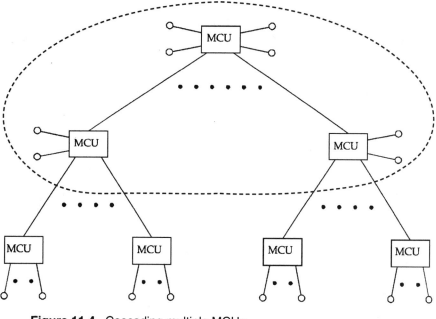

Figure 11.4 Cascading multiple MCUs
(Reprinted with permission of ITU, from Recommendation H.231 (3/96) figure 2.)

ally experienced it and suspect that it should normally be avoided. The dotted line oval in Figure 11.4 indicates this suggested cascading limit.

11.1.1 Audio and Video Mixing

The major function of an MCU, aside from being a hub for the network connections, is to "decide" what signals are to be sent to whom. As discussed in Chapter 5, this decision could be automatic, as in voice-activated switching, or under the control of a meeting chairman. At one extreme, one might wish to send all video and audio signals to each site. At the other extreme, one might decide to send one chosen audio and one chosen video signal to each site. Sending only one audio signal would give much the same aural effect as does a half duplex speakerphone. This is an effect that the industry once labored mightily to overcome, so it must be avoided, making audio mixing imperative. As discussed in Chapter 5, the most straightforward technique is to mix all of the audio signals, then compress and send to each site the summed audio, with each site's own audio signal subtracted. Unfortunately, the noise components from all of these audio signals are added in also—the more sites, the more noise. This raises the noise floor and decreases the signal-to-noise ratio of the summed audio.

Makers of audio bridging equipment for telephone conference calls long ago hit on a satisfactory solution, variations of which have been adopted for MCU use. In large conferences, they may mix in only five or so signals, perhaps chosen as the five (or so) current strongest signals. In a conference with well-mannered participants, there will usually be only one talker at a time, with that signal being by far the strongest. Identifying the talker's site is necessary for voice-activated switching. With this information available, another reasonable algorithm is to mix in the signals from the other four sites that have most recently had the talker. Either of these techniques gives the "ambiance" of a multiway videoconference with fully mixed audio, without raising the noise floor too high.

The nature of video signals and human senses is such that "mixing" video is more difficult. If it were not for bandwidth limitations, the best situation would be to send all video signals to all sites, with users at those sites viewing all signals, or at least choosing which one(s) to view. The most common implementation is to send just one video signal, usually that of the current talker. Another interesting possibility is to decode the video streams at the MCU and assemble a selected number of them as separate "windows" of a single video signal, which is then recoded as an H.320 video stream. Unfortunately, the decoding/encoding cycle can add another 200 milliseconds or more of delay. An interesting special case that might allow us to avoid the MCU decoding/encoding cycle is to have the participating sites transmit QCIF signals, four of which are selected to be assembled into a four-quadrant CIF video bit stream at four times the transmitted QCIF video bit rate. There has been some work on this concept among members of the ITU video coding experts group. However, it appears to require modification of existing H.320 terminals. Also it is not clear that the separate signals can be properly assembled and synchronized without incurring much of the delay caused by the total decoding/encoding method.

11.1.2 Meeting Control

Should a meeting be egalitarian or tightly controlled? This should be up to the users, so manufacturers may want to offer capabilities for a range of control methods. Voice-activated switching, delivering the picture from the site of the current talker, is probably the most used technique, by far. Therefore it is very important to handle the switching smoothly. One doesn't want to switch on a cough or on the crinkling of a potato chip bag. Also, rapid switching back and forth between two loudly arguing sites can be disconcerting. It

do forever
    check all sites for audio signal strength.
    if (loudest_signal – next_loudest_signal)$<\Delta_s$
     then do nothing
    else if loudest_site = old_loudest_site
        then do nothing
        else if time elapsed since last switch$<\Delta_t$
            then do nothing
                else send video from loudest_site to all other sites;
                     send video from old_loudest_site to loudest_site;
                     set old_loudest_site to site of loudest signal;
          fi
       fi
   fi
od

Figure 11.5 An algorithm for voice-activated switching

is probably best to switch to a new site only after a suitable delay, and only after there is clearly only one (new) site "talking loudest." The basic algorithm is shown in Figure 11.5. The ITU recommendations describe how to carry out the switching, but do not describe how to decide when to switch when in the voice-activated mode.[3] This is left to MCU designers, since the decision method is not expected to affect interoperability.

The voice-activated mode is not always the most desirable for a given meeting. Consider a distance learning installation in which a teacher has students in several remote sites. The teacher may want to select which site to view when.[4] For this and other situations where more control is desirable, H.243 describes how a site can "request the floor" and how a meeting can be chaired from a selected site.

11.1.3 Data transmission

Sending files, sending faxes, sharing an electronic whiteboard, and remotely observing the execution of a computer program all require the sending and receiving of data streams. This adds complexity to the MCU, especially since

---

[3] This is also referred to sometimes as "automatic" mode.

[4] At least one MCU manufacturer has provided an "autocycle" mode for this case, so that a teacher can see the other sites on an automatically rotating basis.

many data transmission protocols are designed for two-way communication, not multiway. The more complex issues and techniques are described in the T.120 series of ITU recommendations, and are covered in Chapter 12. However, some data transmission capability is covered in the H.320 family. The frame structure of the data stream transmitted by an H.320 terminal, specified by H.221, includes provisions for three types of data channels to be opened within the stream: high-speed data (HSD), low-speed data (LSD), and Multilayer Protocol (MLP).

MLP was put in to carry T.120 traffic, but can carry H.224 data also. H.224 is entitled "A Real Time Control Protocol for Simplex Applications Using the H.221 LSD/HSD/MLP Channels." It was proposed for the purpose of carrying simplex fax transmissions and camera control signals. As briefly noted in Chapter 4, many videoconferencing systems allow what is commonly called "far-end camera control," that is, someone at the receiving site can select and control cameras at the sending site. Since users get visual feedback about the success of their camera movement requests, it was felt that a simplex command transmission was acceptable.

When such products were first introduced, there was some brief resistance to "letting someone else control my camera." However, it was soon understood to be analogous to the viewing choices that people usually get to make when they all meet in the same physical room. This lets the conference table be "extended 1,000 miles" without totally denying participants the ability to control their own eyes. Of course, this gets more difficult in a multiway environment. H.281, entitled "A Far End Camera Control Protocol for Videoconferences using H.224," specifies how camera control works, allowing each properly equipped camera in a multipoint videoconference to be individually controlled from any properly equipped terminal in the conference. H.224 gives the protocols for determining the identifying tags and capabilities of the cameras at each terminal. H.281 emphasizes the need for minimum delay and minimum variation in delay in order to keep far-end camera control from being too difficult and clumsy. Pan, tilt, zoom, and focus are all supported by the protocol.

As stated in the paragraph on its scope, H.224 describes a protocol "primarily used in multipoint video conference networks using the H.243 broadcast capability of the H.221 LSD/HSD Channels or the H.221 MLP data channel." Since it was conceived as a lightweight protocol to be used where T.120 mechanisms might be too slow and cumbersome, there was some initial argument about whether it should be used over MLP.[5] The final decision was that an H.224-compliant terminal must be capable of operation in LSD

---

[5] To some extent, it was also developed (by Study Group 15) because of concern that the T.120 work (by Study Group 8) would not be completed soon enough.

mode and in MLP mode. HSD is optional. The primary expected use of H.224 is within the LSD channel to transport H.281 camera control commands.

11.2 H.231

Work on the H.320 suite was initially directed toward developing a satisfactory two-way, point-to-point set of standards. H.231, "Multipoint Control Units for Audiovisual Systems Using Digital Channels up to 1920 Kbps," and H.243, "Procedures for Establishing Communication Between Three or More Audiovisual Terminals Using Digital Channels up to 1920 Kbps," were developed later. One might say, with some simplification, that the MCU specification was achieved in large part by defining first how an MCU must work in order to allow an H.320 terminal to operate just as if it were in a two-way call, and then later adding the necessary functions for chairman control, multiway data transmission management, and "requesting the floor." An overall block diagram of an MCU is shown in Figure 11.6, slightly adapted from H.231. An actual MCU implementation may or may not fit neatly into the structure depicted. For instance, an *N*-port MCU may not have *N* physical

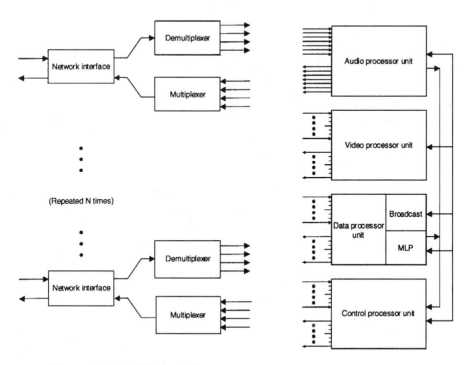

Figure 11.6 MCU block diagram
(Reprinted with permission of ITU, from Recommendation H.231 (3/96) figure 3.)

ports to the network, since a single PRI can provide at least 23 B-channels. In a typical videoconferencing MCU, all of the functions will be present. However, not all are required by H.231. For example, an audiographics MCU need not handle video, nor must a video MCU offer MLP. G.711 audio (basic PCM) is a must, with G.722 (7 KHz, 48 to 64 Kbps) and G.728 (3.3 KHz, 16 Kbps) being optional. Also, audio switching is allowed (though not suggested) in place of mixing, so that no decoding is necessary. Unless both the audio and video are switched, the differences in MCU processing time will desynchronize the audio and video streams. H.231 states that buffers should be used to keep audio delay to less than 30 milliseconds.

Not all terminals in a conference are required to have the same capability, though it is allowable for a given MCU to require it. One important reason for allowing mixed capabilities is so that plain old telephones can be "terminals" in a multiway conference. An MCU that cannot handle terminals whose capabilities differ may choose not to admit a terminal with lesser capabilities, or to negotiate a set of capabilities for the conference that will match those of the least capable terminal.

11.3 H.243 (AND H.242)

In Chapter 10, we gave a brief description of a how H.221 uses a B-channel. Figure 11.7 shows a particular example of the data rate choices that are possible for several bit streams multiplexed together as specified by H.221.[6] When LSD, MLP, or HSD channels are opened, they "steal" bandwidth from the video, since FAS/BAS and audio must stay fixed.[7] In this particular example, HSD is left out since we expect MLP to be generally more useful. H.242, entitled "System for Establishing Communication Between Audiovisual Terminals using Digital Channels up to 2 Mbit/s," describes how two terminals connect with each other after an initial communication link (e.g., an ISDN B-channel) is established, so that they can agree on what subchannels will be created and what each subchannel will carry.

The two terminals must determine their joint capabilities, such as which audio compression can be used, whether CIF or QCIF must be used, or whether MLP is available. In fact, they must negotiate on whether additional communication channels are to be used. For example, a calling terminal dials a receiving terminal via a single B-channel, and as the connection is made it

---

[6] H.221 of course spells out the exact bit positions within the 16 subchannels available within the two B-channels.

[7] It is conceivable that a new audio rate could be negotiated, but this seems unlikely in practice.

video	86.4 Kbps
Audio	16 Kbps
FAS/BAS	3.2 Kbps
LSD	6.4 Kbps
MLP	16 Kbps

Figure 11.7   A possible allocation of data rates

begins transmitting G.711 audio, along with FAS (frame alignment signal) and BAS (bit rate allocation signal). In the BAS channel it continuously sends a list of its capabilities. The terminal being called does the same. In the meantime each terminal searches for FAS in the bit stream it is receiving. Once a terminal determines the FAS position in the multiplexed bit stream, it can then decode the BAS signals that tell it what the other terminal can do. Figure 11.8, taken from Appendix I of H.242, illustrates this process for the case of having 16-Kbps audio and using two B-channels. "A = 0" is transmitted by a terminal when it achieves proper alignment of the signal, indicated in Figure 11.8 by the phrase "Recover MFA."[8]

H.243 adds the necessary protocols for establishing a multiway call. Beyond that, much of H.243 deals with data transmission, cascading, and chair control of conferences, and with the various methods available for terminals to request what video to receive. Terminals must be given ID numbers for many of the control functions to be carried out. For instance, if a user wants to see the video from a particular site, he or she can cause his or her terminal to send a request (video command select), containing the number of the terminal whose video is desired, to the MCU.

H.243 also describes in detail how to set up conferences in which multiple calls are made by each terminal into the same "network address number" (essentially, the phone number). These are called "meet me" calls.

The H.243 concept favors the use of a central decision point for handling

---

[8] MFA stands for multiframe alignment. A multiframe is 16 frames, 80 octets per frame.

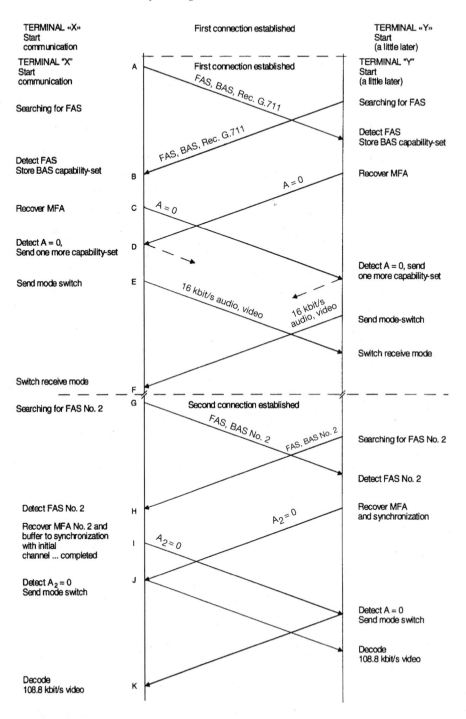

Figure 11.8 Connection and negotiation example
(Reprinted with permission of ITU, from Recommendation H.242 (3/96) figure I.1.)

requests to transmit video, to transmit data, or to be granted the chair control token. Therefore in multiple MCU conferences, one MCU should be designated as the "master" if these functions are to be available.[9] A simple audio/videoconference with automatic switching can be handled relatively easily without a master, since each MCU can make its video follows voice decisions based on the audio levels it is receiving at each port.

H.243 allows each terminal to make requests[10] to the MCU (or to the master in a cascaded conference). In a conference without chair control, the MCU determines when to grant the requests. In a conference with chair control, someone at the "chair site" will make the decisions. A user can "request the floor" by having his or her terminal send a request to broadcast its video to all others. In a chair-controlled conference, the chair site can send a command to the MCU to cause a particular terminal's video to be broadcast to all others. Also, a user can send a request to view any particular terminal's video, but this may conflict with a chair site command. Also, in a cascaded conference, "requests to view" may conflict, since generally only one video signal can be sent from one MCU to another. The resolution procedures for these and similar conflicts are, for the most part, spelled out in H.243.[11] To give the reader a better feel for what is involved, Table 11.1 lists some of the commands and functions available in a multiway conference.

To transmit data on LSD or HSD, a terminal asks the MCU for a token. When it receives it, it can transmit. Opening a data channel takes bandwidth away from the video, not the audio. If a non-data-capable terminal is in the call, it will not be able to receive video from or send video to terminals with the data channel open. For this reason, an MCU is permitted to choose *not* to open the requested data channel if non-data-capable terminals are in the call.

Chair control can be handled either by the procedures of Section 8 of H.243, or by using the MLP channel and the procedures of T.124. Though the use of MLP is covered by the T.120 suite, the MLP channel must be opened under the rules of H.243. One method is to start all conferences that will use MLP with the MLP channel open at 6.4 Kbps, and let T.124 govern it from there. How H.243 and T.124 will work together best in practice has still not been fully resolved.

Section 8 of H.243 describes the procedures for chair control using BAS codes. The MCU performs such tasks as assigning a number to each terminal,

---

[9] The T.120 series uses the similar concept of "top provider."

[10] Terminals must be equipped to do so.

[11] The reader will appreciate that there are often disagreements among the developers of the standards about how such conflicts should be resolved, and also that there are situations that are not properly understood until there is experience with actual use in products.

Table 11.1 Command and control examples

MCV	*Multipoint command visualization-forcing* — Sent by a terminal wishing to force the MCU to transmit its video signal to all other terminals in the conference.
MIV	*Multipoint indication visualization* — Received from MCU to indicate to the terminal that its video signal is being sent to other terminals.
MIZ	*Multipoint indication zero-communication* — Sent by MCU to tell a terminal that no other terminals are yet connected into the conference.
MIS	*Multipoint indication secondary-status* — Tells a terminal that other terminals of higher capability are connected to the conference, so it may miss some signals.
VIN	*Video indicate number* — Sent by MCU to indicate the source (terminal ID) of the video being received.
VCB	*Video command broadcast* — Sent by a chair control terminal to select which terminal's video signal is to be broadcast to the others.
Cancel-VCB	*Cancel video Command Broadcasting* — Returns the conference to automatic mode (video follows voice).
VCS	*Video command select* — Used by a terminal to request viewing a particular site, if this request doesn't conflict with a VCB command.
Cancel-VCS	Transmitted by a terminal to return to viewing in automatic mode.
DCA-L* DCA-H*	*LSD/HSD command acquire-token* — Sent by a terminal to get a token for sending LSD or HSD data. The request must include the desired data rate.

assigning a chair control token to the chair site's terminal, disconnecting a terminal from the conference if so commanded by the token holder, and switching video signals as commanded by the token holder. At least one terminal in the conference must be "suitably enhanced" in order to perform chair control functions and send the required control messages.

Chapter 12

Multipoint Data

Many times, sharing data in a conference is more important than having motion video. Sharing a drawing (and sharing the act of drawing) is one of the most fundamental forms of communication. Exchanging computer files has also become extremely important, and the shared observation of the execution of a computer program is often useful. In the past, various manufacturers have offered some or all of these capabilities in proprietary products. Standardization of such methods is now done through ITU Study Group 8 and is described by the T.120 series of recommendations. In this chapter we first discuss basic capabilities included in both the historical proprietary approaches and the T.120 recommendations. Then we cover the rich capabilities of T.120. Finally, we consider some alternate protocol approaches. Because most current products emphasize shared presentations, we will emphasize them also.

12.1 SHARING IMAGES AND DRAWINGS

In business meetings, classrooms, and elsewhere, it is normal to use an overhead projector to show transparencies outlining the discussion and providing visual stimulation. Correspondingly, in a videoconference, a camera on a stand can be used to capture the image of a transparency or sheet of paper. Displaying the image as a video source is possible, but not entirely satisfactory. Video at 352×288 does not provide sufficient clarity for medium and small fonts to be legible. Transmitting the image as motion video consumes substantially more bandwidth than would be needed to transmit a single still image (even a higher resolution still image). Transmitting the image from the camera stand as video preempts the transmission of video from cameras pointed at the people in the conference.

Rather than transmit a presentation page as live video, it is more effective to transmit a page once, and not retransmit until the page changes. For paper pages, the input source is likely to be a video camera on a stand. If the page is computer generated, then the input can be directly obtained from computer storage. JPEG, or another coding algorithm appropriate to still image, will normally be used to reduce the bandwidth needed for transmitting the image. Bandwidth normally used for video can be briefly diverted for transmitting a still image, potentially losing some frames of video until the still image transmission is complete. If multiple monitors are available, then one can be used for the still image and another for motion video. In a single monitor system, the still image will normally be shown full screen, with a window of the motion video positioned over a less important portion of the still image.

A coded image is still substantial in size, 50 kbytes or more. The coding process produces a descriptor of the coded image and a sequence of bits (the coded image). Since the image is to be transmitted only once, it is necessary to ensure that the bits of the image are delivered to the other end of the conference, in sequence, and with no transmission errors. These requirements can be met with traditional communication protocol mechanisms, which we now summarize. [For detailed discussion of traditional protocols, see, for example, TANE89.] For simplicity, we assume a point-to-point conference between a pair of systems.

The International Standards Organization (ISO) Open Systems Interconnect (OSI) Reference Model distinguishes seven layers of protocol. For our purposes, the layers of interest are the bottom four layers and primarily just the transport layer (layer 4) and the data link layer (layer 2). The bottom layer, the physical layer, is concerned with electrical and mechanical issues that are not relevant to this chapter. The network layer (layer 3) is not relevant to a direct connection between two systems.

The coded image is passed to the transport layer on the sending system. At the receiving system, the transport layer delivers the coded image intact for display. The transport layer cannot expect the lower layers to deal with large chunks of data, so it segments the data into small packets, usually a few hundred bytes each. The transport layer can depend on the data link layer (network layer) to provide reliable delivery of each of these packets. However, the transport layer cannot depend on the packets being kept in order, so it must be prepared to reassemble the packets in the original order, regardless of the arrival order. The descriptor at the beginning of each packet is given a sequence number by the sender so that the receiver can assemble the packets in order. The transport layer software must also ensure that the sending system is not sending packets faster than the receiving system can handle them. For example, the sending transport layer may keep a count of the unacknowledged packets and ensure that count stays below an acceptable limit.

The data link layer is responsible for delivering the packets without transmission errors, lost packets, or duplicates, regardless of the error characteristics of the physical layer. The receiving side returns positive acknowledgment to the sending side when it correctly receives packets and negative acknowledgment when it detects corrupted or missing packets.[1] With negative or missing acknowledgment, the sending side will retransmit the corresponding packets. Corrupt packets are usually identified by a faulty check sum. A check sum is calculated by the sending side and verified by the receiving side, as evidence of error-free transmission. In addition to the data content of the packet, it will have descriptor fields that include the packet's sequence number, the check sum calculated by the sender and other information. For example, a typical packet format, as recognized by the data link layer is

start flag	address	control	data	checksum	end flag

The address field is of limited use in our examples. The control field includes sequence numbering, acknowledgment, and similar information. In addition to true data in the data field, the protocol layers above the data link layer may use the data field for information not needed for the data link layer.

Other types of data, besides still images, can be transmitted with the same protocols. For example, text characters, description of drawn lines, or other annotation of an image may be included in the data field. Conference control information, such as camera positioning, may also be transmitted with these protocols. It is useful to identify separate channels for these different types of data. Thus a channel number field might be included at the beginning of the data field by the transport layer. Looking inside the data field for a text string, we might see

channel	x-position	y-position	font	color	text string

and the data field for a straight line might be

channel	x-start	y-start	x-end	y-end	width	color

With a multipoint control unit and multipoint conferences, numerous complexities are possible, but simplifying assumptions can cover some of the most common cases. For example, with a single MCU that has terminals connected to it in a star topology, a conference may be treated as a collection of

---

[1] "Missing" may mean "too late" or "too far out of sequence."

point-to-point conferences. If there are more than two systems in the conference, it might be the case that a system transmitting data intends that data to go to only a subset of the other systems. More often, the data will be intended for all of the other systems. In this case the MCU can forward the data to all of the systems except the originator. The T.120 recommendations cover a rich collection of the complexities, so we will delve into them as appropriate in discussing T.120.

12.2 ITU-T T.120 RECOMMENDATIONS

In the T.120 framework, T.123 covers the OSI layers up through the transport layer. T.122/T.125 provide a rich set of addressing and control services. T.124 encompasses a primary control application, the node controller, a registry for application and conference information, and additional control mechanisms. T.127 provides file transfer services and T.126 provides a comprehensive set of facilities for sharing still images and drawings. Figure 12.1 illustrates the relationship between these and other components. The following approved ITU-T recommendations are the defining documents:

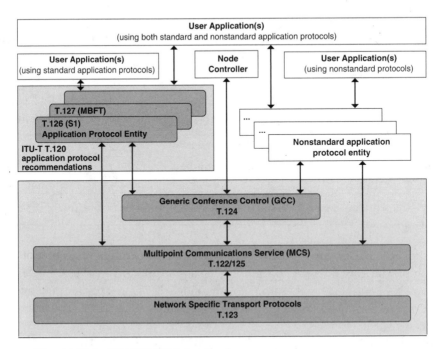

Figure 12.1 ITU-T T.120 infrastructure
(Reprinted with permission of ITU, from Recommendation T.120 (7/96) figure 3.)

ITU-T Recommendation H.221 (1993), "Frame Structure for a 64 to 1920 kbit/s Channel in Audiovisual Teleservices."

ITU-T Recommendation H.242 (1993), "System for Establishing Communication Between Audiovisual Terminals Using Digital Channels up to 2 Mbit/s."

ITU-T Recommendation T.122 (1993), "Multipoint Communication Service for Audiographic and Audiovisual Conferencing."

ITU-T Recommendation T.123 (1993), "Protocol Stack for Audiographics and Audiovisual Teleconference Applications."

ITU-T Recommendation T.124 (1995), "Generic Conference Control for Audio-Visual and Audiographic Terminals."

ITU-T Recommendation T.125 (1994), "Multipoint Communication Service Protocol Specification."

ITU-T Recommendation T.126 (1995), "Still Image Protocol Specification."

ITU-T Recommendation T.127 (1995), "Multipoint Binary File Transfer Protocol Specification."

12.2.1 Transport and Lower Layers (T.123)

The T.123 layer of T.120 encompasses OSI layers 1 to 4. T.123 isolates the upper T.120 layers (shown above T.123 in Figure 12.1) from dependency on the type of network. We will limit attention here to T.123 for H.221 and ISDN, but the T.123 recommendation also covers analog telephone lines, TCP/IP, IPX/SPX, and other types of networks.

Figure 12.2 shows the components of the ISDN profile for T.123. I.430 and I.431 are the physical layer definitions for basic rate ISDN and primary rate ISDN, respectively. The left column of the figure depicts the D-channel, and the Q.921 and Q.931 protocols used for call control and setup. The B- and H-channels are as defined in earlier chapters. H.221 provides multiplexed bit streams for audio, video, and various types of data. The procedures for using H.221 are described in H.242. The focus of T.123 is the multilayer protocol (MLP) data type provided by H.221. (This last is an understatement—the T.120 protocols were originally known as "MLP" when H.320 was defined.)

Looking at the top right column of Figure 12.2, we see layers 2 up through 4 in the OSI model. Recommendation Q.922 provides a specific definition of data link control with the characteristics described in Section 12.1. As suggested in Figure 12.2, network layer 3 is essentially null for T.123. The SCF

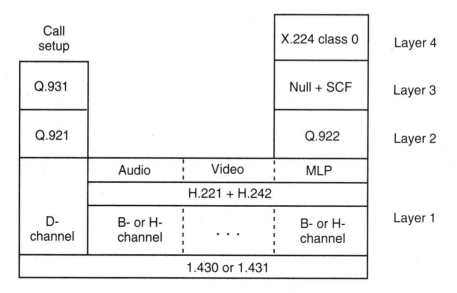

Figure 12.2   T.123 components
(Reprinted with permission of ITU, from Recommendation T.123 (11/94) figure 5.)

(synchronization and control function) manages the establishment and release of network connections within the context of an established physical link. In the T.123 definition, transport layer connections map directly to data link layer connections.

The transport layer, defined by Recommendation X.224, is primarily used for segmentation into packets, as discussed in Section 12.1.

12.2.2 Multipoint Communication Service (T.122/T.125)

The multipoint communication service (MCS) is central to the T.120 recommendations. MCS defines standard procedures for providing the capabilities that vendors have been offering in proprietary ways, and substantial additional capabilities. We do not attempt to cover precisely the breadth and depth of MCS. Rather, we attempt to describe the essence of MCS. Perhaps, in some cases, we will blur some of the formal definitions. The ITU-T documents, particularly the T.122 recommendation, provide precision and formality for implementation. The T.122 recommendation defines the multipoint service, while the T.125 recommendation defines the protocol implementation of MCS.

The nodes of the multipoint environment are referred to as "providers" in MCS. A provider is likely either an MCU or an end-user conferencing system. However, a provider might also be a conferencing system that is serving as an intermediary, or a general-purpose computer that is serving the role of an MCU.

MCS depends on T.123 for connections between providers. T.123 has been defined for a wide variety of physical networks. MCS is independent of the underlying physical network(s); T.123 provides this abstraction and isolation. It is not only possible, but likely, that quite different physical networks will be used concurrently in an MCS-supported conference. For example, an MCU might be connected to several videoconferencing systems by ISDN, and a personal computer (without audio/videoconferencing capability) could be connected by Ethernet to either the MCU or one of the conferencing systems, and participate in the conference for data sharing.

Whether the physical network is point to point, as in ISDN, or shared media, as with classical Ethernet, MCS imposes a tree structure among providers in a conference. MCS defines a tree-structured "domain" of providers, with a domain being essentially equivalent to "conference," or a "side conversation" within a conference. Figure 12.3 illustrates a typical star

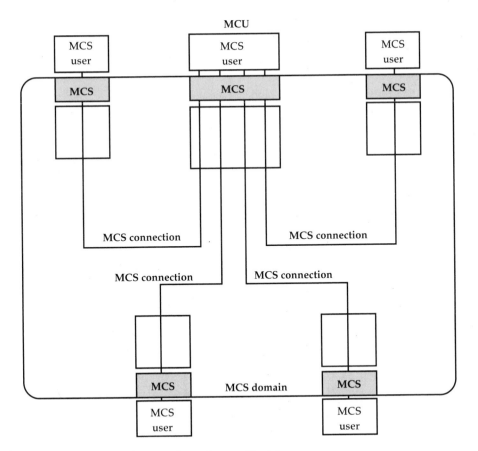

Figure 12.3 Star configuration multipoint
(Reprinted with permission of ITU, from Recommendation T.122 (3/93) figure 1.)

connection of conferencing systems to an MCU. The shaded boxes indicate MCS providers. The "MCS users" are applications and other software dependent on MCS.

The provider at the root of the tree is called the "top provider" for the domain. The top provider manages the domain's resources, such as the channels and tokens that we discuss in subsequent paragraphs. As defined in MCS, the hierarchical domain structure is necessary for management of these resources, and for the enforcement of the "uniform send" option (also to be discussed later).

Figure 12.4 illustrates a slightly more complex configuration, with a provider that is neither the root nor the leaf of the tree. This provider might either be another MCU, "cascading" to the root MCU, or a conferencing system. In the latter case, the conferencing system might be a room system, with the leaf provider being a notebook computer carried into the conference by one of the attendees. Figure 12.5 depicts a conference with two domains. Figures 12.3, 12.4, and 12.5 illustrate a few of the most basic configurations possible. Deeper trees, more severely unbalanced trees, and other configurations are supported in the recommendation and are of value in practice.

A domain, the top provider for the domain, and the tree structure are established when connections are initially established. It is possible for additional connections to the domain to be established later, or for connections to be terminated, as long as the top provider remains intact. When a provider initiates connection to another provider, a field in the request indicates whether this connection to be attached is going up to a higher level, or down to a lower one.

The provider receiving the connect request can choose to reject the re-

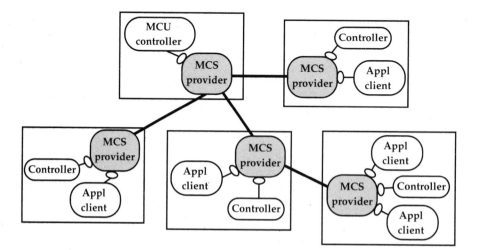

Figure 12.4 MCS providers, clients, and controllers
(Reprinted with permission of ITU, from Recommendation T.122 (3/93) figure 3.)

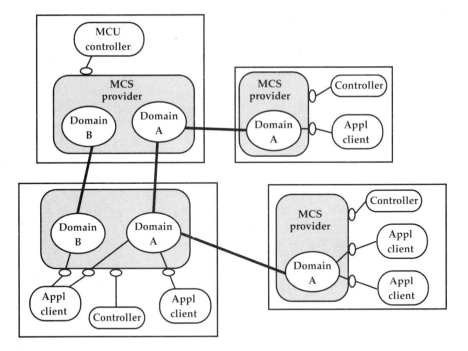

Figure 12.5 Multiple domains
(Reprinted with permission of ITU, from Recommendation T.122 (3/93) figure 4.)

quest. A user data field in the *connect provider* message can be used to exchange passwords or other data to negotiate the connection.

User applications also attach to the domain, but without affecting the connections and domain structure. A unique user identifier is established as part of the application attachment.

MCS uses *channels* as domain-wide addresses. Applications use channels to transmit data. An application joins a channel to receive data being sent to that address. Channels are *multicast* in the sense that data on the channel is only sent to those applications desiring to receive the data. If an application does not join a given channel, then it does not receive the data for that channel. An application does not need to join a channel to send to that channel. Channel membership is maintained in a distributed fashion, with partial membership information recorded at each level of the hierarchy in a multiple provider domain.

It is conventional for a user application to join a channel with the same number as the application's user identifier. Other applications in the domain can then use a user identifier as a channel number to reach a specific application.

In addition to the public channels managed by the top provider, individual user applications may establish private channels. The establishing application can invite other applications to join the channel and expel applications from the channel.

With "simple send" (in MCS terminology) of data, it is possible, if not likely, that providers near the sender in the domain tree will receive data sooner than those more distant in the tree. With multiple senders, it is likely that different providers will receive data interleaved in different sequences.

With "uniform send," all the *uniformly sequenced send data* requests are routed to the top provider and from there sent in the same order to all the receiving sites.

MCS provides "tokens" to allow exclusive access to resources. An application associates a token with the resource to be controlled. When an applications site wishes to use the specific resource, it must ask for the associated token. When no other site is holding the token, it may be granted to the requesting site.

The discussion of T.127 in Section 12.2.4 illustrates usage of MCS channels and tokens.

12.2.3 Generic Conference Control (T.124)

Generic conference control (GCC) provides services to complement and enhance MCS. There are services for conference establishment and termination, managing a *conference roster*, managing an *application roster*, for an *application registry*, and for conference *conductorship*. Each MCS provider has an associated GCC provider that provides GCC services to the local *node controller* and local *application protocol entities*, if any exist (see Figure 12.6). The node controller is closely related to GCC, but is separate, as defined by T.124.

When a new conference is created, a *conference profile* is specified by its creator. The conference profile includes such things as the conference name, whether the conference has restricted access by means of a password, whether it is open (*unlocked*) or restricted to be joined by invitation only (*locked*).

An existing conference may be expanded by the site wishing to join, or by a conference *convener*. If a conference is locked, only the convener can add more sites. GCC provides a means of transferring participants from one conference to another. This function may be used to achieve the effect of merging two conferences, or splitting a conference into more than one conference.

At any time a site may disconnect from the conference, leaving the other sites to continue the conference. The convener may also unilaterally terminate the entire conference at any time, or disconnect a particular site from the conference.

GCC provides an application roster for identifying which *application protocol entities* (APEs) are available at each node. The roster provides necessary

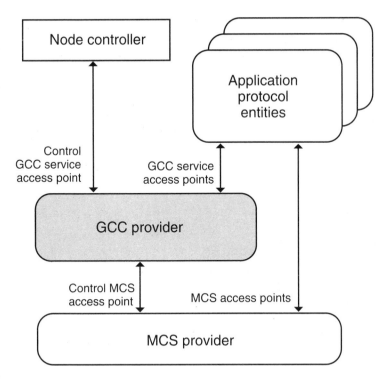

Figure 12.6 GCC provider and related components
(Reprinted with permission of ITU, from Recommendation T.124 (8/95) figure 6-2.)

information for peer APEs to communicate with each other. Upon joining a conference, each site sends to all other nodes its local list of APEs—its *local application roster*. As the roster changes, when applications begin or end execution, the roster should be updated and re-sent. From the merging of the local rosters, the top provider forms the *conference application roster* and sends this global roster to all sites.

The *application registry* is a database residing at the top provider that may be used to manage channels, tokens, and other shared resources used in a conference. The information in the application registry can be used by applications to establish communication with compatible sites.

GCC provides a method for allowing a node to become a conductor for a conference. An MCS token is used by GCC to determine whether a conference is conducted or nonconducted. The node that grabs the conductor token becomes the conductor of the conference. A node may also request conductorship or accept conductorship from the current conductor. Upon request, GCC provides the identity of the current conference conductor. On creation of a conference, it may be specified that conducted mode is not permitted for the duration of the conference.

A GCC method is provided for coordinating timed conferences. A GCC mechanism is provided for a site to find out how much time is remaining in a timed conference, as well as a mechanism for announcing to all sites how much time is remaining. Such an announcement would usually come when the allowed time is nearly elapsed. A site may request more time, but there is no guarantee that such a request will be honored. A GCC method is also provided to request assistance from an operator.

12.2.4 File Transfer (T.127)

T.127, "Multipoint Binary File Transfer (MBFT)," defines protocols and application services for file transfer. Since the files are binary, T.127 does not address byte order, character sets, etc. These issues of representation, where they are important, are left to the applications using T.127.

T.127 services and protocols support a rich variety of file transfer applications. The transfers may be broadcast, where the files are sent to all sites in the conference. With broadcast transfers, all sites are expected to receive the file, even when the file is not of interest to some of the receiving sites. A receiving site is free to discard the file after receiving it, but it must at least receive the file. Transfers may be *directed*, which means that only a subset of the sites in the conference are designated as recipients. In this case, a site only need receive a file if it has stipulated that it wishes to receive the file.

T.127 defines a *session* as a peer-to-peer relationship between two or more file transfer applications. The peer applications of a session use one MCS channel for control purposes, and one or more MCS channels for data transfer purposes. Only one file can be transmitted on each data channel at a time, but additional data channels can be used to allow distribution of multiple files simultaneously. The number of data channels in use at any given time depends on the number of concurrent file transfers in progress.

Broadcast data channels are used for broadcast transfers to all sites. *Acknowledged* data channels are used for directed transfers to sites choosing to receive the transferred files. The creator of an acknowledged data channel specifies whether only the creator may send files on the channel, by defining the channel to be "exclusive," or whether all sites may send files on the channel, by defining the channel to be "shared" (see Figure 12.7).

A sender may desire a file to be directed to only one site or a subset of sites in the conference. For example, an instructor or a particular student might wish to transfer course work without visibility to other students. In T.127, this can be accomplished by establishing a private session between the desired sites. This can also be accomplished, with less overhead, by establishing a private *subsession* within an existing session. A subsession inherits capabil-

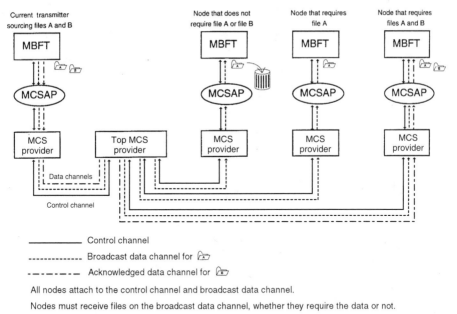

Control channel

------------- Broadcast data channel for 📂

-- -- -- -- Acknowledged data channel for 📂

All nodes attach to the control channel and broadcast data channel.

Nodes must receive files on the broadcast data channel, whether they require the data or not.

Nodes only join an acknowledged data channel if they wish to receive the file currently being offered on it.

MCSAP is an MCS "access point."

Figure 12.7 T.127 channel usage
(Reprinted with permission of ITU, from Recommendation T.127 (8/95) figure 2.)

ities and participants from the parent session and is not visible to GCC, thus the lower overhead. A subsession has a single control channel and one or more data channels, but is not required to have a broadcast data channel. See Figure 12.8 for an illustration of subsessions, and Figure 12.9 for the overall structure of sessions.

Other capabilities of T.127 include capabilities for sites to request files from known locations on another site, and to specify priority of transfers via the control channel. Provision is made for sites to request a file from other nodes to allow information retrieval from databases, bulletin boards, etc.

T.127 uses an MCS token to limit file request access to the control channel and an MCS token to limit file transmit access to the data channel. In other words, an application must acquire a file request token before requesting a file (releasing after the request process is completed) and a file transmit token before sending a file.

12.2.5 Still Images (T.126)

T.126 defines services for primary modes of data conferencing, sharing still images, and annotations. The visual model is based on a collection of over-

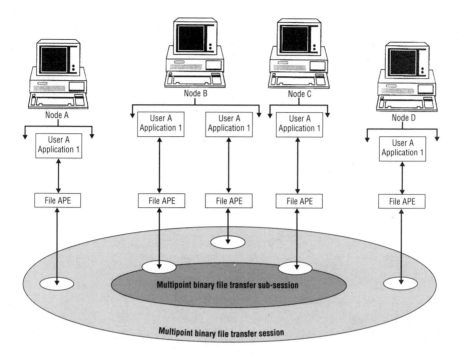

Figure 12.8   Session and subsession relationships
(Reprinted with permission of ITU, from Recommendation T.127 (8/95) figure 3.)

laid two-dimensional planes, called a *workspace*. A plane typically consists of a bitmap or of annotation. The overlapping planes are depth ordered, with visibility controls. A specially designated virtual pointer plane may exist in front of the other planes (see Figure 12.10). When a new site joins a conference, GCC notifies the other sites. As soon as a new workspace is created, the sites are then required to delete all prior workspaces. The T.126 recommendation suggests that workspaces be created frequently, so that all workspaces are kept up to date.

When a workspace is created, the pixel dimensions are fixed for all sites in the conference. The coordinate space of each plane has the origin (0,0) in the upper left corner. The pixels in the workspace proper have square aspect ratio (1:1). In the workspace framework, it is the responsibility of the sites of the conference to convert to and from their native pixel aspect ratio, if it is other than square. It is also possible for sites to exchange bitmaps in non-square pixel formats, outside of the workspace framework.

A workspace is made visible through one or more rectangular views of the workspace. A T.126 session may consist of multiple workspaces, each with multiple views. Exactly one of all of these views is designated as the *focus* view at any given time.

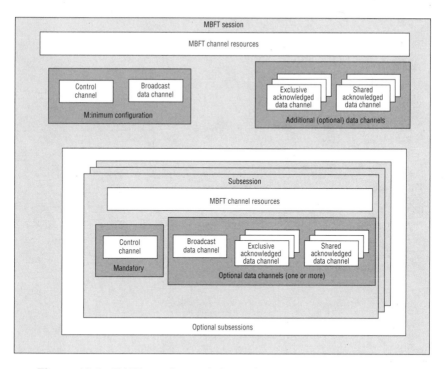

Figure 12.9 T.127 session and channel structure
(Reprinted with permission of ITU, from Recommendation T.127 (8/95) figure 4.)

A site may choose (or may only be able) to display a portion of the view, in which case it may use scrolling or some other mechanism to accommodate the mismatch. Similarly, a site may choose to scale a view to a size larger than the logical pixel resolution. In any case, the coordinate space of the workspace is used for operations on the workspace.

The T.126 operations are intended to be independent of processor and operating system. The operations are primarily bitmap, annotation, and pointer oriented. Text is not dealt with directly; text operations can be implemented using the bitmap support.

The most important bitmap formats are uncompressed, Group 3 fax, and JPEG. Other standard and proprietary formats can be negotiated in the capabilities exchange at session establishment.

The annotation support is equivalent to many classical two-dimensional drawing packages. The basic shapes supported include points, open and closed polylines, rectangles, and ellipses. In drawing these shapes, the specifiable attributes include pen shape, line thickness, line style, line color, and fill color. Custom shapes are supported by use of bitmaps.

Pointers are treated specially, with the virtual pointer plane being in front

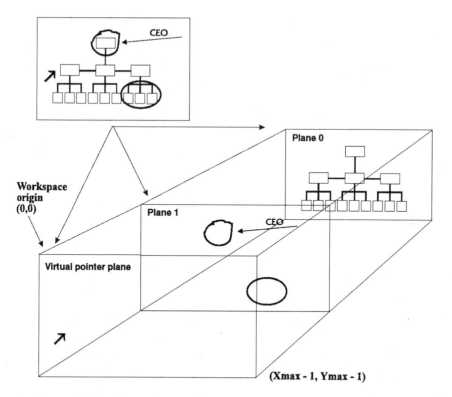

Figure 12.10   Planes in a workspace
(Reprinted with permission of ITU, from Recommendation T.126 (8/95) figure 5.3.)

of the other planes. The cursor shapes for pointers are specified as bitmaps. A pointer is controlled exclusively by the site that created the pointer.

12.2.6 Other Recommendations and Work in Progress

Four other sets of recommendations in the T.120 series are worthy of note:

T.121, "Generic Application Template," describes how a proprietary application might use MCS and GCC. Such an application would not interoperate with distinct applications, but would interoperate with other instances of the same application. ITU-T approval of T.121 is expected in 1996.

"T.AVC," for audio/video control, is a group of recommendations (T.130, T.131, T.132, and T.133) that specifies how the audio and video portions of a multimedia call need to work together with the data portions of a call. T.AVC addresses such issues as multimedia conference start-up, real-time audio/video stream control, audio/video/data bandwidth control and throughput issues, and remote device (cameras, microphones, VCRs, video focus, etc.) control. When completed, T.AVC will supercede H.243. ITU-T approval of the T.AVC recommendations is expected in 1997.

T.RES, for Reservation control, is split into three recommendations that specify the interface and protocols used between

- A user terminal and a reservation system,

- An MCU and a reservation system, and

- Two different reservation systems.

ITU-T approval of these recommendations is expected in 1998.

T.SHARE defines protocols that support multipoint program sharing in the sense of the discussion in Section 3.4. We expect ITU-T approval of this recommendation in 1998.

12.3 DISTRIBUTED DATA IN LARGER CONFERENCES

T.120 has achieved widespread support among equipment manufacturers, software developers, end users, and others. It is reasonable to expect that T.120 will be the preferred standard for many years to come. However, there are environments that T.120, especially T.122/125, does not address well, and either T.120 will need to adapt to these environments or manufacturers will propose alternatives to T.120.

The most notable restriction of T.122/125 is in conferences with large numbers of participants, say, 100 or so. In such a conference,

- It is likely that the conference will be asymmetrical, in that most participants will be largely listening/viewing, and

- It is likely that some of the advanced features of MCS, for example, uniform send and token management, will not be needed or, at least, will not be practical.

The hierarchical structure of MCS and the notion of a top provider are primarily present to support uniform send and token management. In large conferences without need for these functions, it will be desirable to use distributed control functions rather than the centralized control required by the hierarchy and notion of a top provider.

REFERENCE

TANE89   Tanenbaum, A. S., *Computer Networks*, 2nd ed., Prentice Hall, Englewood Cliffs, NJ, 1989.

PART 3

Down the Road

Chapter 13

Barriers Breaking Down

Several technologies and a multitude of products make videoconferencing attractive and practical now. But videoconferencing is not yet "mainstream." Videoconferencing is still thought of as a future consideration by the majority of potential users. Achieving pervasive videoconferencing requires overcoming a variety of technical barriers, followed by social and cultural adoption. Now is the time to discuss these barriers, how they may be overcome, and when they are likely to be overcome.

13.1 FIBERS AND ROPES (CONNECTING SYSTEMS)

Today, the biggest barriers to videoconferencing are the difficulties surrounding the establishment of appropriate connections between conferencing systems. To paraphrase the real estate cliché, the three most important considerations in videoconferencing are connections, connections, connections. The connection barriers begin with the available physical networks. As discussed in the earlier chapters, there are two primary network orientations, circuit switched, such as basic rate ISDN (BRI), and packet switched, as typified by Ethernet for local areas and frame relay for longer distance connections. Circuit-switched networks have been used almost exclusively in videoconferencing until recently. Conferencing with packet-switched networks is rapidly gaining in popularity. This is evident in sales of commercial products from companies such as InSoft, Intel, and RADVision, and in several experimental systems gaining much attention on the Internet and related environments. The ITU-T is rapidly progressing on recommendations to standardize packet-based videoconferencing and gateways between circuit- and packet-based systems. H.323 was "decided," i.e., sufficiently finished to proceed to final balloting, in May 1996. Several companies have already announced products based on the H.323 recommendations.

We are consciously omitting discussion of conventional analog telephone service for connections for videoconferencing. POTS (plain old telephone service) is marginally usable for videoconferencing. This has been achieved partly by limiting video frame rate and resolution even more than is usual in H.320 systems. With the establishment of the ITU-T H.324 recommendations for POTS videoconferencing, we expect that there will be a large number of personal computers capable of H.324 videoconferencing. There will likely be more H.324 systems than all other videoconferencing systems combined. However, we believe the limited video capabilities of these systems will be insufficient for "serious" videoconferencing, for the sorts of applications we have discussed in Chapters 1 and 6. We consider BRI bandwidth to be the minimum for "mainstream" videoconferencing. [See SCHA96 for comprehensive discussion of H.324 videoconferencing.]

BRI is a natural match for the audio and video technologies typically used in videoconferencing, and it is a natural technology for the telephone companies to offer, since it efficiently uses most of their existing copper wiring and digital network equipment. After more than a decade of doubt, BRI is becoming a popular technology that seems to be succeeding in the marketplace. The availability and popularity of BRI bodes well for videoconferencing, because BRI is a sufficient solution for effective videoconferencing. Figure 13.1 shows an ISDN PBX.

However, BRI is probably *not* the long-term solution for videoconferencing. First, the bandwidth of BRI, 128,000 bits per second, is not sufficient for transmission of audio and video with quality comparable to broadcast television. This is certainly true with existing technology for coding audio and

Figure 13.1   Northern Telecom Meridian 1 ISDN switch, capable of supporting hundreds of B-channels

video. It is likely to remain true with the coding technology of a decade hence. At minimum, several BRI lines (say, 6 B-channels) are required to get sufficient resolution and frame rate to approach television quality. Second, the telephone companies are interested in providing substantially higher capabilities than BRI, in order to attain higher revenues and profits than traditional telephony and BRI enable. Third, BRI is not yet pervasively installed, even where BRI is readily available. Most offices and homes do not yet have BRI connections. In some areas, especially less densely populated areas, it is still difficult to obtain BRI service.

Of the circuit-switched options, the most attractive near-term alternatives to BRI are other forms of ISDN, such as primary rate ISDN (PRI), which provides 23 B-channels in the United States and 30 B-channels in many other countries. PRI also allows efficient use of much of the existing telephone wiring and equipment, with the obvious advantage of more than 10 times the bandwidth of BRI. The pricing of PRI might be assumed to be many times higher than BRI, given the bandwidth is more than 10 times greater, but this is not necessarily the case. The costs to the telephone companies for local PRI connections are similar for both BRI and PRI. PRI connections need two pairs of wire, versus one pair for BRI, and the customer equipment cost for PRI is no more than twice the cost of BRI, so the total cost ratio is on the order of 2 or so, not 10. In one of the largest metropolitan areas in the United States, local PRI service is available at prices comparable to BRI. With increasing availability of even higher bandwidth services, at bandwidths of 45 megabits and 155 megabits, it is likely that PRI pricing will become attractive in more areas, since it will not be likely that 1.5 megabits will justify much of a price premium (over 128 kilobits).

Higher bandwidths, 155 megabits per second and much higher, will inevitably become available with fiber optic connections. Fiber optics provides enormously more transmission capability than copper wire, at essentially the same costs in terms of physical size, material costs, and installation costs. It is estimated that more than 10 million kilometers of fiber strands have already been installed, with each strand physically capable of many *billions* of bits per second.

In anticipation of very high bandwidth physical connections, asynchronous transfer mode (ATM) has been and is being developed as a comprehensive approach to requirements of both circuit-switched and packet-switched applications. Because ATM is still being developed, and because it includes characteristics of both circuit- and packet-switched networks, there is often confusion about ATM characteristics, especially the circuit versus packet characteristics. ATM has several alternate modes of operation, called "adaption layers." ATM adaption layer 1 (AAL 1) is most like traditional circuit-switched environments and allows for allocation of fractions of the total bandwidth, to be designated for particular constant bit rate usage, such as audio and video. Connections using AAL 1 are effectively circuit-switched connections. ATM adaption layer 5 (AAL 5) connections provide variable bandwidth, without the guarantees of AAL 1. AAL 5 connections are effectively packet-switched connections available for a variety of uses, including audio, video, and data.

For bandwidths above 155 megabits, ATM depends on fiber optics, but for 155 megabits and below it is also feasible to use twisted-pair copper wiring. ATM adapters and switches are readily available for use within a local area, in lieu of Ethernet. Wide-area (long-distance) ATM connections are available in some pilot environments. Broad availability of wide-area ATM seems likely to be achieved between the years 2000 and 2005. Figure 13.2 shows an ATM switch designed for both local- and wide-area connections.

Though demand for higher bandwidth circuit-switched connections will continue to grow, it seems that the strongest demands for high bandwidth are coming from data networks and computer applications. Local-area networks are transitioning to 100 million bit per second capability. Wide-area

Figure 13.2 ATM switch supporting 155-megabit connections (*ForeRunner* ASX-200BX and *ForeRunner* ASX-1000 ATM Switch Photos printed with permission from FORE Systems, Inc., a worldwide leader in the design, development, manufacture, and sale of high-performance networking products based on ATM. FORE Systems and *ForeRunner* are registered trademarks of FORE Systems, Inc.)

connections between internets of local-area networks are transitioning to higher bandwidths, 45 megabits per second and more. It may well be today, and almost certainly will be so in the future, that the highest bandwidth connections available for videoconferencing are packet-switched connections.

13.2 WEB THREADS

For those steeped in circuit-switched networks and, especially, those immersed in videoconferencing using circuit-based connections, the thought of using Ethernet or other packet-based networks for audio and video is usually baffling at first. How can audio be acceptable with packets of audio getting lost (or out of sequence) all the time? How can video coding algorithms cope with all of the lost packets? The answers are twofold: First, audio will not be acceptable and video coding will not work when many packets are lost, and, second, not many packets get lost. The second answer is the important one: Though Ethernets do suffer collisions, the collisions are infrequent, and the Ethernet protocol masks the collisions. Even when Ethernet collisions occur, packets are usually not lost. Packets are sometimes lost by routers connecting Ethernets and other internets, but such loss is usually a small fraction of the overall traffic.

For those responsible for managing packet-switched data networks, the thought of audio and video saturating those networks evokes expressions such as "over my dead body." However, audio and video traffic is likely already on their networks, due to World Wide Web browsers capable of playing live or stored audio and video. When efficient coding techniques are used for the audio and video, the load on the network is likely less noticeable than the load for viewing the rapidly proliferating still images on Web pages.

Further, a technique known as "multicasting" can gain efficiency in multipoint conferences, using network connection resources more efficiently than would be the case in a circuit-based conference. In a multipoint circuit-based conference, the resources are always reserved for the conference, whether all the participants are speaking or all the sites are listening to a speaker at one site, and whether the video for a site is being transmitted to other sites or not. If the same audio and the same video are being sent to multiple sites, they are sent on separate connections.

In a packet-switched environment, efficiency can be gained by not transmitting audio and/or video unnecessarily, and by routing audio and video by multicasting instead of one-to-one transmission. The term "multicasting" is derived from "broadcasting" in the common sense, transmitting to all who wish to receive, and from "unicasting," transmitting from one site to one site (see Figure 13.3). Multicasting is transmitting from one site to several

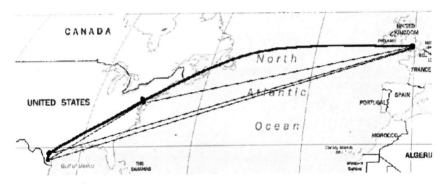

Figure 13.3 Logical routes, multicast (thick lines), and unicast (thin lines)

selected sites. Multicasting is specifically supported in Ethernet and Internet protocols.[1]

Suppose there is to be a videoconference between systems in London, Philadelphia, Austin, and San Antonio. Each site is responsible for mixing the audio from the other sites, and selecting which video streams it wishes to display. With unicasting, connection bandwidth would be redundantly used between each pair of sites. For example, London to Austin and London to San Antonio would use separate connection bandwidth, even though the physical path is nearly identical, and even though the same content is being sent from London to each city. With multicasting, the content is multicast addressed to Austin and San Antonio. It can be expected that the content will take one physical path from London to Austin (or San Antonio), and be forwarded from Austin to San Antonio (or vice versa). Multicasting is especially attractive in situations where one site is the primary source of audio and video, and many other sites are primarily listening and viewing, with occasional audio/video transmissions.

Along with the rapid increase in number of Internet sites has been rapid increase in sites capable of participating in the multicast backbone, the MBone [MACE94, HUIT95, KUMA96]. In October 1995, there were 3,000 subnetworks (each with multiple video systems) capable of participating in the MBone. In addition to the MBone, unicast prototypes and products, such as CU-SeeMe [DORC95] are proliferating on the Internet. Growth of both Internet bandwidths and usage of the Internet for conferencing are likely to accelerate more growth of bandwidth and usage. It is easy to estimate that the numbers of users and conferences with MBone and CU-SeeMe conferencing

---

[1] Many installed Internet protocol routers do not yet support multicasting. However, router manufacturers are generally supporting multicast in their products, so it is reasonable to anticipate widespread support for multicasting.

are of the same order of magnitude as numbers of users and conferences with circuit-based desktop and group conferencing systems.

The experience with the MBone has led to two related standardization efforts. The first has been the definition of RTP (real-time protocol) and related standards by the Internet Engineering Task Force (IETF). The second has been the H.323 family of recommendations from the ITU-T, which adopt much of the definition from RTP and add substantial further capabilities, particularly with regard to gateways to H.320 systems.

13.3 QUILTS AND FUTURE FABRIC

There is little doubt that there are now, and will be many more, useful connection "fibers," including basic rate ISDN, primary rate ISDN, Ethernet, and some "ropes" of fiber optic strands, that will provide more than adequate raw capability for videoconferencing. However, it often seems that individual communities of users are separate patches of fabric that need to be stitched together. One community of users, where BRI is readily available, may be using 128-kilobit circuits for conferencing using "traditional" circuit-switched products. Another community with good enterprise internet support is used to depending on using a couple hundred kilobits, more or less, for conferences, using either commercial or experimental packet-based systems. Yet another community of users has dedicated circuits for 1.5-megabit connections, yet another uses satellites, and yet another has 155-megabit ATM. Mixing in the real estate analogy, those "located" in a given community are fine until they need to reach someone in a different type of community or even a similar but separated community. Attempts at "intercommunity" conferences fail as a result of the lack of gateways between the communities. Videoconferencing technology, especially videoconferencing usage of connections and approaches to interoperability, needs to quilt these communities together.

Just as semiconductor technology has enabled and spurred the computer industry with the advance of the microprocessor, it is likely that fiber optics will advance communication capacity far beyond traditional telephony. From the Intel 8086 to the Pentium Pro, a period of roughly 15 years, the effective processor performance per clock cycle has increased by a factor of 10s, and the typical clock frequency has increased by a factor of 40. A personal computer with a Pentium Pro is hundreds to over a thousand times faster than the initial IBM PC (at a lower price, after adjusting for inflation). Fiber optic transport will continue to deliver comparable, or even more dramatic, increases in connection performance in the coming years. Once the strands of fiber are put in place, they can support enormous transmission capacity, gigabits per second and more. Even though it may be a decade or more before fiber optic is the normal transport, ATM and other fiber optic-based connections are in use today and will rapidly increase in usage.

Therefore, the real challenge is to sew together the patchwork of current and evolving technologies that must fit together until communications bandwidth is as freely available (and as affordable) as microprocessor computation. In addition to the technologies already mentioned, connections using modems, cable modems, and wireless and emerging technologies, such as alternate satellite designs, will be used for videoconferencing.

With most of these technologies, both circuit-switched and packet-switched connections can and will be supported. However, with several of them, most noticeably, local-area networks, cable modems, and some wireless technologies, only packet-switched connections can reasonably be supported. It is routine to support packet switching on underlying circuit-switched networks, using telephony circuitry to establish long-distance connections between routers and packet switches. On the other hand, it is usually impractical to support circuit switching efficiently on packet switching. There are a number of approaches, including quality of service protocols and the "next generation" Internet Protocol (IP), that can be used to make packet networks more like circuit-switched networks, but even with these approaches, the primary network characteristics are those of packet switching.

Two fundamental changes in videoconferencing connections are in progress: First, dramatically better, but diverse, connection bandwidth is becoming available. Second, circuit-switched connections are being superseded by packet-switched connections. This change is inevitable, both because of the technology issues and because of the dominance of data communications. There is little doubt that the preferred connection method for videoconferencing will inevitably become packet-switched connections.

13.4 CLEARER PICTURES

What happens with dramatically higher connection bandwidth? When ATM is commonplace, what will the videoconferencing be like? A frequent misconception is that video coding will go away! Video coding strategies are certainly different in different bandwidth ranges, but video coding is far too valuable to disappear. Though it would be possible to send uncoded video on a 155-megabit connection, this is not likely to be done. Uncoded full color RGB video at CIF resolution (352×288) takes roughly 73 megabits/second, but it is possible to use coding to send the same video, without perceptible artifacts, in less than 2 megabits/second. Except in limited circumstances, it will continue to be significantly more expensive to use 73 megabits than to use 2 megabits. As long as this is true, some level of coding will be very cost effective.

Even if cost is not an issue, picture quality probably is (see Figures 13.4, 13.5, and 13.6). Higher resolutions are easily supported with higher bandwidths. From a television equipment perspective, 720×480 is a natural step in resolution. From a computer perspective, 640×480 is a natural step in resolution. In either case (1) the enhanced clarity will be valuable to many conferencing situations and necessary to some, and (2) uncoded video at higher resolution would not fit in a 155-megabit connection. Using less computation than current videoconferencing products, such resolutions can be transmitted in well under 10 megabits per second.

Most of today's higher resolution, higher bandwidth products use "motion JPEG" for video coding. Motion JPEG codes each frame independently, that is, without any motion estimation, temporal filtering, etc. Each frame is coded using the same JPEG algorithms commonly used for still images. Motion JPEG is thus conceptually simpler than many other video coding approaches. The JPEG "Q factor" can be set to trade off between level of compression and image quality. By selecting a lower Q factor, it is possible to attain substantial compression without visible artifacts.

The other contender for higher bandwidth, higher resolution video coding is MPEG2. The original MPEG has finally gained widespread commer-

Figure 13.4 Image stored at 160×120 resolution

Figure 13.5   Image stored at 320 × 240 resolution

cial usage for one-way video, in computer games and in television products such as the Digital Satellite System. MPEG2 development has enabled higher resolutions, notably the HDTV (high-definition television) resolutions of 1,280 × 720 and 1,920 × 1,080, and lower latencies for interactive applications such as conferencing. Numerous manufacturers are developing integrated circuits optimized for MPEG2, so implementation of MPEG2 products is likely to be inexpensive. The ITU-T is formulating the H.262 recommendations for using MPEG2 in videoconferencing. Thus MPEG2 will likely be the dominant coding approach for higher bandwidth, higher resolution environments.

13.5 SOUNDING BETTER

Audio is critical to the success of videoconferencing. Some of the critical issues, and expectations for improvement include the following:

- *Available communication bandwidth:* For 128 kilobits or less total bandwidth, the common practice is to allocate 16 kilobits for coded audio. At higher total bandwidths, up to 64 kilobits may be allocated for audio. As total

Figure 13.6 Image stored at 640 × 480 resolution

bandwidths increase, more bandwidth can be allocated to audio, enabling improved sound quality.

- *Nominal frequency response:* In current practice, the nominal audio frequency response is either 3.3 or 7 KHz. In comparison with human hearing, and with radio and television, these are narrow frequency ranges, and the loss of low- and high-frequency response is noticeable to most people. As full frequency response, to 20 KHz, becomes more and more pervasive in entertainment and computer products, the expectation is set for conferencing for frequency response above 7 KHz.

- *Number of audio channels:* Most conferencing products use a single channel. More audio channels may enhance realism, as evidenced by entertainment systems progressing from two channels to five or more channels for theatrical environments. Multiple channels may also be needed for functional purposes, for example, a separate private channel might be needed for an observer in medical diagnosis or educational situations.

- *Coding:* Techniques for audio coding are continuing to improve dramatically, for example, enabling 3.3-KHz audio bandwidth in very narrow communication channels (just over 5 kilobits), as in G.723.1, and 7-KHz audio bandwidth in 16-kilobit channels. The Dolby AC-3 coding used in entertainment achieves five full frequency channels in 384 kilobits.

- *Echo cancellation:* As frequency response and the number of channels increase, echo cancellation becomes far more challenging. It is likely that trade-offs against frequency response and number of channels will be necessary to preserve full duplex capability.

- *Noise reduction:* To pick up all of the desired sounds of a group, extra microphones and microphones with broad directional characteristics are desirable. However, undesirable sounds are likely to be accumulated by using more microphones and fewer directional microphones. Signal processing techniques similar to echo cancellation techniques can be used to remove much of the extraneous noise.

13.6 FREE MIPS MEET FREE BAUDS

Today's fastest processors are priced under $2,000 each, and are capable of hundreds of "MIPS" of processing. Some less capable processors are already priced at less than a dollar a MIP. Advances in processor architecture and semiconductor processes are continuing without apparent obstacles to the historical trend of performance doubling every 18 months or so. In real terms, and, especially, compared to historical price/performance levels, processor power seems almost "free." Even if the MIPS are not literally "free" in a monetary sense, the MIPS are "free" in the sense of availability. With massive computation power available at low cost, processor cycles can be allocated to video coding, audio coding, echo cancellation, noise reduction, and so on. The computational power may be from the main processor of a desktop computer or from additional processors added to enhance video and audio.

Bauds (a measure of communication bandwidth) are becoming "free," in the availability sense, as ISDN, Fast Ethernet, ATM, etc., dramatically increase the bandwidth available, compared to the analog modems and classical Ethernet that have been dominant. Free MIPS and free bauds in desktop computing make videoconferencing practical with minimum (or no?) added components.

Processors and networking are two of the most visible facets of personal computing, but the entire culture and industry of personal computing is facilitating videoconferencing. This is not a conscious, organized phenomenon, but the benefit is real, nevertheless. Hardware and software put in place for games (enhanced audio and graphics), for multitasking, for presentations, and other purposes fit naturally into conferencing. Technologies specifically designed for conferencing, notably application sharing and the

T.120 data conferencing protocols, are being included in popular operating systems such as Microsoft Windows.

After decades of research and development, speech recognition is finally becoming effective enough for general use. Speech recognition capabilities for personal computers seem to be sufficient to enable voice-activated control of conferencing equipment. Perhaps the *Star Trek* style of videoconferencing will soon be a reality!

13.7 BETTER THAN BEING THERE

With enough connections, connections, connections, the biggest barrier to conferencing will be gone. Improvement in audio, video, and ease of use will at least match expectations from television. Mainstream videoconferencing equipment will sufficiently sustain the key illusion—that of being in the same place.

The next barrier to fall will be familiarity. You may not yet be used to videoconferencing, but as Tom Selleck says in the AT&T commercials, "you will." Basic videoconferencing capability will be a common capability of personal computers. This is not to say all computers will have this capability, but the cost and price characteristics will be similar to those in place when CD-ROM drives became a typical part of a personal computer, and the mass acceptance characteristics will be similar.

Familiarity and enjoyment will follow availability. Many times it will be more fun to travel a digital highway than a real one. Video meetings will often be used instead of face-to-face meetings. Working at home will become practical more often for more people. New patterns of meeting and working will evolve as they have with other communication capabilities such as electronic mail, faxes, and express delivery services. Entertainment and social use of videoconferencing will likely become even more prevalent than business usage. Almost as soon as CU-SeeMe began to proliferate, entertainment became a significant fraction of usage. Without the current barriers, enjoyment of videoconferencing will catalyze further acceptance.

13.8 MAIN STREAMS

This chapter has focused on the technical issues that will be overcome as videoconferencing becomes mainstream, from the perspective of those involved in videoconferencing. What about the perspective of those watching the trends but not yet involved?

One of the clear trends is the assumption of individual, desktop systems being dominant. In some senses, this is inevitable. The cost of basic videoconferencing, beyond the cost of a full-featured personal computer, is primarily the cost of the camera. The cost of a video camera is low enough that video cameras will increasingly be bundled with personal computers. So, in the years ahead, there will be millions, perhaps, tens of millions of videoconferencing-capable systems. From this perspective, it would be easy to assume that larger scale systems would be displaced by desktop units.

However, larger systems will continue to have capabilities that make them attractive, certainly for groups and even for some individuals. Perhaps an analogy to printers is appropriate. With the advent of inexpensive, high-quality ink-jet and laser printers, it is economically feasible to have a printer with every personal computer. However, in most organizations, it is usually desirable for a group to share even more capable printers, that are faster and have higher resolution and other features. Though many personal computers will have videoconferencing capability, many groups will want to have group-oriented video systems, with interoperability among all the systems, desktop and group.

The other dominant trend is the explosion of the Internet and the dominance of the Internet in electronic communication. From strictly the perspective of audio and video, the Internet and packet switching are not necessarily optimal. However, the Internet and packet-switched networks are *the* communication fabric that have and will dominate computer-based communication, covering the vast majority of computer users. Assuming this fabric is adequate for current and future needs for data communication, it will be adequate for videoconferencing. Because it is the communication vehicle most widely used by computer users, it is the one they will use for videoconferencing.

REFERENCES

DORC95   Dorcey, T., "CU-SeeMe Desktop VideoConferencing Software," *ConneXions 9*, 3 (March 1995).

HUIT95   Huitema, C., *Routing in the Internet*, Prentice Hall, Englewood Cliffs, NJ, 1995.

KUMA96   Kumar, V., *Mbone: Interactive Multimedia on the Internet*, New Riders Publishing, Indianapolis, IN, 1996.

MACE94   Macedonia, M. R., and Brutzman, D. P., "Mbone Provides Audio and Video Across the Internet," *IEEE Computer 27*, 4, pp. 30–34 (April 1994).

SCHA96   Schaphorst, Richard, *Videoconferencing and Videotelephony: Technology and Standards*, Artech House, Norwood, MA, 1996.

Chapter 14

Things to Come

Let us anticipate a few years in the future when connections, connection bandwidth, and processor power are plentiful. We will see conference environments that are far more natural and engaging. We will use bandwidth, processor power, and other technology to provide virtual equivalents of the capabilities we expect when we are all in the same room.

Some of the virtual equivalents are already quite practical. For example, high-quality projection displays, capable of providing bright images in normal lighting, have recently become available and affordable. Instead of smaller than life images on a CRT monitor, projection displays allow remote images to be life size and larger than life. A larger than life image of a remote person can have more impact than the person's physical presence.

Other enhancements are obviously feasible, based on results of prototypes, but not quite ready for everyday usage. We can anticipate having these capabilities and having successful results of research in progress. In this concluding chapter we extrapolate the future capabilities based on work in progress and likely extension of that work.

14.1 HOW TO STRETCH THE TABLE BETTER

A consistent design goal has been to "stretch the conference room table 1,000 miles" while giving up as few as possible of the benefits of a face-to-face meeting. This has led to the inclusion of full duplex, hands-free audio, shared whiteboards, and shared computer screens, along with efforts to make such features easier to control. Videoconferencing system developers will continue to "stretch the table" and this will continue to lead to incremental advancements such as better microphone designs and camera control efforts.

14.1.1 Microphone Arrays

The placement of microphones has been and continues to be an annoying problem. In earlier years, one would find microphones stuck almost anywhere in a conference room (including ceilings) as desperate technicians tried to compensate for inadequate equipment design, poor acoustics, and poor aesthetics. Improvements in echo canceling have improved overall audio performance greatly, but the best microphone placements, acoustically, are not always the best microphone placements, aesthetically. Some users like having a microphone on the conference room table. To them, it is an appropriate part of the milieu—they may in fact be more comfortable knowing where the microphone and camera are located. Others are annoyed by the clutter on the table—the microphones get in the way of their briefcases, papers, and coffee cups, or just don't look quite right on their handsome, carefully chosen tables. Moving the microphones to the ceiling or embedding them into the table-top control panels has not proven to be particularly effective.

One very promising technique for eliminating the physical microphones on the conference table is to use a phased array of microphones that can dynamically adjust sensitivity and directionality. A microphone array might have a few or a few hundred microphones, but configurations with as few as eight microphones seem well suited to videoconferencing. Audio signal processing techniques similar to those used for echo cancellation and noise reduction are used to combine the microphone signals, effectively steering the microphone array, to "point" at the current person speaking.

Microphone arrays may eventually allow "virtual microphones" to be placed, electronically and adaptively, anywhere in the room. Similar concepts have been used for decades to steer radar antennas and sonar arrays electronically—that is, to adjust the direction of maximum sensitivity electronically without physically moving the radar antenna or the sonar array. (This is particularly important for submarines which have sonar arrays mounted along their flanks. They can't be physically steered without moving the boat itself.) Large amounts of processing power are necessary, and engineering details remain to be worked out, but the computational processing is becoming affordable and research and development is progressing [see BRA93, SIL92, and `http://www.is.cs.cmu.edu/ISL.multimodal.mic.html`]. Further development should allow microphone arrays to be mounted in the front of a room (or perhaps also along the sides), electronically steering in real time to place a "virtual microphone" in front of the lips of the person (or persons) speaking. Figure 14.1 illustrates an array mounted on both sides of a camera. Another useful arrangement will be to mount the array in the (now) traditional roll-about cabinet. When such a conferencing system is rolled into a new conference room, classroom, or lab, the array can be unfolded and automatically configured, avoiding current tasks of microphone placement and cabling (see Figure 14.2).

Figure 14.1 Microphone array and camera

14.1.2 Camera Management

If a microphone array can point itself at a voice, the same information can be used to point a camera at the sound source. The microphone array must compute the location of the person speaking in order to place its virtual microphone (or microphones). This information can be used to direct a camera to pan, tilt, and zoom to the current person speaking. Several variations on this are possible. One might use several fixed cameras, and switch among them, to avoid the delay of panning, tilting, and zooming (PTZ). One might also use two PTZ cameras, delaying switching to the new camera until it has been set to the desired coordinates and focal length. It is likely that microphone arrays will be useful for camera management even before they are developed well

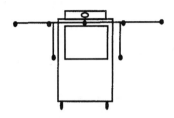

Figure 14.2 Unfolding microphone array

enough to act as virtual microphones. PictureTel and VTEL have announced camera management products based on microphone array technology.

In some senses, an ideal group videoconference would be conducted with each group in a television production studio. Of course, this is likely to be an unnatural setting for the participants, being in a studio instead of a conference room or classroom, but it would enable audio and video "production" that would best capture the participants for listening/viewing at the other sites. It is even better to keep the participants in their natural settings, but with microphone and camera management comparable to a fully staffed television studio. Further, the microphone and camera control should not be visible, so as to not interfere with the participants' primary activities.

In an alternative approach, the motion estimation information from video coding can be used to point the camera. See `http://www.is.cs.cmu.edu/ ISL.multimodal.face.html`.

Neither of these approaches will be 100% accurate in camera positioning, but laboratory prototypes suggest that these technologies will be sufficient to automate camera management in many conferences. Combination of the approaches is likely to increase their applicability.

Future camera and microphone array techniques will be combined and refined in other ways. A very wide angle lens can have most of the conference room in its field of view. With a sufficiently dense light sensor array (say, 4,000 $\times$ 4,000 pixels), one might also "steer" an electronic PTZ camera, or even have it act as a set of cameras, by constructing the 352 $\times$ 288 pixel output of a virtual camera of the desired focal length and orientation. The distortions of the wide-angle lens can be removed automatically. This requires more computation and denser pixel sensor arrays, which will inevitably evolve, along with a great deal of engineering work, but could make installation and use simpler than ever.

14.2 TABLE STRETCHING VARIATIONS: BREAK ROOMS, OFFICES, AND HALLS

In the mid 1980s, researchers at Xerox PARC set up a continuous audio link and a continuous 56-Kbps video link connecting break rooms in buildings in two different cities. This bit rate gave a low-quality video connection. Part of the idea was to allow the kinds of casual meetings that often result in serendipitous problem solving among researchers and other coworkers. Some years later, the idea was tried again at Bellcore [see FIS90], with much higher quality equipment. The Bellcore goal was to "split the [break]room into two parts," moving one part "50 miles down the road." To approximate having a lifelike interaction, their VideoWindow teleconferencing system used a screen three feet high and eight feet long, producing approximately life-sized images. The audio subsystem used four independent, full duplex channels, arranged across the plane of the screen to maintain spatial correlation between images and sounds. Free coffee was provided in the areas visible to the windows. Those who experimented with the system felt that it gave an increased sense of shared space among remote coworkers, but not as much as some might have expected. Fish, Kraut, and Chalfonte [FIS90] wrote ". . . we believe that the current VideoWindow system lacks something due to factors we do not understand." One must keep in mind that the authors were trying to determine whether the system promoted increased social closeness through casual interaction, and were not studying its usefulness for holding business meetings at a distance.

As an entertainment variation of this kind of connection, video systems have been set up at famous tourist sites. For example, one can[1] dial up a video codec and camera at the Tower of London. Another variant is the multitude of World Wide Web sites that show periodic snapshots from the corner of Hollywood and Vine, views of the Golden Gate Bridge, or a panorama of Cambridge, England.

Bellcore's experiments with more casual video interaction have not been limited to VideoWindows. For several years, there have been variations on an experimental system at Bellcore, called Cruiser™ that uses a "cruising the halls" metaphor for controlling a desktop-to-desktop conferencing system [FIS92]. Users are able to wander the halls electronically to see which of their colleagues are available for casual conversation, are busy but interruptible, or want complete privacy. In one variation, three calling methods are used: *Cruises, Autocruises,* and *Glances.* In the *Cruises* mode, when the caller dials, a two-way audio/video connection is opened immediately, but if the called party doesn't explicitly "answer" within three seconds, the connection shuts down. In *Autocruises* mode, the three-second connections are generated by the system itself at random times and to random locations. In *Glances,* a caller is afforded a one-second glance at the called party's office, during which the caller can also be seen. The caller may then choose to use the *Cruises* mode to call. Any user could select a *privacy* mode, in which all callers are notified that the called party is busy.

14.3 TIME/SPACE QUADRANTS

Another valuable model of how people interact is shown in Figure 14.3. Meetings can be thought of as being of four types: same time and place (traditional conferences), same time but different place (traditional

---

[1] Or could the last time we tried. We cannot know which particular sites might stay in existence.

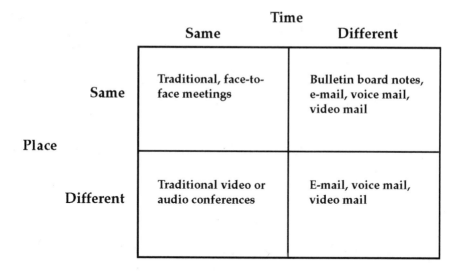

Figure 14.3 How people interact

videoconferencing), different time and place (voice mail, e-mail, and video mail), and different time but same place (voice mail, e-mail, video mail, bulletin board, Post-it™ notes, and so on).

One might think of collaborative software (groupware) such as Lotus Notes as fitting mostly in the "different place" row, but some aspects of some groupware products can be useful in all four situations.

One example fostered by Figure 14.3, and not by "stretching the table," is the extra value of video mail. This is especially so when the mail is broadened to include the other media, such as whiteboards and annotation, which are used in full-featured systems.

Consider the following hypothetical videomail use scenario:

Tuesday evening, 9:00 P.M. (Texas)   Bob, the director of the wrist video project, needs to send a detailed message, with supporting documentation, to his counterpart, Jacques, at his company's European partner. Bob has artist's renderings of three possible designs, prepared by RazorSharp Studios. He also has a spreadsheet file with preliminary product cost estimates, along with a spec sheet for a new microcamera that looks appropriate for two of the designs.

Bob enters his conference room, arranges his materials, and dials Jacques' conferencing system, which automatically answers, since there is no one there to talk to. Bob selects the VidMail option from his menu and enters his password. At this point Jacques' system checks its available disk space (and Jacques' preference settings) and reports the information to Bob's system. Bob's system displays the maximum allowable message length, in minutes, and can count down in real time to let Bob know how much time he has left in which to finish his message. When Bob is ready to begin, he selects "Start Message," whereupon Jacques' system begins storing the received bit stream to its hard disk (or perhaps it demultiplexes and stores audio, video, and data channels separately). Bob delivers a short greeting and, as he begins outlining the message content, puts the camera spec in his scanner and begins transmitting it.

Continuing to chat about what is going on, Bob selects the copy stand, previewing the first of the three artist's renderings, then selecting it to be sent as a JPEG slide. The slide is also displayed on the LCD graphics tablet. There Bob uses a stylus to annotate the slide and highlight the important features, while explaining how the camera described in the spec sheet might fit in. Similarly, Bob then sends, annotates, and comments on the next two drawings. He then brings up the cost estimate screen from a network server, sends it and describes it briefly, pointing out the key items both verbally and by on-screen annotation. He also sends a copy of the spreadsheet workfile. Having spent about 15 minutes delivering his multimedia message, Bob hangs up.

Wednesday Morning, 4 A.M. (Europe)   Jacques' conferencing system receives and stores the message, and sends e-mail notification to Jacques.

Wednesday Morning, 9 A.M. (Europe)   Jacques reads the notification of a received message from Bob. He sits down at the conferencing system,[2] enters the password, and begins viewing the message. He sees it just as if he had been present at 4 A.M., except that he can pause it while he gets a cup of coffee, or can rewind it to view a section again. He can store the slides for later review, separate from the received bit stream. Also, after the complete message is viewed, the spreadsheet workspace will have been decoded and stored separately on Jacques' system, so he can work with it later.

14.4 INTERNET AND VIRTUAL REALITY INFLUENCES

14.4.1 MOOs and MUDs

The ideas presented in earlier sections are merely logical extrapolations of current technological trends in videoconferencing combined with useful ways of looking at what problems videoconferencing has been trying to

---

[2] He might also choose to have the message file routed to his desktop computer for decoding and viewing, depending on the capabilities there.

solve. However, neither the "stretch the table" guideline nor the delineation in Figure 14.3 necessarily leads to MUDs (Multiuser dungeons, multiuser domains, or, even less game-like, multiuser dimensions), MOOs (MUD, object oriented), virtual meeting spaces, or other new directions. Let us look briefly at how these might be radically new and different in videoconferencing.

MUDs grew out of text-based adventure games, such as ZORK, and online chat rooms. Users interact with both the environment and with other users. MUDs have been used overwhelmingly for entertainment, but have some characteristics of interest for business communication. MUD encounters occur in real time, are scalable to varying numbers of participants, and a permanent record is easily produced. MUDs have traditionally been text based. While a text description of an environment has its merits from an entertainment point of view, allowing users to create their own mental pictures of the MUD environment, it is inappropriate for most (all?) business use. The MOO concept is more oriented toward useful work.

The oldest and best known MOO seems to be LambdaMOO at Xerox PARC. It has been largely text oriented, but the move to add other communication media is under way. CUR93 describes work and plans at PARC to add GUIs, audio, and video to a MOO system. Users in a "multiroom" MOO will hear all the sounds associated with that room, and when they speak, all other users in that room will hear it. The system may also be configured so that sounds from an adjoining room are heard faintly. The plan for video is to "make it easy" for users to view video from other users in the same (virtual) room, or to view output associated with that room itself. The latter case is useful for a MOO setup to allow remote users to attend a meeting that is taking place in an actual, physical conference room. One of the systems in which these concepts will be realized is called "Jupiter." Jupiter is a MOO that, while otherwise text based, will incorporate audio and video and be used at both PARC and EuroPARC in England. One of the Jupiter goals is to facilitate casual interaction. Plans include virtual break rooms with newspapers and games, along with audio and video devices in actual break rooms, perhaps inspired by the earlier efforts at PARC and Bellcore that were described earlier.

14.4.2 VRML

The Virtual Reality Modeling Language is likely to be the standard for 3D modeling on the World Wide Web. As of this writing, VRML 1.0 is the current specification, but VRML 2.0 is nearing completion [WIL96]. VRML 1.0 is a text-based language for describing 3D "world models," which can later be rendered according to the user's point of view. For example, ASCII strings such as "Sphere {radius .1}" are used. The user's computer connects to a server with the desired VRML model and then copies the VRML file. The VRML program running on the user's computer allows the user to dynamically change his point of view, so that the user can travel through the 3D world described by the VRML file. Up until now, most VRML models have been simple, sparse, and toy-like. VRML 2.0 should allow much better modeling, and should be completed well before the end of 1996. Most VRML work seems to have in mind that the scenes will usually be rendered into 2D views displayed on a normal computer monitor. That is, users are not expected to be required to wear "virtual reality helmets" or glasses, though their use is not precluded.

The first announced VRML 1.0 site may have been WAXweb [MEY9X]. Its URL is `http://bug.village.virginia.edu`. Based on a short film by David Blair, WAXweb 2.0 has been said to be the first interactive, intercommunicative feature film on the World Wide Web (Variety, 2.16.95, as cited in the VRML FAQ at `www.oki.com/vrml/VRML_FAQ.html`). WAXweb is an experiment in combining MOOs and VRML.

14.4.3 3D Interactive Virtual Worlds

Several projects and services using interactive 3D worlds are under way, some adhering to VRML and some proprietary, with the usual struggles within the standards committee about whose extensions and techniques are to be incorporated into the next version of the standards.[3] 3D body icons, typically called "avatars," are a common concept among on-line 3D worlds. In many systems, each user is represented by an avatar that is visible to other users. Developers want to provide users with the opportunity to use accurate renditions of themselves, though some users may want to make other choices. For instance, at a public demonstration[4] of the Starbright Foundation's plans, Steven Speilberg chose, unsurprisingly, to use an avatar that looked like his movie character ET. Some of the proprietary extensions to VRML are to handle avatars and interactions among them.

Worlds, Inc. [`http://www.worlds.net`] and Black Sun Interactive [`http://www.blacksun.com`] are two examples of early 3D, entertainment-oriented meeting environment providers. The Starbright World project of the Starbright Foundation [`http://www.starbright.org`] uses both 3D worlds and videoconferencing technology to allow children in different hospitals to communicate with each other and play together.

---

[3] Some readers may be familiar with the "standard joke": "Standards are wonderful; that is why we have so many of them."

[4] Digital World 95, Los Angeles, June 1995.

We are confident that virtual 3D conference rooms and other virtual meeting spaces will be combined with videoconferencing in useful and perhaps unexpected ways, even though most of the current efforts are entertainment oriented.

14.5 REVISITING THE MEETING ROOM

With progress among these individual pieces, we will be able to recombine them in offices and meeting rooms where "telepresence" is normal. Two explorations in this direction are British Telecom's "Electronic Agora" project and Sun Microsystems' "Starfire" project. David Travis [TRAV95] writes:

> In Athens, the Agora was the marketplace, but also a venue where citizens met to talk and gossip. We use this as a metaphor for a business meeting environment that is highly interactive and sociable, and which exploits the wealth of interpersonal skills that people already have. Compare the Agora with traditional video meetings: these are polite, with few interruptions. People wait their turn before speaking. The traditional face-to-face view in videotelephony makes it difficult to judge the body language of remote conferees. Issues such as these are responsible for the fact that users rate video meetings more akin to telephone meetings than to real meetings.
>
> We argue that this is because conventional video support for remote collaborative work, including relatively sophisticated Media Spaces, offer restricted spatial access to local and remote users, limited possibilities to share documents, and are based on the misconception that collaborative work amongst business and professional people primarily involves face-to-face communication. In the Electronic Agora, video is ubiquitous and used to support the social and psychological elements of meetings. The aim is to provide remote conferees with many of the key proxemic cues that they would receive if physically present. We attempt this by using "electronic surrogates" comprising a display, camera and speaker. These are placed in the positions normally occupied by physically present people: by the door, at the table, at the whiteboard, next to the overhead projector. This provides the remote user with a sense of the physical space, and shows different views of the meeting room, just as the user would get if physically present in the room carrying out these various tasks. Because the remote user can easily change position, users that are physically present gain a sense that the remote user is in the room, that is, they gain a stronger sense of the other's social presence. In addition, remote conferees also have full access to the technological facilities in the meeting room, such as the

whiteboard and the overhead projector. For example, remote users can contribute to a brainstorming session on a whiteboard, and present slides and video footage from their local computer onto the overhead projector in the Agora.

Figure 14.4 provides a view from a doorway into an Electronic Agora meeting room, with "electronic surrogates" located at the television monitors.

Sun's Starfire (`http://www.sun.com/tech/projects/starfire/`) project is a film envisioning the office and meeting environments of the year 2004, where videoconferencing, computing, and large displays are an integrated part of the business environment. Figure 14.5 depicts a "desk-size" computer. In the film, a leader of one automotive division is taken by surprise in a board meeting by a rival's attempts to discredit her division's latest project. The board members are in multiple meeting rooms. As the meeting progresses, she is able to consult with her staff and rebuff the challenge by inquiry into a remote information server.

By the year 2000, the features we have described in this chapter will be

Figure 14.4 Electronic Agora meeting room

Figure 14.5   Starfire desk-sized computer
(The Starfire desk-sized computer URL site is used with permission from Sun Microsystems, Inc.)

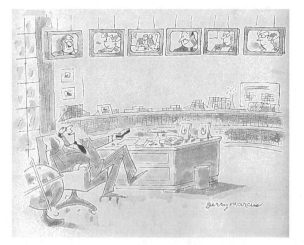

Figure 14.6   "Before we get our Saudi Arabian representative to give his report, I'd like to ask Harris what's the night life like in Paris these days?" (Printed by permission of Jerry Marcus.)

part of typical meetings. Video will be life-size and ubiquitous. Microphones and cameras will be capable of self-positioning using beam forming and motion detection technology. Computers and other information sources will be integrated with the rest of the meeting room technology. We will soon be far beyond the cartoon of Figure 14.6.

REFERENCES

BRA93   Brandstein, Michael S., and Harvey F. Silverman, "A New Time-Delay Estimator for Finding Source Locations using a Microphone Array," TR LEMS-116, Division of Engineering, Brown University, March 1993.

CUR93   Curtis, Pavel, and David A. Nichols, "MUDs Grow Up: Social Virtual Reality in the Real World," Xerox PARC, `ftp://ftp.parc.xerox.com/pub/MOO/papers/MUDsGrowUp`, May 1993.

FIS90   Fish, Robert S., Kraut, Robert E., and Chalfonte, Barbara L., "The VideoWindow System in Informal Communications," in *Proceedings of the Conference on Computer-Supported Cooperative Work,* October 1990, pp. 1–11.

FIS92   Fish, Robert S., Kraut, Robert E., Root, Robert W., and Rice, Ronald E., "Evaluating Video as a Technology for Informal Communication," in *CHI '92 Conference Proceedings,* May 1992, pp. 37–48.

MEY9x   Meyer, Tom, Blair, David, and Connor, D. Brookshire, "WAXweb: Toward Dynamic MOO-based VRML," `http://www.cs.brown.edu/people/twm/waxvrml.html`, Brown University.

SIL92   Silverman, Harvey F., and Kirtman, Stuart E., "A Two-Stage Algorithm for Determining Talker Location from Linear Microphone Array Data," *Computer Speech and Language 6,* pp. 129–152 (1992).

TRAV95   Travis, D. S., "The Electronic Agora," in Emmott, S.J., Ed., *Information Superhighways: Users and Futures,* Academic, London, 1995.

WIL96   Wilcox, Susan, "VRML 2.0 Takes Flight," *New Media 6,* 5, pp. 36–40 (April 1996).

Appendix I

Summary of ITU-T Standards

THE INTERNATIONAL TELECOMMUNICATION UNION

The International Telecommunication Union (ITU), a United Nations organization headquartered in Geneva, Switzerland, is the main international standards body for videoconferencing equipment and services. About 170 countries participate as voting members of the ITU. Each country has one vote. Other organizations may participate in the work of the ITU but do not have voting rights. Examples include telecommunications operating agencies (AT&T, British Telecom, KDD), scientific or industrial organizations (IBM, CLI), and certain other international organizations (Intelsat).

The part of the ITU that develops telecommunications standards is known as the International Telecommunication Union—Telecommunication Standardization Sector (ITU-T). The ITU-T was formerly known as CCITT but underwent a name change in early 1993. The work of the ITU-T is split into 15 study groups. Every four years, each study group is given approximately 30 areas of study (called questions) that result in a number of internationally agreed-on standards, called recommendations.

Videoconferencing is covered most directly by Study Group 15 (Transmission Systems and Equipment) and Study Group 8 (Terminals for Telematic Services). Study Group 15 (SG15) is responsible for producing the H-series and G-series of recommendations covering videoconferencing terminals, multipoint control units, and video and audio processing techniques. SG8 is responsible for developing a standardized set of protocols (the T.120 and T.130 series of recommendations) that supports multimedia applications such as fax, still image transfer, annotation, file transfer, etc., in multipoint as well as point-to-point videoconferences. It appears that there will be some reorganization of the study groups for the four-year period beginning in 1997, with an additional study group formed to address "Multimedia Services and Systems" topics currently considered in Study Groups 1, 8, 14, and 15.

The equivalent U.S. national standards body to ITU-T SG8 is the

Telecommunications Industry Association TR29.3 group. The U.S. group that corresponds to ITU-T SG15 is known as T1A1.5 and is sponsored by the Alliance for Telecommunications Industry Solutions. TR29.3 and T1A1.5 are both accredited by the American National Standards Institute, and are allowed to develop ANSI standards.

The ITU has been formed by treaties among governments. Individual companies, trade associations, and groups like TR29.3 and T1A1.5 cannot officially make submissions directly to ITU-T study group meetings. The U.S. State Department has set up its own study groups to forward contributions to ITU meetings. U.S. Study Group C handles submissions to ITU-T SG15, and U.S. Study Group D handles ITU-T SG8. Submissions usually come from individual U.S. companies. They may come directly to a State Department study group meeting or be approved and forwarded by standards groups such as T1A1.5 or TR29.3. Depending on the degree of support, a submission may be allowed to go to the ITU as either an official U.S. contribution or as a company contribution. Usually a contribution from a country is seen as more important than a contribution from an individual company.

H.320, H.321, H.323, and H.324 are the "top-level documents" for the basic suite of standards for videoconferencing. Figure 11.2 in Chapter 11 provides a good outline of the relationship between the various H.320 recommendations concerning videoconferencing. Similar figures apply to H.321 and H.323. Figure I.1 applies to H.324.

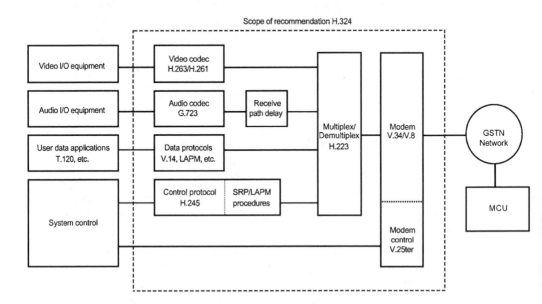

Figure I.1   H.324 component recommendations
(Reprinted with permission of ITU, from Recommendation H.324 (3/96) figure 1.)

STUDY GROUP 15 G-SERIES RECOMMENDATIONS (AUDIO)

Recommendation	Title/Description
G.711	**Pulse Code Modulation (PCM) of Voice Frequencies**
	3-KHz audio at 48, 56, or 64 Kbps.
G.722	**7 KHz Audio-Coding within 64 kbit/s**
	7-KHz audio at 48, 56, or 64 Kbps.
G.723	**Dual Rate Speech Coder for Multimedia Communications Transmitting at 5.3 and 6.3 kbps**
G.728	**Coding of Speech at 16 Kbit/s Using Low-Delay Code Excited Linear Prediction**
	3-KHz audio at 16 Kbps.
G.729	**A Speech Codec for Multimedia Telecommunications Transmitting at 8/13 Kbit/s**

STUDY GROUP 15 H-SERIES RECOMMENDATIONS

Recommendation	Title
H.221	**Frame Structure for a 64 to 1920 Kbit/s Channel in Audiovisual Teleservices**
	Defines how to multiplex video, audio, control, and user data into one serial bit stream. Used with H.320.
H.223	**Multiplexing Protocol for Low Bit Rate Multimedia Communication**
	Multiplex used with H.324.
H.224	**A Simple Data Link Layer Protocol for Use in Multiway Conferences**
	A simplex data protocol for use in multipoint conferences.

H.225   **Media Stream Packetization and Synchronization on Non-Guaranteed Quality of Service LANs**

Multiplex used with H.323.

H.230   **Frame-Synchronous Control and Indication Signals for Audiovisual Systems**

Defines simple multipoint control systems procedures and describes network maintenance functions.

H.231   **Multipoint Control Unit for Audiovisual Services Using Digital Channels up to 2 Mbit/s**

Defines a set of MCU functions and operational requirements.

H.233   **Confidentiality Systems for Audiovisual Services**

Defines how encryption can be applied to an H.221 bit stream but does not define the actual encryption algorithm.

H.234   **Authentication and Key Management for Audiovisual Systems**

Specifies the encryption key management procedures used in conjunction with H.233.

H.242   **System for Establishing Communication Between Audiovisual Terminals Using Digital Channels up to 2Mbit/s**

Defines initiation of communications between systems and capabilities negotiation procedures.

H.243   **Procedures for Establishing Communication Between Three or More Audiovisual Terminals Using Digital Channels up to 2Mbit/s in Multiway Conferences**

Defines initiation of communications between systems and capabilities negotiation procedures in multiway conferences.

H.244   **Synchronized Channel Aggregation**

Specifies how to combine (IMUX) up to 128 channels of 64 Kbps using H.221 procedures.

H.245   **Control Protocol for Multimedia Communication**

Defines initiation of communications between systems and capabilities negotiation procedures. Successor to H.242.

H.261   **Video Codec for Audiovisual Services at p × 64Kbit/s**

Defines the p × 64 video coding algorithm. Annex D describes a technique for 4 × CIF still image transfer between systems.

H.262   **Video Coding for ATM Environments**

Defines a video coding algorithm for use over cell-relay packet networks, in H.310.

H.263   **Video Coding for Low Bit Rate Communication**

Defines a coding algorithm for use with H.324. Also used with H.323, and with H.320.

H.281   **A Far End Camera Control Protocol for Videoconferences Using H.224 (H.DLL)**

The first multipoint data application that uses the H.224 protocol.

H.310   **Broadband Video Conferencing Systems and Equipment**

The broadband (ATM) equivalent to H.320.

H.320   **Narrow-Band Visual Telephone Systems and Terminal Equipment**

Defines how the H-series video conferencing recommendations work together for ISDN.

H.321   **Adaptation of H.320 Terminals to B-ISDN**

Defines how H.320 terminals should operate when connected to a broadband ISDN network.

H.322   **Visual Telephone Systems and Terminal Equipment for Local Area Networks That Provide a Guaranteed Quality of Service**

Defines how H.320 terminals should operate when connected to an isochronous LAN, e.g., isoEthernet.

H.323	**Visual Telephone Systems and Terminal Equipment for Local Area Networks That Provide a Non-Guaranteed Quality of Service**
	Defines conferencing on conventional LANs, e.g., Ethernet.
H.324	**Terminal for Low Bit Rate Multimedia Communication**
	Analog telephone line videophone standard.

STUDY GROUP 8 T.12X AND T.13X RECOMMENDATIONS

Figure 12.1 in Chapter 12 shows how the various T.120 series of recommendations can be used as the building blocks for multipoint and multimedia applications. These protocols run in the multilayer protocol (MLP) channel. The T.120 recommendations were designed to work with prior ITU-T recommendations such as I.430, H.221, Q.922, and X.224, as shown in Figure 12.2. T.13x recommendations are newer recommendations evolving from the T.120 efforts.

Recommendation	Title/Description
T.120	**Protocols for Multipoint, Multimedia Data Transfer**
	Overview of the T.120 series.
T.121	**Generic Application Template**
	Guidance for developing T.120-compliant applications.
T.122	**Multipoint Communication Service for Audiographic and Audiovisual Conferencing**
	Provides a description of how the multipoint communications service protocol operates.
T.123	**Protocol Stack for Audiographic and Audiovisual Teleconference Applications**
	Specifies what protocols are to be used on what types of networks.

T.124	**Generic Conference Control for Audio-Visual and Audiographic Terminals**

Defines how data applications should operate in a multiway conference.

T.125	**Multipoint Communications Service Protocol Specification**

The companion recommendation to T.122.

T.126	**Still Image Protocol Specification**

Defines how to do JPEG, JBIG, and fax still image transfer and annotation in a multiway conference.

T.127	**Multipoint Binary File Transfer Protocol Specification**

Defines how to accomplish a multipoint file transfer.

T.131	**Network Specific Mappings**
T.132	**Real Time Link Management**

Management of network connections used to distribute real time streams.

T.133	**Audio-Video Control**

T.13x specifications are expected to displace H.243.

Appendix II

Web Resources

Products in the videoconferencing industry are changing rapidly, just as in the computer and communications industries, which provide the basis for videoconferencing. Manufacturers and suppliers of videoconferencing equipment, networking vendors, telecommunications companies, standards organizations, and others are likely to be the appropriate sources of "how to" information in this dynamic environment. This appendix, which we intend to update periodically at `http://www.aw.com/cp/duran-sauer.html`, consists of pointers to many of these sources. Since the URLs for these resources are likely to change, we do not show the URLs in the following text, but assume the reader will find them through the links at `http://www.aw.com/cp/duran-sauer.html`. The URLs are intended to be videoconferencing specific, but in many cases point to home pages of companies with broader interests. The categories and categorizations are somewhat arbitrary. For example, Intel has roll-about group conferencing system products, but their product efforts seem to be dominated by desktop conferencing systems (and their processors and other products), so we have chosen not to list Intel with the group conferencing suppliers.

GENERAL RESOURCES AND STANDARDS ORGANIZATIONS

- ADSL Forum
- ATM Forum
- Frame Relay Forum
- International Multimedia Teleconferencing Consortium
- International Telecommunication Union (ITU)
- Internet Engineering Task Force (IETF)
- Dan Kegel's ISDN Page

- Matrix Information and Directory Services
- National Institute of Standards and Technology (NIST)
- Telecom Information Resources

SUPPLIERS OF DESKTOP VIDEOCONFERENCING SYSTEMS

- Apple Computer
- Compression Labs (CLI)
- Creative Labs
- Diamond Multimedia
- Intel ProShare
- Multimedia Access Corporation
- PPD—PicturePhone Direct
- PictureTel
- Silicon Graphics
- Sun Microsystems
- VCON
- VTEL
- Zydacron

SUPPLIERS OF GROUP VIDEOCONFERENCING SYSTEMS

- British Telecom
- Compression Labs (CLI)
- Matsushita (Panasonic)
- NEC
- PictureTel

- Sony

- Videoconferencing Systems, Inc.

- VTEL

SUPPLIERS OF VIDEOCONFERENCING SOFTWARE AND SOFTWARE COMPONENTS

- CU-SeeMe Welcome Page

- Data Connection Limited

- DataBeam

- Future Labs

- InSoft

- Microsoft ActiveX Conferencing

- Netscape

- Precept Software, Inc.

- Softwright

- Vivo

- VDOnet

- White Pine

SUPPLIERS OF MULTIPOINT CONTROL UNITS

- Accord Video Telecommunications

- Lucent

- Madge Networks

- Multilink

- PictureTel

- Sony

- Tektronix
- VideoServer
- VTEL

SUPPLIERS OF NETWORKING EQUIPMENT AND SOFTWARE

- 3Com
- ADC Kentrox
- Amati
- Ascend Communications
- Bay Networks
- BBN
- CableLabs
- Cisco Systems
- First Virtual
- Fore Systems
- General Datacomm
- Incite
- Madge Networks
- Memotec Communications
- NetManage
- Newbridge
- Nortel (Northern Telecom)
- Novell

- Promptus Communications

- RADVision, Ltd.

SUPPLIERS OF CONFERENCING AND NETWORK SERVICES

- Ameritech

- AT&T

- Bell Atlantic

- Bell South

- British Telecom

- Cable and Wireless

- Compunetix

- ConferTech International

- Deutsche Telekom

- France Telecom

- GTE

- KDD

- MCI

- MPR Teltech

- NTT

- NYNEX

- Olivetti

- Pacific Bell

- PTT Nederland

- SITA

- Southwestern Bell

- Sprint
- Stentor
- Tele Danmark, KTAS
- Telefonica de Espana
- Telstra
- U S West
- WorldLinx

SUPPLIERS OF VIDEOCONFERENCING SYSTEM COMPONENTS

- 8 × 8
- AMX
- Bitfield
- Canon
- C-Cubed
- Connectix
- Digital Equipment Corporation
- IBM
- Liveworks
- Lucent
- Madge Networks
- Mentec
- Motorola
- Nokia
- ParkerVision
- Polycom, Inc.
- Precept Software, Inc.

- Ricoh
- SAT-SAGEM
- Samsung
- Sharp
- SMART Technologies
- Telenor
- Teles GmbH
- Texas Instruments

RESEARCH ORGANIZATIONS AND COMPANIES

- Bellcore
- Carnegie Mellon Interactive Systems Laboratories
- ETRI
- GMD-FOKUS
- ITRI
- Microsoft Research Telepresence Group
- MIT Media Lab

MISCELLANEOUS

- Tom Brinck's Video Communications Bibliography
- Dave Hawley's isoEthernet Page
- DT-5 / Desktop Videoconferencing Product Survey
- Hendricks and Steer Videoconferencing FAQ
- Howard Enterprises, Inc. Home Page
- MBone Information Web
- NetWatch!
- Pacific Bell Videoconferencing for Learning
- ReSerVation setup Protocol (RSVP)

Glossary

In the body of the text, we have underlined the first occurrence of each of the following terms. In the summaries of each term in this glossary, cross-references are also underlined.

352 × 288 is the resolution of the Common Interchange Format (CIF), the most frequently used resolution for motion video.

640 × 480 is the base resolution used for VGA on PC-compatible computers and on the Macintosh. 640 × 480 is usually used in computer displays to avoid the cost of higher resolution display. 640 × 480 is also frequently used for still images in videoconferencing.

1024 × 768 is the most common resolution used for desktop PCs and Macintoshes.

10BaseT is the most frequently used wiring scheme for Ethernet. The "10" indicates 10 million bits per second. The "T" indicates use of twisted-pair wires of the sort used for telephone circuits. 10BaseT uses two pairs between the computer interface and the "hub," one pair for transmitting and one for receiving.

100BaseT is the family of wiring schemes used for Fast (100 million bits per second) Ethernet.

Aliasing is the perception as noise of high-frequency sounds or visual components, due to insufficient sampling frequency. Proper filtering avoids aliasing.

Analog signals have voltage directly analogous to the strength of the corresponding physical signal, that is, the loudness of a sound or the brightness of a light source. The voltage of the signal alternates (between positive and negative) at the frequency of the sound or light source.

Aspect ratio is the ratio of the pixel width of the visible display to the height of the display area.

Audiographics is a means to augment telephones with graphics such as shared documents.

Basic rate ISDN (BRI) is the most common form of ISDN. BRI provides two B-channels with one 16,000 bit per second D-channel for signaling, using ordinary telephone wiring.

B-channel is a 64,000 bit per second digital telephone circuit. B stands for "bearer." A 56,000-bit channel is "restricted." A typical telephone line in urban areas is capable of transmitting a pair of B-channels.

BRI stands for "basic rate ISDN."

Cathode-ray tube (CRT) is the type of picture tube used in televisions and for computer displays.

CCITT is the former name of the ITU-T.

Chair control (see conducted conferences).

Chrominance refers to the color components (hue and saturation) of a luminance-based representation of color.

CIF stands for Common Interchange Format.

Circuit switching is what the telephone network is based on, which means that once a call is established, there are circuits (B-channels) dedicated to the call.

Codec is a term for coder/decoder.

Coder is a device for coding.

Coding is one of two terms, along with "compression," used almost interchangeably in referring to processes for reducing the bit rate.

Composite video is the most common form of electrical signals used to transfer video between components. Luminance, hue, and saturation are multiplexed together on a single signal wire on the sending end and separated at the receiving end. Most inexpensive cameras, VCRs, and televisions use composite video. Composite video usually uses single-pin "phono" connectors, the same as the ones that are typically used for audio connections.

Compression is an alternate term for coding.

Conducted conferences allow one site to be designated as the conductor of the conference. Conducted conferences are sometimes called "chaired" or "chair controlled."

Continuous presence refers to the capability in a multipoint conference to make video from many of the sites continuously present on the screen.

CRT stands for <u>cathode-ray tube</u>.

D-channel is an <u>ISDN</u> circuit used for dialing and other signaling.

DCT stands for <u>discrete cosine transform</u>.

Digital signals are a representation of physical signals using numbers, usually called "<u>samples</u>," to represent amplitude or intensity. The range of the numbers in a sample is the major determiner of the signal-to-noise ratio.

Discrete cosine transform (DCT) is a key step in many video <u>coding</u> techniques. See Chapter 9.

Document sharing is a conferencing capability to allow the participants to view and manipulate the same document.

Document stand is a device with a built-in video camera for capturing images of paper documents and similar items. See Figure 4.11.

E1 is a dedicated telephone circuit, similar to <u>T1</u>, but with a 1,928,000 bit per second bandwidth. E1 is used instead of <u>T1</u> in Asia and Europe.

Echo cancellation is used in speakerphones and videoconferencing to eliminate echoes caused by microphones capturing sounds produced by corresponding microphones. Echo cancellation works by "remembering" what signal has been put through the speaker, and then subtracting it, appropriately attenuated and delayed, from the signal entering the microphone. The difficulty is in attenuating and delaying the correct amount. Echo cancellation requires much computation, and likely adds cost for processor capability to perform the cancellation algorithms. Echo cancellation is discussed in depth in Section 10.2.

Ethernet is the most widely used form of <u>local-area network</u> (LAN). In the original form, signals are broadcast on coaxial cables, analogous to radio transmission through the mythical "ether." <u>10BaseT</u> wiring is now preferred over coaxial cable in most environments.

Filtering is the removal of undesired frequencies. Most commonly, filtering is used to remove high-frequency audio and video signals to avoid <u>aliasing</u> in <u>sampling</u>. From a digital perspective, the filtering has not reduced the amount of data, since there are the same number of samples, each with the same number of bits, as without filtering. The filtering, if done properly, results in output signals sounding or looking better.

Focal length is the distance from the optical center of a lens to the point where light rays converge (are in focus). Shorter focal lengths correspond to a wider field of view and vice versa, i.e., a "telephoto" lens has a longer focal length.

Frequency is the number of cycles per unit of time (of a sound or radio wave, for example).

Full duplex is simultaneous bidirectional transmission, as opposed to alternating bidirectional transmission (half duplex).

G.711 is the default audio representation used in H.320, providing roughly 3.5-KHz frequency response in a 64,000-bit communication channel. See Section 10.1.

G.722 is an optional audio representation used in H.320, providing roughly 7-KHz frequency response in a 48,000-, 56,000-, or 64,000-bit communication channel. See Section 10.1.

G.723 is an audio representation used in H.324, providing roughly 3.5-KHz frequency response in a 6,300-bit communication channel. See Section 10.1.5.

G.728 is an optional audio representation used in H.320, providing roughly 3.5-KHz frequency response in a 16,000-bit communication channel. See Section 10.1.

Graphics tablet is a device for computer input of physical coordinates, commonly used in computer-aided design. See Figure 4.6.

Grayscale refers to monochrome representation of light with multiple intensity values (more than on and off, corresponding to white and black).

H.221 "Frame Structure for a 64 to 1920 Kbit/s Channel in Audiovisual Teleservices" defines the usage of P B-channels to transmit multiplexed audio, video, other data and control signals. We discuss aspects of H.221 in Chapters 3, 8, and 12.

H.261 "Video Codec for Audiovisual Services at $P \times 64$ Kbit/s" has been known informally as "$P \times 64$" because it defines video coding based on P 64,000-bit per second channels. (P is typically two or more.) We consider H.261 in Chapter 9.

H.263 "Video Coding for Low Bit Rate Communication" is the coding method designed for H.324, using the techniques of H.261 plus significant enhancements. We consider H.263 in Section 9.2.9.

H.320 "Narrowband Visual Telephone Systems and Terminal Equipment" is the summary ITU-T recommendation for standard videoconferencing using ISDN or similar telephone circuits.

H.323 "Visual Telephone Systems and Terminal Equipment for Local Area Networks which Provide a Non-Guaranteed Quality of Service" is the summary ITU-T recommendation for standard videoconferencing with conventional local-area networks.

H.324 "Terminal for Low Bit Rate Multimedia Communication" is the summary ITU-T recommendation for standard videoconferencing using POTS.

Half duplex is bidirectional transmission in alternating (not simultaneous) directions.

Hue is the relative proportion of green and red in a luminance-based representation. The hue control on a television is often called "tint."

Internet is the proper name for the worldwide computer network that evolved from the 1970s ARPANET.

Interframe coding is coding among related video frames.

Intraframe coding is coding within a video frame.

Inverse multiplexor (IMUX) is a device for separating one higher bandwidth communication channel to appear as multiple B-channels.

IP stands for Internet Protocol, the network level protocol used in the Internet and other computer networks.

IPX/SPX stands for "Internet Packet eXchange/Sequenced Packet eXchange," the family of protocols originally used on NetWare networks. (Some NetWare networks use TCP/IP instead of IPX/SPX, and many NetWare networks use both families of protocols.)

Iris is the device behind a camera lens that controls the amount of light admitted, and thus controls brightness of images.

ISDN stands for "Integrated Services Digital Network." ISDN is a standardized approach to providing digital service from digital telephones.

ITU-T is the International Telecommunications Union—Telecommunication Standardization Sector, which establishes "recommendations" for standard protocols.

JPEG is the Joint Photographic Experts Group standard for coding of still images.

Local-area network (LAN) is a computer network, designed for a small geographic area, that is capable of higher speed connections than typical networks for wider geographical areas.

Luminance is the brightness intensity of a visual image. The luminance control on a television is often called the "picture."

MCU (see Multipoint control unit).

Modem (MOdulator/DEModulator) is a device used to transmit digital data across analog telephone circuits.

Motion estimation is the estimation of which pixels in a frame are different from those in the previous frame.

Motion Picture Experts Group (MPEG) is a standard form of coding used for stored video and television.

Multimedia is data that include multiple forms of natural media, typically including audio and video.

Multiplexing is the process of combining separate streams or channels into one logical stream of data.

Multipoint is the usual term for conferencing with more than two sites.

Multipoint control unit (MCU) is a device for implementing multipoint conferences.

Noise-gated microphone is one that can effectively turn itself off when the sounds entering the microphone are below a predetermined threshold (and thus likely to be "extraneous") and turn itself on (instantly) when louder sounds are present (when someone is speaking near the microphone).

NT1 (network terminator one) is a device for BRI that converts the two off-premises signal wires to four-wire connections suitable for an ISDN telephone. An NT1 is often designed to support more than one of these four-wire connections, for example, one for a telephone and one for a fax machine.

NTSC (National Television Standards Committee) is the standard for television broadcasting in North America.

Overlaying video (see video overlay).

Packet switching is the approach used in most computer networks for carrying different logical streams of data on the same shared physical network.

PAL (phase alternating lines) is the standard for television broadcasting in Europe and other countries.

Pixel ("picture element") is one of many small dots used to represent a picture.

Plain Old Telephone Service (POTS) is a common term for conventional analog telephony.

PRI stands for primary rate ISDN.

Primary rate ISDN (PRI) is a high-bandwidth form of ISDN. A PRI circuit has 23 B-channels and a 64,000-bit D-channel for signaling (1,536,000 bits per second) in the United States, and 30 B-channels in Europe and Asia.

Private branch exchange (PBX) is a telephone switchboard designed for private use (as opposed to a "central branch exchange" used in telephone company offices).

Program sharing is a conferencing mechanism allowing more than one person, each on different computers, to use the same copy of the same program, working with the same document, and seeing the same displays on screen.

$P \times 64$ is an informal name for H.261.

QCIF (Quarter Common Interchange Format) is a variant on CIF with 176 × 144 resolution.

Radiographic is a term for computerized radiology (diagnostic "X-rays").

Resolution is a measure of detail in a digital visual image, measured either in number of pixels in the horizontal and vertical directions, or in pixels per unit of physical measure of the display device.

RGB is a representation of color using the intensities of the primary colors of light, red, green, and blue. Appropriate mixtures of these primary colors can be used to represent any color. For example, black is represented by R(ed), G(reen), and B(lue) all at zero intensity, white is R, G, and B all at one (full intensity), yellow is B at zero, R and G at one, etc. This representation facilitates design of both hardware and software for manipulation of images and colors at the pixel level.

Roll-about is a medium-scale videoconferencing system intended for use by small groups in typical meetings. It can be transported from room to room, as long as the room has appropriate connections to telephone or local-area networks.

Router is a device in packet-switched networks for routing packets from one subnetwork to another.

Sample is a number representing the strength of a signal at a particular time, used with other samples in digital signal representation.

Saturation is the overall intensity of color in a luminance-based representation of a color image. On a television, the saturation control is often called "color."

Scaling is the process of converting resolution.

Scan converter is a device used to convert the computer video output to a television representation, or vice versa. This device must perform the appropriate scaling to convert between square pixels and rectangular pixels. See the discussion in Section 4.3.

Student response terminals is a device, typically a keypad, for a student to communicate to an instructor.

S-Video is a form of electrical signal used to transfer video between components. S-Video keeps the luminance and chrominance component signals separate on separate signal wires, using multipin connectors. S-Video leads to higher image quality, compared to composite video, because the degradation that results from combining and separating the components is avoided.

Switched 56 is a 56,000-bit per second circuit, designed for dial-up customer use, which became available in the United States before ISDN. Though similar to BRI, Switched 56 is harder to attach to than BRI, because of the equipment needed at the customer premises. A typical videoconference requires two Switched 56 circuits versus one BRI to get comparable bandwidth. As BRI becomes readily available it is expected that use of Switched 56 will diminish.

T1 is a higher speed telephone circuit used in the United States for dedicated connections, capable of 1,544,000 bits/second. The electrical connection uses two pairs of telephone wires. T1 circuits are widely used for connecting PBXs to central telephone offices. T1 circuits are also used to connect distant LAN segments.

T.120 "User Data Transmission Using a Multi-Layer Protocol (MLP)" is a comprehensive ITU-T recommendation for data conferencing.

TCP/IP (Transmission Control Protocol/Internet Protocol) is the name usually used for the family of protocols used on the Internet and in many other networks.

Telecommuting is the practice of working at home but "commuting" to an office by computer networking and/or videoconferencing.

Telemedicine is the practice of medicine across a distance by computer networking and/or videoconferencing.

Temporal filtering is the process of dropping frames and otherwise filtering excess detail across successive frames as part of video coding.

Terminal adapter (TA) is an ISDN device to manage dialing and answering the call (using the D-channel) and convert the bit-serial data on the B-channels to and from a form suitable for management by the conferencing software.

Touch panel is a touch-sensitive display device for controlling equipment.

VGA stands for "video graphics array." VGA first appeared on the IBM PS/2 in 1987 and subsequently became the *de facto* standard for graphics subsystems in PCs. The default resolution for VGA is 640×480. Higher resolutions of 800 by 600, $1,024 \times 768$, and $1,280 \times 1,024$ are known as "super" VGA.

Video follows voice is the concept of a videoconferencing system that automatically points the camera at the person speaking.

Video overlay is the combining of multiple images in mosaic fashion. In broadcast television, a common example is that of showing a forecaster in front of a weather map. In computer-based videoconferencing, a common example is that of showing a video image of people "in front of" a computer-generated image.

Virtual circuit is a logical connection across a packet-switched network that temporarily has the appearance of a dedicated physical circuit.

Visual artifacts is a term for discrepancies between a coded image and the original source.

Voice-activated switching refers to multipoint conferences where the sites generally display the video from the site with the strongest audio signal, with that site seeing the video from the previously selected site.

World Wide Web is one of the most commonly used applications on the Internet, providing hyperlinked access to data in a convenient fashion.

YIQ is the luminance-based representation of color used in NTSC.

YUV is the luminance-based representation of color used in PAL and in many video coding approaches.

Index

n after page number = footnote reference

A

Accunet 56™, 109, 111
Adaptive differential pulse code modulation (ADPCM), 171–76
Addressing and delivery, 33–36
Agora project, 244–45
A-law, 39, 170–71
Aliasing, 37, 39, 95–96
  anti, 97
America Online, 24
Analog signals, 7, 8
  conversion back to, 97
  conversion to digital, 93–97
  low-cost terminals and high-cost transmission, 97–99
Antialiasing, 97
Apple, 24
Application protocol entities (APEs), 210–11
Application registry, 210, 211
Application roster, 210, 211
AppsView™, 58–59
Arithmetic coding, 141–43, 165
ARPANET, 31n
Aspect ratio, 50
Asynchronous transfer mode (ATM), 111–12, 127, 223–24
AT&T, 3, 23, 109, 111, 129, 187
Audio
  issues regarding, 230–32
  in multipoint videoconferencing, 71–73, 169
  practical considerations, 184–86
Audio compression
  adaptive differential pulse code modulation, 171–76
  codebook excited linear prediction, 176–77
  echo canceling, 179–84
  pulse code modulation, 169–71
Audioconferencing, personal computers and, 37–39
Audiographics systems, 6
Automatic gain control (AGC) microphones, 186

B

Bandsplitting, 184
Barrel effect, 184
Basic rate ISDN (BRI), 18, 32–33, 107, 116, 117
  connecting to, 119–20, 222–23
  group videoconferencing and, 54–55
Bauds, free, 232–33
B-channel, 8, 108, 116
Bearer channel, 108, 116
Bell Atlantic Corp., 80, 113, 129
Bellcore, 129, 238–39
B-frames, 165
Bit allocation signal (BAS), 162, 197
Bit rate compression, 131
Black Sun Interactive, 243
Blocking artifacts, 163
BONDING (Bandwidth ON Demand Interoperability Group), 121–22
BRI.ISDN *See* Basic rate ISDN
British Telecom, 244
Broadcast data channels, 212, 213
Business meetings, 12–13, 77–79
Butterfly technique, 136

C

Cameras
  group videoconferencing and, 48–50
  management of, 237–38
  television, 98–99, 103–5
  video, 103–5
Candide model, 143
Cathode-ray tubes (CRTs), 50, 99
CCIR 601, 102
CCITT, 25
CELP. *See* Codebook excited linear prediction
Chaired/chair-controlled conferences, 74, 199–200
Channels, 209
Charge-coupled device (CCD) sensors, 103–4
Check sum, 203
Chrominance, 21, 101, 102